D1715892

Tax Systems

Zeuthen Lecture Book Series
Carl-Johan Dalgaard, editor

Modeling Bounded Rationality
Ariel Rubinstein

Forecasting Non-stationary Economic Time Series
Michael P. Clements and David E. Hendry

Political Economics: Explaining Economic Policy
Torsten Persson and Guido Tabellini

Wage Dispersion: Why are Similar Workers Paid Differently?
Dale T. Mortensen

Competition and Growth: Reconciling Theory and Evidence
Philippe Aghion and Rachel Griffith

Product Variety and the Gains from International Trade
Robert C. Feenstra

Unemployment Fluctuations and Stabilizations: A New Keynesian Perspective
Jordi Galí

Tax Systems
Joel Slemrod and Christian Gillitzer

Tax Systems

Joel Slemrod and Christian Gillitzer

[Zeuthen Lecture Series]
The MIT Press
Cambridge, Massachusetts
London, England

MIT Press books may be purchased at special quantity discounts for business or sales promotional use. For information, please email special_sales@mitpress.mit.edu.

This book was set in Palatino, by Toppan Best-set Premedia Limited, Hong Kong. Printed and bound in the United States of America.

Library of Congress Cataloging-in-Publication Data

Slemrod, Joel.
Tax systems / Joel Slemrod and Christian Gillitzer.
pages cm. — (Zeuthen lectures)
Includes bibliographical references and index.
ISBN 978-0-262-02672-7 (hardcover : alk. paper) 1. Taxation. I. Gillitzer, Christian.
II. Title.
HJ2305.S695 2014
336.2—dc23
2013018522

10 9 8 7 6 5 4 3 2 1

Contents

Series Foreword   vii
Acknowledgments   ix

I   **Introduction and Motivation**

1   **The Need for Tax-System Analysis**   3

2   **Standard Optimal Tax Models**   13

II   **Building Blocks of Tax Systems**

3   **Multiple Behavioral Margins**   23

4   **Multiple Sources of Costs**   69

5   **Tax Base Elasticity**   79

6   **Multiple Tax-System Instruments**   93

III   **Optimal Tax Systems**

7   **General Model**   115

8   **Standard Instruments with New Costs**   121

9   **Endogenous Elasticity**   137

10   **Optimal Observability and Complexity**   145

11   **Notches and Optimal Line Drawing**   157

IV   Future Directions and Closing Thoughts

12   Future Directions   171

13   Conclusion   185

Notes   189
References   197
Index   215

Series Foreword

The Zeuthen Lectures offer a forum for leading scholars to develop and synthesize novel results in theoretical and applied economics. They aim to present advances in knowledge in a form accessible to a wide audience of economists and advanced students of economics. The choice of topics will range from abstract theorizing to economic history. Regardless of the topic, the emphasis in the lecture series will be on originality and relevance. The Zeuthen Lectures are organized by the Institute of Economics, University of Copenhagen.

The lecture series is named after Frederik Zeuthen, a former professor at the Institute of Economics.

Karl Gunnar Persson

Acknowledgments

In October 2008 Professor Slemrod delivered the Zeuthen Lectures at the University of Copenhagen. This series of lectures has been given since 1996 in honor of the renowned Danish Professor in Economics, Frederik Zeuthen, who was on the faculty at the University of Copenhagen from 1930 to 1958. As part of the lecture series, Slemrod gave a public lecture on the topic of tax systems.

Zeuthen Lecturers receive the opportunity to publish with the MIT Press a monograph based on the public lecture's theme. After a few years of procrastinating, Slemrod enlisted the collaboration of an outstanding economics PhD student at the University of Michigan, Christian Gillitzer, who had excelled in the graduate class on taxation on which this book is loosely based. The two of us worked together closely to expand the lectures into this book.

We have several people to thank. First is Jane Macdonald, the MIT Press editor who patiently but persistently kept inquiring about the status of the Zeuthen Lectures book. Next are the University of Michigan graduate students who, over the past years, have discussed these ideas in Slemrod's tax class. We are very grateful to the people who read some or all of the draft manuscript and offered comments and suggestions for improvement: James Alm, James R. Hines Jr., Claus T. Kreiner, Wojciech Kopczuk, Emmanuel Saez, Agnar Sandmo, Steven M. Sheffrin, Shlomo Yitzhaki, and especially Louis Kaplow, who provided extensive comments on the entire manuscript. Yulia Paramanova, an economics graduate student at the University of Michigan, checked the math, and Mary Ceccanese, the program manager at the Office of Tax Policy Research, edited the text and prepared it for publication in her usual highly competent way. Slemrod especially wants to thank the many people he has worked with over the years on these issues, and frankly acknowledges that many of the ideas and insights in this book were developed in close collaboration with those colleagues, and often originated with them. Special acknowledgment goes out to Slemrod's long collaboration with Shlomo Yitzhaki, which began in 1975 in graduate school at Harvard University and has lasted with almost no interruptions until this day. Slemrod also thanks Martin Feldstein, the late Oswald Brownlee, Roger Gordon, Louis Kaplow, Wojciech Kopczuk, and the many other people from whom he has learned much over the years.

Part I   Introduction and Motivation

1   The Need for Tax-System Analysis

1.1   Tax Phenomena

• A new type of motorcycle with three wheels and long benches at the back seating up to eight passengers, and a redesigned panel truck with glass windows instead of wood panels and upholstered seats in the back—both designed to avoid high taxes on cars.
• Income taxes based not on income but, for restaurants, the seating square footage and number of tables.
• Simplified tax rules—or no tax at all—levied on businesses below a size threshold.
• The IRS commissioner testifying before a congressional appropriations committee that an additional dollar added to its budget will generate $7.30 in additional tax revenue, and will therefore *decrease*, not increase, the deficit.
• Tax experts declaring a value-added tax as a self-enforcing administrator's dream, while deriding the textbook-equivalent retail sales tax as not acceptable under usual standards of equity and intrusiveness.
• In the United States, the self-employed remit only 43 percent of their true tax liability, while wage and salary earners remit 99 percent.
• US corporations making substantial real investments in Puerto Rico in electronics, pharmaceutical, and high-fashion production, not generally considered activities in which Puerto Rico has a comparative advantage.

To those who find tax to be a fascinating subject—and there are many of us—one source of fascination is how it reflects so many very human qualities. One is human ingenuity, as shown by the creative ways people find to avoid, and sometimes evade, their tax liability. Another is the heterogeneous attitude toward authority, as some people bridle at the very idea of owing tax to the government, while others view taxpaying as a civic duty that honest people like them should not even consider shirking. To economists, tax is fascinating and important because it affects just about every corner of a modern economy. Taxation changes the reward to working, saving, investing, leaving a bequest, and buying a house. It can change the price of giving to charity, smoking cigarettes, and doing basic research. It affects the choice of religion, the timing of marriages, births, and even deaths. It tempts some people into breaking the law, and others into blowing the whistle on people suspected of same. While some people expend considerable time and money to learn details of the tax code so as to take advantage of the legal loopholes, others know very little, forgoing tax benefits they are entitled to and making decisions according to misperceived, or unperceived, tax-related incentives. Through its effect on individuals' and firms' choices, the tax system affects the level and growth of national income. Through the progressivity of the tax burden, it affects the distribution of welfare in society. And through its collection of revenue, it funds the provision of public goods and social insurance that can contribute to individuals' well-being.

The clash between the deep and mind-numbingly practical and detailed makes taxation especially intriguing. What reflects such profound issues as the proper limits of the state is often fought out on the prosaic battlefield of, for example, whether blood donors can deduct the cost of their groceries as a cost of doing business. In a democratic system it also becomes a clash over the minds of voters, so that the arguments become stylized and simplified (and even distorted and obfuscated), and these issues get framed as a detergent marketer might do—packaged to appeal to cognitive biases and shortcuts.

1.2 · Modern Tax Theory and Its Limitations

Beginning in the first half of the 1970s, the modern normative theory of taxation, known as optimal taxation, placed the evaluation of taxation on a rigorous footing, replacing mostly vague arguments about what makes one tax system better than another, an approach that did not lend itself to intellectual progress. Optimal taxation is an elegant theoretical structure that enabled economists to characterize what tax system would best achieve explicit objectives under carefully delineated conditions. For example, in one of the fundamental contributions to optimal tax theory, Diamond and Mirrlees (1971) established that although in the absence of lump-sum taxes there will certainly be distortions from raising revenue, under some conditions the second-best optimum will always feature production efficiency: whatever goods and services are consumed should be produced (or obtained, when imports are an option) in a social cost minimizing way. As a second example, all taxed goods should, in general, be taxed differentially, or in other words, uniform commodity taxation is optimal only under very strong assumptions.

Although the rigor of the approach greatly facilitated intellectual progress, as with all economic models the standard models of optimal taxation had to be stylized and had to abstract from some aspects of the tax environment. Some important limitations of the standard optimal tax model include:[1]

· Little attention paid to the administrative and compliance costs of taxation.
· A focus on tax rates and, to a lesser extent, tax bases, to the relative exclusion of all other tax-system instruments, such as enforcement tools.
· A focus on what might be called real behavioral responses to taxation, to the relative exclusion of avoidance and evasion responses.
· A recognition of the central role of asymmetric information between the government and private citizens, but extreme assumptions regarding what is measurable without cost and what is not measurable at any cost.
· No meaningful role for firms.
· No concern with the details of tax remittance.
· An assumption that people understand and react rationally to the tax system, implying that the government has no reason to manipulate citizens' perceptions.

To be sure, some research has addressed one or more of these issues. Moreover, for some issues in taxation, these characteristics are not central and do not critically mislead. But, for many issues in taxation, they are crucial.

1.3 Toward Tax Systems

The premise of this book is that in order to address many critical tax policy issues—including the issues mentioned at the start—tax analysis must move beyond these aspects of the standard model. This approach, which we dub a tax-systems approach,[2] addresses much more than the optimal tax base (e.g., income or consumption) and the optimal rates to apply to that base. It addresses such things as what fraction of tax returns to audit, how to choose the audited returns, and what structure of penalties to apply to detected evasion. It addresses whether to have consumers or retailers remit retail sales taxes, and whether employers should remit labor income tax, or employees. It addresses what compromises to the ideal (in the absence of avoidance and evasion) base, such as the taxation of capital gains upon realization rather than accrual, the taxation, or nontaxation of the imputed income from owner-occupied housing, the use of statutory depreciation schedules rather than the true decline in value of capital assets, and so on.

A tax-systems approach takes tax evasion seriously, recognizing that people break the law all the time. They murder, steal, extort, scam, break contracts, and smoke marijuana. Some crimes are violent, some are not; some are done for money, others not. Some have obvious victims, while others harm no one and nothing except other people's sensibilities, morals, or religious beliefs. Some people never knowingly violate any law, but end up doing so because the law is uncertain or unknown to them. Given this, it should be no surprise that some people cheat on their taxes. Tax evasion is not a violent crime. It is not, however, a victimless crime, although the victims are neither identifiable nor iconic.[3] It is done for financial gain, although in some cases it may arguably be motivated by, or rationalized by, a cause, such as disapproval of what the government is doing with the money, or in protest of the right of the government to collect taxes in the first place. It is large, by IRS estimates $385 billion in 2006, or about 14.5 percent of what should be collected.

Because of the specter of evasion, no government can announce a tax system and then rely on taxpayers' sense of duty to remit what is owed. Some dutiful people would undoubtedly pay what they owe at first, but many others will not. Over time the ranks of the dutiful will shrink, as they see how they are being taken advantage of by the others. Thus paying taxes must be made a legal responsibility of citizens, with penalties attendant on noncompliance. But even in the face of those penalties, substantial tax evasion exists—and always has. And every government has methods in place to deal with evasion, including information collection, audits/surveillance, and penalties.

The tax-systems approach revisits the issue of tax remittance—who writes the checks to cover the tax liability—which is ignored or dismissed in the standard approach. For example, our textbooks assert that a uniform value-added tax (VAT) and a retail sales tax (RST) are really equivalent tax systems. But in reality they are not, because the remittance system—who writes the checks to the government—is different, and this turns out to be a crucial difference that in large part explains why the VAT is the world tax success story of the last half century, adopted by over 140 countries, and why almost no country levies a RST at a rate exceeding 10 percent. In the presence of costly information acquisition (i.e., in all real tax systems), which leads to avoidance and evasion, the cost of administration and enforcement varies depending on the identity of the remitter.

Moving beyond the standard model requires recognition of administrative and compliance costs, and their incorporation into optimal tax analysis. Administrative costs (all those costs incurred by the tax authority in operating a tax system) and compliance costs (those costs imposed on taxpayers by tax-system rules and procedures) affect the operation of tax systems and the set of tax policies that is both feasible and desirable. These costs are not trivial, amounting in the US income tax to as much as 10 percent of the revenue raised.

The broader perspective recognizes that there are multiple margins of behavioral response to tax rates. Moreover, under some assumptions, all are symptoms of excess burden. When higher tax rates send taxpayers to the Internet looking for state tax-free cigarettes, to unscrupulous tax professionals looking for income tax loopholes, or to the Cayman Islands looking for undetectable credit card accounts, the marginal revenue collected relative to private cost is lower. When the tax in question is an income tax, all of these responses (labor supply, avoidance, evasion, etc.) to income tax rate changes are usefully summarized by what has come to be called the elasticity of taxable income (ETI). But the concept applies to *all* tax-rate changes, summarizing all behavioral responses in a tax base elasticity. Under certain assumptions, this tax base elasticity is a sufficient statistic for the marginal efficiency cost of higher tax rates. This is because, at the margin, a taxpayer is willing to sacrifice utility valued at one dollar in order to reduce tax liability by one dollar. This sacrifice can take many forms, such as additional risk bearing due to evasion, expending real resources to identify and execute avoidance schemes, or substitution to activities that are more lightly taxed but otherwise provide less utility. Under some assumptions, we do not need to know whether the behavioral response—which causes the leakage in revenue—is due to evasion, due to avoidance, or due to substitution in order to evaluate the costs to society. All one needs to know is potential tax revenue (assuming no behavioral change) from a change of a parameter of the tax system, and the actual change (taking into account all behavioral responses) in order to evaluate the marginal efficiency cost of raising revenue.

We show that the usual injunction to equate the marginal social cost of net revenue raised across tax instruments extends beyond the choice of tax rates to nonstandard instruments—such as tax base breadth and enforcement effort. In real-world tax systems, governments trade off the social cost of raising revenue from a broad tax base with low tax rates against a narrow tax base with high tax rates. For commodities, broadening the tax base and lowering tax rates reduces the distortion in consumption choices but increases administrative cost, because some goods and services are by their nature harder to tax than others.

The tax-systems perspective recognizes that tighter enforcement is sometimes a more socially desirable way to raise revenue than an increase in statutory tax rates. Increased enforcement raises administrative costs but does not impose a greater burden on compliant taxpayers. It recognizes that equating the marginal cost of enforcement with marginal revenue raised always results in an excessive level of enforcement. Spending a dollar in administrative costs to raise a dollar of revenue can never be optimal. Such a policy raises no revenue on the margin but takes a full dollar of income from taxpayers.

Recognizing that the tax base elasticity can be controlled yields new insight. Avoidance opportunities that could be eliminated at little cost can be desirable if the loss in revenue is small compared to the distributional benefit to a favored group—such as low-income earners. On the other hand, avoidance opportunities exploited predominantly by high-income earners can limit the feasibility of otherwise socially desirable redistribution. Incurring resource cost to eliminate income tax avoidance opportunities is desirable if it reduces the tax base elasticity enough to yield larger net gains in social welfare from increased redistribution because of lower excess burden.

Complexity is of central importance in real-world tax systems. Sometimes it creates an unnecessary compliance burden for taxpayers, but it may also be exploited by taxpayers to obfuscate their affairs and minimize tax liability. However, some complexity is tolerable. It may be preferable to simple tax instruments that lead to capricious tax assessments. Just as retailers use coupons to discriminate between price-sensitive and price-insensitive consumers, complexity in the tax/transfer system can be a powerful policy tool to discriminate between deserving and undeserving transfer program recipients.

In real-world tax systems cognitive limitations affect taxpayers as decision makers. Governments may be able to control taxpayer behavioral response by manipulating the presentation of taxes, for example, by requiring that retailers notify customers about sales taxes at the register rather than at the aisle. Whether or not governments should try to manipulate taxpayer perceptions is a fascinating open question.

The tax-systems approach to taxation recognizes the central role of firms in tax collection, and that it is cost efficient for the tax authority to deal with a small number of business entities with relatively sophisticated accounting and financial expertise rather than a much larger number of employees or providers of capital.

Information is at the heart of modern tax systems—governments seeking to avoid capricious tax burdens can only tax what they can observe—and firms play the main role in modern economies gathering information and making it easily accessible. The low rates of evasion on wage and salary income are due mainly to information reports on employee earnings provided by firms to tax authorities. Inter-firm trade involves market transactions whose observability restrict opportunities for tax evasion (although transactions conducted in cash are much less monitorable). The VAT has been an administrative success in large part because it requires information reports for both sales and purchases. Because one firm's revenues (generating sales tax liability) are another firm's costs (a tax-deductible business expense), evasion incentives are mutually inconsistent.

While what is taxable, and at what rate, is unambiguous in the standard model, the real-world, in-the-trenches scuffling about taxation, as any tax lawyer will know, is all about drawing and interpreting lines. For example, although optimal commodity taxation prescribes a different tax on each good, this is obviously infeasible, especially because modern economies produce a vast amount of different goods, and the set of available goods is constantly evolving. When selective commodity taxation is called for, a non-capricious tax system must have procedures for distinguishing among goods subject to different tax rates. Real-world consumption tax systems do that by appealing to the characteristics of the commodities. For example, the retail sales taxes of US states often exempt food but not restaurant meals, requiring the tax law to draw a line between the two categories; the line can be fine when, for example, grocery stores sell pre-prepared meals that may or may not be eaten on the premises, or set up in-store salad bars.

We recognize that technological progress has the potential to fundamentally change what can be observed and what can be taxed. Electronic smart cards tracking consumer purchases may make feasible a progressive tax on consumption (or at least on purchases). Computer technology has the potential to dramatically simplify tax filing, expanding the degree to which governments can personalize tax burdens at tolerable compliance and administrative cost. However, technology is not a one-way street. Electronic sales suppression software has been used by some firms to evade sales taxes, and the ability of firms and governments to track ever greater aspects of our lives as taxpayers is, to some, an intolerable intrusion into our privacy.

1.4   What Is a Tax System?

A tax system is a set of rules, regulations, and procedures that (1) defines what events or states of the world trigger tax liability (tax bases and rates), (2) specifies who or what entity must remit that tax and when (remittance rules), and (3) details procedures for ensuring compliance, including information-reporting requirements and the consequences (including penalties) of not remitting the legal liability in a timely fashion (enforcement rules).

As suggested above, much of modern economic analysis of taxation, and certainly the seminal contributions, presumes that tax liability can be ascertained and collected costlessly, in which case 2 is irrelevant and case 3 is unnecessary. But this way of modeling taxation misses much that is important about taxes. It cannot address many current tax policy issues—should Greece raise revenue to meet its bailout conditions by raising tax rates, or by cracking down on tax evasion?—explaining why there is often a disconnect between topical tax issues of the day and the economic theory of taxation. And, in our view, it misses much of what is intellectually fascinating about taxes.

This book is motivated by the aspects of reality that the standard model ignores. We began the book with a list of tax phenomena that standard tax analysis struggles to explain. We can state these blind spots more generally now:

1. Although some individuals may remit their tax liability dutifully, others view compliance as a tactical decision and will evade their liabilities if the odds of success seem favorable.

2. Taxpayers will re-arrange their affairs to legally reduce their tax liability, including efforts to reduce their tax liability without altering their real activities, which we will refer to as avoidance.

3. Limiting avoidance and evasion is costly, and tax authorities have limited administrative resources.

4. Tax authorities have limited policy instruments.

5. Taxpayers (and tax policy makers) have cognitive limitations.

6. The world is complex, complicating the collection of non-capricious taxes. Some of the complication is manufactured by taxpayers to obfuscate their affairs, and some exists because the tax system is used to achieve specific social goals in addition to raising revenue.

These issues are especially critical in developing countries, so much so that a former IMF official[4] once opined that in developing countries, "Tax administration *is* tax policy." They are also critical in developed countries, where the operative issue is generally not the feasibility of certain taxes, but rather the comparison of alternative imperfect tax structures. For example, while in many developing countries an income tax that relies on self-reporting cannot be administered with tolerable cost and equity, in a developed country the question is to what extent optimal tax design should reflect the reality of evasion, the necessity of enforcement, and the costs of collection. In addition, an important set of generic aspects of income tax structure, such as the absence of taxation of imputed rents from consumer durables, taxation of capital gains (if at all) on a realization basis, and pre-set depreciation schedules, are undoubtedly largely driven by practical concerns of administrability. For these reasons consideration of evasion, avoidance, and administration is essential to the positive and normative analysis of taxation in *all* jurisdictions.

1.5   Organization and Objectives of the Book

In this book we organize, explicate, and evaluate the modern literature that incorporates these considerations into the economics of taxation. We do not attempt a comprehensive literature review of this topic, and inevitably overemphasize the contributions of the book's authors. Along the way we address both the positive and normative aspects of tax theory, and assess the empirical evidence that sheds light on the theory. To the extent possible, we adopt a common analytical framework that is compatible with modern theory to clarify the relationship

among the various contributions to this field. Part I provides an introduction and motivation, and then goes through some standard results
in optimal tax theory as a framework for what follows.

In part II we lay out the building blocks of tax systems, extending
the standard model in four main ways. In particular, we examine (1)
the implications of there being various types of behavioral responses,
including not only labor supply and choice of consumption goods, but
also evasion and avoidance; (2) the multiple sources of the cost of taxation, looking beyond the standard distortion costs; (3) the promise of a
tax base elasticity as a summary measure of the marginal cost of raising
revenue through higher tax rates; and (4) the central role of information
in taxation, including institutions that economize on it and the implications of limiting tax instruments to retain simplicity.

Part III of the book uses these building blocks to extend our understanding of optimal tax systems. We examine how the considerations
raised in part II affect the standard tax instruments, such as optimal
commodity taxation in the presence of administrative cost, and investigate the optimal use of new tax instruments, such as enforcement
effort. In addition, we investigate the use of these new tax-system
instruments to affect behavioral elasticities—such as the elasticity of
taxable income, the optimal observability and complexity of the tax-
and-transfer system, as well as optimal line drawing in the tax system.

Part IV focuses on the implications for tax policy of rapid changes
in the environment that have important consequences—the information revolution and globalization—and a possible backlash in taxpayer
concerns about privacy. We address some potential new directions in
tax-systems research, and then conclude.

2 Standard Optimal Tax Models

2.1 Preliminaries

Although in this book we expand the scope of tax analysis in many dimensions, we adopt analytical techniques that are standard to public economics. Thus, in our positive modeling, we assume that individuals maximize utility, or expected utility, subject to constraints. In doing so, for the most part we leave aside the fascinating questions raised by behavioral economics, although we refer to these issues in chapter 10. In our normative modeling, we characterize tax systems that maximize the well-being of citizens, either via a stylized representative individual or as a function of all citizens' well-being that obeys the Pareto principle. Readers who are familiar with the basics of optimal tax theory can skip to chapter 3, although at the possible cost of having to return to this chapter to pick up the notation we use.

A benevolent tax-system designer should seek to achieve its objectives with minimal possible damage to the otherwise-efficient functioning of the economy, and subject to the existence of externalities and the distributional objectives of society. This damage goes by many names—efficiency cost, excess burden, distortion, or deadweight loss. In the standard model (without externalities) all taxes other than lump-sum taxes (for which liability is independent of behavior) undermine efficiency because they change relative prices, which in turn induce consumers to select socially suboptimal consumption baskets, or induce firms to produce goods using a socially suboptimal mix of inputs. Consumers and firms substitute away from relatively highly taxed goods and activities to those that are relatively lightly taxed, including leisure. The canonical optimal taxation exercise does one of two things: it (1) describes the tax system that minimizes these costs, subject to constraints on the tax instruments available, or (2) describes the trade-off between these costs and the distribution of welfare among individuals.

The efficiency cost of a tax system is the burden to taxpayers in excess of that imposed by revenue-equivalent lump-sum taxes. The total burden of a tax system is the unavoidable burden—that would be imposed even by nondistorting lump-sum taxes—plus the excess burden. Lump-sum taxes affect behavior via an income effect but do not affect behavior through changes in relative prices. In characterizing optimal policy, we will focus on the social planner's utility maximization problem, noting that with a representative agent this is the same as minimizing the equivalent variation measure of excess burden (denoted EB below)—the amount in dollars a taxpayer would be willing to give up in addition to revenue raised to return to a world without taxes. To see this, first note that following Auerbach (1985), the equivalent variation measure of deadweight loss is

$$EB_{ev}(\theta) = E(0, v(0, A)) - E(0, v(\theta, A)) - R(\theta), \tag{2.1}$$

where $E(0, v)$ is the minimum expenditure needed to achieve the utility level v in a world without taxes, $v(\theta, A)$ is the taxpayer's indirect utility under the tax-system policy vector θ, with exogenous income (e.g., a demogrant) of A, $v(0, A)$ is the taxpayer's indirect utility in the absence of taxes, and R is revenue raised.

The tax-system policy vector that minimizes efficiency cost subject to the exogenous revenue requirement G, that is, the one that solves

$$\min_{\theta} EB_{ev}(\theta) \equiv \min_{\theta} \left[E(0, v(0, A)) - E(0, v(\theta, A)) - R(\theta) \right] \quad \text{s.t.} \quad R(\theta) \geq G, \tag{2.2}$$

is the same policy vector that maximizes the representative taxpayer's utility subject to a revenue requirement

$$\max_{\theta} v(\theta, A) \quad \text{s.t.} \quad R(\theta) \geq G, \tag{2.3}$$

assuming that the expenditure function is strictly increasing in final utility and that the revenue constraint $R(\theta) \geq G$ holds with equality.[1] The revenue constraint binds at an optimum if there exists at least one tax instrument for which a marginal increase in its use raises revenue and reduces the representative taxpayer's utility.[2] Thus minimizing the excess burden of a representative taxpayer yields the same solution as maximizing utility subject to a revenue constraint.

2.2   The Canonical Optimal Taxation Model

With a representative taxpayer, the Lagrangian for the social planner's problem is:

$$L = v(\theta, A) + \lambda[R(\theta) - G]. \tag{2.4}$$

The first-order condition (FOC) for any tax instrument θ_i that has an interior solution is then

$$[\partial \theta_i] \quad \frac{\partial v(\theta, A)}{\partial \theta_i} + \lambda(\theta, A) R_{\theta_i} = 0. \tag{2.5}$$

This simple first-order condition contains the key building blocks of normative tax analysis. First, R_{θ_i} is the derivative of revenue with respect to a tax instrument θ_i. Second, $\lambda(\theta, A)$ is the decline in utility due to a marginal increase in the revenue requirement, often referred to as the social marginal utility cost of public funds.

Next we introduce the function T, which specifies tax liability taking tax policy θ and agents' choice variables as arguments. Now we can rewrite the FOC (2.5) for θ_i as

$$[\partial \theta_i] \quad \frac{\partial v(\theta, A)}{\partial \theta_i} + \lambda[T_{\theta_i} - (T_{\theta_i} - R_{\theta_i})] = 0, \qquad \frac{\partial v}{\partial \theta_i} = -\lambda[T_{\theta_i} - B_{\theta_i}] \tag{2.6}$$

where T_{θ_i} represents the marginal revenue from increasing tax instrument θ_i given no behavioral response by taxpayers. This is sometimes referred to as the "mechanical" relationship between revenue and an aspect of the tax system. Accordingly, $B_{\theta_i} \equiv (T_{\theta_i} - R_{\theta_i})$ measures the marginal revenue consequences of any and all uncompensated behavioral responses to a marginal change in the tax instrument θ_i.

By the envelope theorem, the marginal effect of tax instrument θ_i on utility is simply the direct revenue effect, $\partial v/\partial \theta_i = -\alpha T_{\theta_i}$, where $\alpha \equiv \partial v/\partial A$ is the marginal utility of exogenous income. Hence we can write equation (2.6) and define the marginal efficiency cost of funds (MECF) as

$$[\partial \theta_i] \quad MECF(\theta_i) \equiv \frac{\lambda}{\alpha} = \frac{T_{\theta_i}}{(T_{\theta_i} - B_{\theta_i})} = \frac{1}{1 - (B_{\theta_i}/T_{\theta_i})}. \tag{2.7}$$

In words, the MECF is the social marginal cost of funds, λ, divided by the marginal utility of exogenous income, α. This representation (see Slemrod and Yitzhaki 1996) makes clear the dependence of the social marginal cost of public funds, λ, on the amount of taxpayer behavioral response, B_{θ_i}. If a marginal change in tax instrument θ_i causes no behavioral response, then $B_{\theta_i} = 0$ and MECF(θ_i) is exactly one: θ_i corresponds to a lump-sum tax. The larger the behavioral response, the larger the social marginal cost of public funds. Thus $B_{\theta_i}/T_{\theta_i}$ is a sufficient statistic for the marginal excess burden.

   This general formulation encompasses as special cases the Ramsey commodity tax problem and the optimal linear income tax problem, as we show next. The general rule expressed by equation (2.7) is that, for any tax instrument used, at an optimum its MECF should equal a common value. be Tu sAmL.

2.3   Optimal Commodity Taxation

One of the workhorse models of optimal tax theory characterizes the optimal pattern of taxation of a set of commodities. Although modern optimal tax theory dates from about 1970, this is often called the Ramsey tax problem, because the brilliant polymath Frank Ramsey laid out the solution in an article published in 1927. In the Ramsey problem the goal is to find the set of commodity tax rates that minimizes excess burden, with lump-sum taxes (including uniform ones) excluded by assumption, making the task a problem of the second best.

   Formally, the problem requires finding the commodity taxes on a set of goods $1, 2, \ldots, n$, that minimize excess burden, with good 0 the untaxed numeraire (e.g., leisure). The producer price for good k, q_k, is assumed to be fixed, so the consumer price is $p_k = q_k + t_k$ after the tax has been imposed.[3] This formulation abstracts from administrative or compliance costs, so the only source of excess burden is the distortion in the representative consumer's consumption bundles due to the change in relative prices when taxes are imposed. Letting $\theta = (t_1, \ldots, t_n)$ denote the tax policy, and $c = (c_0, c_1, \ldots, c_n)$ the taxpayer's chosen consumption bundle, the mechanical burden from a marginal increase in the tax rate on good k is $T_{t_k} = c_k$, while the marginal revenue consequence of the behavioral response is $B_{t_k} = -\sum_{i=1}^{n} t_i \left(\partial c_i / \partial t_k \right)$. Using the Slutsky formula, we can decompose the behavioral response further as

$$B_{t_k} = -\sum_{i=1}^{n} t_i \left(s_{ik} - \frac{\partial c_i}{\partial A} c_k \right),$$ (2.8)

where the Slutsky substitution effects $s_{ik} \equiv \partial c_i^h / \partial p_k$ measure the utility–constant marginal change in demand for good i in response to a marginal change in the price of good k. Substituting these expressions into equation (2.7) and re-arranging terms yields

$$-\left[\left(1-\frac{\alpha}{\lambda}\right) - \sum_{i=1}^{n} t_i \frac{\partial c_i}{\partial A}\right] \equiv -\Theta = \sum_{i=1}^{n} \frac{t_i}{c_k} s_{ik} \quad \forall k = 1, \ldots, n. \tag{2.9}$$

Using the symmetry of compensated-demand substitution effects, $s_{ik} = s_{ki}$, we get

$$-\Theta = \sum_{i=1}^{n} \frac{t_i}{c_k} s_{ik} = \sum_{i=1}^{n} \frac{t_i}{c_k} s_{ki} = \frac{\Delta c_k}{c_k} \quad \forall k = 1, \ldots, n, \tag{2.10}$$

where Δc_k is the tax-induced change in demand for good k. This is the Ramsey formula for optimal commodity tax rates. Equation (2.10) states that an optimum requires a set of tax rates θ that equalizes the relative changes in compensated demand for all taxed goods, which follows from the fact that, at an optimum, the marginal excess burden per dollar raised must be equal across all taxed goods. When there are no cross-price demand responses ($\partial c_i / \partial p_k = 0, i \neq k$), the rule reduces to the familiar and simple inverse elasticity formula:

$$\frac{t_k}{p_k} = \frac{1}{\varepsilon_{kk}} \left(\frac{\alpha}{\lambda} - 1\right) \quad \forall k = 1, \ldots, n, \tag{2.11}$$

where ε_{kk} is the uncompensated demand elasticity for good k with respect to an own price change. Note that relative tax rates do not depend on α/λ, but only on the relative value of own elasticities.[4] To minimize excess burden, taxes should be higher on goods with relatively inelastic demand because the behavioral response—the source of excess burden—is lower. But not all tax should be collected from the most inelastically demanded good, because the marginal excess burden per dollar raised increases with each tax rate.

As first shown by Corlett and Hague (1953), further insight can be gained by analyzing the Ramsey problem when there are only three goods: untaxed leisure (good zero) plus two taxed commodities. Specializing equation (2.10) to a three-good world yields

$$\begin{aligned} t_1 s_{11} + t_2 s_{12} &= -\Theta c_1, \\ t_1 s_{21} + t_2 s_{22} &= -\Theta c_2, \end{aligned} \tag{2.12}$$

which, with some rearrangement, becomes

$$t_1 = \Theta\left[\frac{s_{12}c_2 - s_{22}c_1}{s_{11}s_{22} - s_{12}s_{21}}\right],$$

$$t_2 = \Theta\left[\frac{s_{21}c_1 - s_{11}c_2}{s_{11}s_{22} - s_{12}s_{21}}\right]. \tag{2.13}$$

Taking the ratio of the expressions in equation (2.13), replacing the Slutsky substitution terms with compensated elasticities, and using the normalization $p_i = 1 + t_i$ for $i = 1, 2$ leads to the first equality in the following expression:

$$\frac{t_1/(1+t_1)}{t_2/(1+t_2)} = \frac{\varepsilon_{12}^c - \varepsilon_{22}^c}{\varepsilon_{21}^c - \varepsilon_{11}^c}$$

$$= \frac{-(\varepsilon_{11}^c + \varepsilon_{22}^c) - \varepsilon_{10}^c}{-(\varepsilon_{11}^c + \varepsilon_{22}^c) - \varepsilon_{20}^c}, \tag{2.14}$$

with the second equality in (2.14) following from the homogeneity of degree zero in prices of the compensated demand function.[5] Supposing good one is more complementary with leisure than good two $(\varepsilon_{10}^c < \varepsilon_{20}^c)$ leads to an optimal tax rate on good one that is higher than that on good two $(t_1 > t_2)$. For example, good one may be skis and good two food. Taxing skis provides an indirect means of taxing leisure because their demand is more complementary with leisure than is food consumption.[6]

Clearly, the same tax rate on goods one and two is optimal only in the special case where $\varepsilon_{10}^c = \varepsilon_{20}^c$. For this to be true, either labor is in fixed supply $(\varepsilon_{10}^c = \varepsilon_{20}^c = 0)$, or the representative consumers' utility function is homothetic and separable between taxed and untaxed commodities, so the marginal rate of substitution between taxed commodities does not depend on the amount of leisure consumed; in other words, the cross-substitution of leisure is identical for the two taxable goods, $\varepsilon_{10}^c = \varepsilon_{20}^c$. In this case there is nothing to be gained by introducing a distortion between them.

2.4 Optimal Linear Income Tax

The general formulation of this chapter can also yield an expression for the optimal linear income tax rate. To derive this, we must introduce heterogeneous taxpayers, and we make them different on only one dimension, their ability level, and posit that they have otherwise identical utility functions.[7] Letting w_n denote the wage rate for a taxpayer of ability type n, the planner's problem is to choose the vector of tax instruments θ to maximize a social welfare function $W(u_1, u_2, \ldots)$ that is assumed to be individualistic, and strictly increasing and concave in each individual's utility, where the concavity of W determines the social trade-off between the distribution of u_i and the sum of u_i. The Lagrangian for the planner's problem is:

$$L = \int W(v(\theta, A, n)) + \lambda [R(\theta) - G] dF(n),$$ (2.15)

where $F(n)$ is the population cdf of n. Solving the FOC for θ_i yields an expression for the optimal setting of tax instrument θ_i, assuming an interior solution:

$$[\partial \theta_i] \quad \frac{\int (\alpha/\lambda) W' T_{\theta_i} dF(n)}{\int T_{\theta_i} dF(n)} = 1 - \frac{\int B_{\theta_i} dF(n)}{\int T_{\theta_i} dF(n)}.$$ (2.16)

Letting l_n denote labor supply for a type-n taxpayer, suppose the vector of tax instruments θ comprises a linear tax rate on labor income, t, and a demogrant, A, so that a higher t (and therefore generally a higher A) implies a more progressive tax system. Revenue collected from a type n taxpayer is equal to $t w_n l_n - A$. The expressions for the mechanical and behavioral responses to these tax instruments are

$$T_A(n) = -1,$$

$$B_A(n) = -t w_n \frac{\partial l_n}{\partial A},$$

$$T_t(n) = w_n l_n,$$ (2.17)

$$B_t(n) = -t w_n \frac{\partial l_n^c}{\partial t} + t w_n^2 l_n \frac{\partial l_n}{\partial A},$$

where l_n^c is compensated labor supply for a taxpayer of type n, and we have made use of the Slutsky formula. Substituting these expressions into equation (2.16), yields FOCs for A and t:

$$[\partial A] \quad \int \left(W' \frac{\alpha}{\lambda} + t w_n \frac{\partial l_n}{\partial A} \right) dF(n) \equiv \int b_n dF(n) = 1,$$ (2.18)

$$[\partial t] \quad \int w_n l_n \left(W' \frac{\alpha}{\lambda} + t w_n \frac{\partial l_n}{\partial A} - 1 \right) dF(n) = \int t w_n \frac{\partial l_n^c}{\partial t} dF(n),$$ (2.19)

where b_n denotes the social marginal valuation of income, and comprises the effect on social welfare of an exogenous dollar, taking into account the tax consequences of the income on labor supply. Combining these expressions gives the Atkinson and Stiglitz (1980) implicit formula for the optimal linear income tax rate:

$$t = \frac{\int w_n l_n (b_n - 1) dF(n)}{\int w_n (\partial l_n^c / \partial t) dF(n)} = \frac{-\mathrm{cov}(b_n, w_n l_n)}{\int - w_n (\partial l_n^c / \partial t) dF(n)}.$$

(2.20)

The greater the social planner's preference for equality, the more negative is the covariance between the social marginal valuation of income, b_n, and labor income, $w_n l_n$, which implies that the optimal tax rate, t, is higher: more progressivity is optimal. The smaller is the response of (compensated) labor supply, l_n^c, to a change in the marginal income tax rate, the bigger is the optimal linear income tax rate. Equation (2.20) is a concise representation of the inescapable trade-off between (vertical) equity and efficiency in the determination of tax progressivity. Redistribution requires a higher marginal tax rate (that funds a larger demogrant), but the higher marginal tax rate distorts decisions (in this model just labor supply), depending on how large is the (compensated) behavioral response. Ceteris paribus, optimal progressivity is higher the more equality of outcomes is valued by society, and the lower is the behavioral response to the reduced incentive to earning income that a higher marginal tax rate implies. We will refer back to these classic contributions to the optimal taxation literature in part III when we consider jointly setting standard tax instruments together with non-standard tax-system instruments, such as tax base breadth, enforcement effort, and audit probability. Before doing so, in part II we introduce and discuss this new·set of tax-system instruments.

Part II   Building Blocks of Tax Systems

3 Multiple Behavioral Margins

In the standard optimal tax problems of chapter 2, taxation generates efficiency cost, an excess burden, because it distorts what consumption bundle (and perhaps how the consumption goods are produced) is chosen, including how much leisure. Individuals make choices according to relative prices that, because of tax distortions, do not reflect the true social trade-offs. A utility-maximizing consumer naturally substitutes toward relatively low-taxed goods, where leisure is completely untaxed. Although this is privately optimal, it is an unintended consequence of the unavailability of nondistorting, or lump-sum ways, to raise revenue. When taxpayers are heterogeneous and society has distributional concerns, some excess burden may be tolerated as the cost of a more desirable distribution of well-being.

[handwritten marginal note: also to pay for socially desired public inputs]

In what follows we extend that framework to accommodate a particular set of margins that taxes affect but are not emphasized in the classic problems—evasion (illegal means of reducing tax liability) and avoidance (legal means of reducing tax liability).[1]

3.1 Theory of Tax Evasion

No government can expect dutiful compliance with the tax laws by everyone. The history of taxation is in fact replete with episodes of evasion, often notable for their inventiveness. During the third century, many wealthy Romans buried their jewelry or stocks of gold coin to evade the luxury tax, and homeowners in eighteenth-century England temporarily bricked up their fireplaces to escape notice of the hearth tax collector (Webber and Wildavsky 1986). In more modern times some businesses install software "zappers" that randomly exclude sales for the electronic record made by cash registers or other point-of-sale devices.

3.1.1   The Deterrence Model of Tax Evasion

In the presence of tax evasion we need to enrich both the positive model of taxpayer decision-making and the normative model of optimal government behavior. The natural starting point for the former is to consider the costs and benefits of tax evasion. And indeed the standard framework for considering an individual's choice of whether and how much to evade taxes is a deterrence model. This was first formulated in the context of a flat income tax by Allingham and Sandmo (1972), who adapted Becker's (1968) model of criminal behavior to the economics of tax evasion. In this model, which we will refer to as the A-S model (after Allingham and Sandmo), a risk-averse taxpayer decides whether and how much to evade taxes in the same way she would approach any risky decision or gamble—by maximizing expected utility. Note that in this model people are influenced by possible legal penalties no differently than any other contingent cost: there is nothing per se about the illegality of tax evasion that matters. Nor is there any intrinsic willingness to meet one's tax obligations, sometimes referred to as "tax morale."

In the basic A-S model, labor income, wl, is held fixed; the risk-averse taxpayer chooses only what income to report to the tax authority. The taxpayer chooses the amount of understatement, e, to maximize expected utility:

$$\max_{e} (1-p)u(wl(1-t)+te)+pu(wl(1-t)-\pi e), \tag{3.1}$$

where von Neumann-Morgenstern utiv lity, u, is concave, p is the probability that evasion is detected and triggers a penalty of π times the taxable income understatement, $wl(1-t)$ is the taxpayer's true after-tax income, and t is the tax rate. In this model the choice of whether and how much to evade is akin to a choice of whether and how much to gamble. Each dollar of taxable income understatement offers a payoff of t with probability $(1-p)$, along with a penalty of π with probability p. If and only if the expected payoff to this gamble, $(1-p)t-p\pi$, is positive, a risk-averse taxpayer will engage in some evasion, with the amount depending on the expected payoff and the taxpayer's risk preferences. This leads to a FOC of optimal tax evasion:

$$\frac{u'(c_l)}{u'(c_h)}=\frac{t}{\pi}\left(\frac{1-p}{p}\right), \tag{3.2}$$

where c_h is income in the nonaudited state and c_l is income in the audited state. When the expected payoff is positive, imperfect enforcement of the tax law (i.e., $p < 1$) induces the taxpayer to assume risk, which is privately optimal but implies that a given revenue requirement will be collected with a lower expected utility—causing an "excess burden of tax evasion," in the words of Yitzhaki (1987). With income held fixed, the excess burden of tax evasion is the cost of paying taxes with uncertainty rather than certainty:

$$EB = u\big((1-p)c_h + pc_l\big) - \big[(1-p)u(c_h) + pu(c_l)\big]. \tag{3.3}$$

Setting $p = 1$ would eliminate this excess burden but is costly to implement; later we investigate the optimal setting of p.

Soon after the seminal A-S model was formulated, Yitzhaki (1974) pointed out the importance of assuming that the penalty for discovered evasion depends on the *income* understatement, as A-S assume, or on the *tax liability* understatement, as more accurately reflects practice in many countries. In the latter case, the taxpayer's maximand is

$$(1-p)u\big(wl(1-t)+te\big) + pu\big(wl(1-t)-\tilde{\pi}te\big), \tag{3.4}$$

and the expected payoff per dollar of evaded income becomes $(1-p)t - pt\tilde{\pi}$. This is an important change because it implies that the tax rate has no effect on the terms of the tax evasion gamble; as t rises, the reward from a successful understatement of a dollar rises, but the cost of a detected understatement rises proportionately. The first-order condition for optimal evasion becomes

$$\frac{u'(c_l)}{u'(c_h)} = \frac{1}{\tilde{\pi}}\left(\frac{1-p}{p}\right). \tag{3.5}$$

Note that t does not appear in equation (3.5), other than via an income effect in the definition of c_h and c_l. Compare this to equation (3.2), where t is a multiplicative factor in the numerator on the right-hand side, implying that increases in t would increase the reward to getting away with understating income, relative to the penalty, making evasion more attractive.

Regardless of whether the penalty depends on the tax understatement or income understatement, more risk-averse individuals will, ceteris paribus, evade less. Individuals with higher income will evade more as long as absolute risk aversion is decreasing; whether higher income individuals will evade more as a fraction of income depends on relative risk aversion. Evasion relative to income will decrease, increase, or stay unchanged as a fraction of income depending on whether relative risk aversion is an increasing, decreasing, or constant function of income. <u>Increases in either p or the penalty rate will decrease evasion. The theory does not pin down how big these effects are, so it becomes the task of empirical analysis.</u>

Increasing t has both an income effect and, possibly, a substitution effect. If the taxpayer has decreasing absolute risk aversion, the income decline makes a less risky position optimal. An increase in t has a substitution effect, increasing the relative price of consumption in the audited state of the world, and thereby encouraging evasion, if the penalty is related to income rather than tax avoided. Under the Yitzhaki assumption that the penalty is related to the tax evaded, a tax increase has no substitution effect, so that an increase in t *reduces* evasion as long as there is decreasing relative risk aversion.[2] To most people, this is a profoundly unintuitive notion, one that has undoubtedly inspired further theoretical development and empirical analysis.

The assumption of a fixed probability of detection and penalty rate implies that the marginal expected return to evasion is also fixed. In this case a risk-neutral person would either not evade at all or evade as much as possible (report zero tax liability, assuming no tax refunds are provided for reports of negative income), and it is only risk aversion that generates other than all-or-nothing outcomes. In practice, <u>the probability of detection is not fixed, and arguably increases with more aggressive noncompliance because</u> more evasion is more likely to attract the attention of the tax enforcement authorities (and it is probably rational for the authorities to devote more attention to apparently large incidences of evasion).[3] Now risk aversion is no longer needed to generate an interior solution. Assuming risk neutrality simplifies analysis considerably, at the cost of ignoring what is certainly a relevant factor (risk aversion) in tax evasion, especially in explaining across-individual variation.

<u>The basic model does not address the crucial fact that the probability of detection varies by the *type* of evasion contemplated.</u> For example, in many countries with effective third-party information-reporting systems, p is close to one for unreported employee wage income. It is generally much lower, but increasing with the magnitude, for underreported self-employment income. For someone with multiple sources of income, p would rise with the total amount of income evaded as one first underreports those sources with the lowest p, and then moves on to underreport those types of income with higher p.

Depending on the other assumptions about the probability of detection, the penalty structure, and risk aversion, the risk-bearing costs of evasion may be a continuous function that increases with the tax rates. These costs are in addition to the compliance costs voluntarily incurred by an individual attempting to minimize the expected cost by camouflaging the evasion or shifting to an otherwise less remunerative occupation. If taxpayers' evasion behavior responds to changes in marginal tax rates, then any additional risk-bearing cost incurred by taxpayers needs to be taken account of in measuring the deadweight cost of taxation. Chetty (2009) argues that the standard measure of the elasticity of taxable income does not incorporate this additional cost, and so mis-measures welfare cost; we focus on this issue in chapter 5.

When there are private costs incurred for *any* amount of evasion, such as social stigma or social conscience, then the level of evasion is lower than predicted by the A-S model. A fixed cost of compliance may induce some people to not file at all, which usually implies noncompliance but also may deter some individuals from claiming benefits, including tax refunds, they are entitled to. The Allingham–Sandmo model has been extended along many dimensions, some of which we address in what follows.

3.1.2 Labor Supply and the Informal Economy

Of particular interest is the relationship between labor market decisions and tax evasion. It is reasonable to presume that the decision of how much to work is made simultaneously with (or before) the decision about how much income to report, so that it is impossible to adjust labor supply and earned income based on whether one is caught evading.

There are two alternative ways to model this simultaneous choice. One way to proceed is to consider homogeneous labor, and consider the joint problem of how much to work and how much income to report. This is equivalent to simultaneously choosing one's consumption basket (i.e., a goods and leisure pair) and exposure to risk. Then the additional income from working more may come in one of two states of the world—evasion undetected or evasion detected. Thus the first-order condition for labor supply differs from that in a model without tax evasion because it contains mean marginal, instead of marginal, utilities. Whether mean marginal utility is bigger or smaller than marginal utility depends on the sign of the second derivative of marginal utility, which is the sign of the third derivative of the utility function. On top of that, if utility is nonseparable, the marginal utility functions depend on the sign of cross-derivatives, which further complicates the problem.

Even assuming separability between consumption and labor supply—so the cross-derivatives are equal to zero—the effect of a change in the audit probability on labor supply is ambiguous when making standard assumptions about a taxpayer's utility function.[4] Changes in the audit probability affect both the return to work, and the risk of a taxpayer's evasion gamble. The risk aspect is likely to be important when the evasion gamble is large, which in the A-S model occurs when the audit probability and/or penalty rate is low. If the second derivative of utility is negative and the third derivative positive—so taxpayers are both risk averse and "prudent," in the sense of Kimball (1990)—an increase in the audit probability may cause a reduction in labor supply. Intuitively, a prudent taxpayer supplies additional labor to limit the extent to which marginal utility in the audited state exceeds marginal utility in the nonaudited state; an increase in the audit probability reduces the equilibrium amount of uncertainty over after-tax income borne by the taxpayer, and so the amount of precautionary labor supplied. This is closely related to the desirability of cheating incentives in the tax system, which we discuss in chapter 8. In general, labor supply responds to enforcement of the income tax, so identifying labor supply elasticities from tax-rate changes will be biased if simultaneous changes in enforcement are ignored.

A second way to proceed is to recognize that much tax evasion is tied to the underground, or informal, economy. In situations where labor income in the formal sector is reported by the employer to the tax enforcement agency as a matter of course (so p is close to one), the only way to evade tax may be by "moonlighting"—working extra hours for oneself at a different job—or by switching completely to the informal sector. The A-S model can be easily modified to yield a stylized description of the choice between formal and informal sector work. Supposing that the taxpayer receives a wage rate w_f for formal sector work and $w_i < w_f$ for informal sector work, and that the total amount of labor she supplies to the formal and informal sectors is inelastic, the taxpayer's choice reduces to how much labor to supply to the formal sector, l_f, and how much to supply to the informal sector, l_i. Income in the formal sector is taxed at the statutory rate, t, and cannot be evaded, while informal sector income is untaxed unless detected by a random audit, in which case it is subject to taxation and penalty. The taxpayer's maximization problem is

$$\max_{\{l_f, l_i\}} (1-p)u(w_f l_f (1-t)+w_i l_i)+pu(w_f l_f(1-t)+w_i l_i (1-t)-\pi w_i l_i), \quad (3.6)$$

subject to the constraint $l_f + l_i = l$. Substituting in the constraint, the taxpayer's problem can be relabeled to resemble a standard A-S model:

$$\max_{e} (1-p)u(w_f l(1-t)+\hat{t}e)+pu(w_f l(1-t)-\hat{\pi}e), \quad (3.7)$$

where $w_f l$ is income when the full labor endowment is employed in formal sector work, informal sector work is relabeled as evasion, $e = l_i$, $\hat{t} = w_i - w_f (1-t)$ is the tax saving on evasion via informal sector work, and $\hat{\pi} = (1-t)(w_f - w_i)+\pi w_i$ is the effective penalty rate on evasion. This representation closely resembles the standard A-S maximization problem of equation (3.1), making it straightforward to analyze a taxpayer's informal sector labor supply decision. Provided that $(1-p)\hat{t} > p\hat{\pi}$, the expected value of evasion via informal sector work is positive and a risk-averse taxpayer will engage in at least some informal sector work. However, because $\hat{\pi} > 0$, informal sector work raises income risk, so a risk-averse taxpayer will in general not be driven to a corner solution, working only in the informal sector, and instead will split her labor supply between the two sectors.

The formal and informal sectors may differ in other ways. Kesselman (1989) develops a set of general equilibrium models in which there are two sectors—aboveground and underground—that produce two distinct goods. Workers are homogeneous in their gross productivity in each sector of the economy (and in their consumption preferences), but must work only in one sector or the other. The workers, though, have differential risk aversion and inherent distaste for tax evasion, as well as differential efficiency in concealment and other skills needed to operate successfully in the underground economy. Although the precise results are model-dependent, three general conclusions obtain: (1) much of the gain from evasion may be shifted from the evaders to the consumers of output through lower prices, and the "marginal" evader gains nothing; (2) relative price effects tend to dampen the impact of tax-rate changes on the extent of evasion; and (3) the effects of evasion on the marginal revenue response to tax-rate changes will depend on consumers' elasticity of substitution between the sectoral outputs.

A key aspect of the foregoing model is that the act of tax evasion is tightly tied to the production of a distinct good.[5] This need not be true, as is indicated by the simultaneous presence of formal and informal housepainters, repair people, and so on. Still there is certainly evidence that evasion is concentrated in particular sectors, such as those that supply services directly to homeowners, because of the small scale of production that can aid concealment and the lesser need for receipts compared to services provided to businesses.[6]

3.1.3   Business Tax Evasion

How much of this framework applies to tax compliance decisions made by businesses? Most of it does for the case of small, single-owner businesses, and indeed the A-S model has been applied to business tax compliance and its relationship to output decisions in, for example, Lee (1998). Interestingly, Joulfaian (2000) finds evidence that corporate income tax evasion is related to managerial preference. For a 1987 sample of firms with assets less than $10 million chosen at random for audit, he finds that noncompliant firms were three times more likely to be managed by executives understating their personal income taxes than were compliant firms.

The applicability of the A-S model to big business is less clear. Arguably, large public companies should act as if they are risk-neutral, rather like the risk-averse decision makers in the A-S model. If true we must look elsewhere for what constrains positive-expected-value evasion. Some firms might be concerned that publicized tax aggressiveness might turn off some potential customers who would prefer to deal with civic-minded companies. Facing public pressure over its alleged corporate tax minimization practices, Starbucks announced in December 2012 that it would voluntarily remit about $16 million more to the United Kingdom tax authority than legally required.[7] Starbucks probably hoped for a more positive reaction to their announcement than the protests it sparked at several dozen stores.

On the other hand, some investors might take tax aggressiveness as a signal that a company is optimally aggressive both in its dealings with the tax authority but also with suppliers and customers (but not investors themselves). Hanlon and Slemrod (2009) look at the stock-market response to publicized tax aggressiveness to sort out empirically these two concerns of public corporations, finding that on average stock prices decline when news about involvement in tax shelters becomes public. Stock price falls tend to be larger for retail-sector firms, which Hanlon and Slemrod (2009) suggest may be due to a possible consumer/taxpayer backlash, while the reaction is less negative for firms with higher cash-effective tax rates, which they see as being consistent with the market rewarding tax aggressiveness.

Furthermore, in large, publicly held corporations, decisions about tax compliance are not made by the shareholders directly, but instead by their agents: a chief financial officer or the vice president for taxation. To align the incentives of the decision makers and the shareholders, a corporation should tie the agent's compensation to observable outcomes that affect after-tax corporate profitability. But because a given effective tax rate can be achieved by both (legal) avoidance or (illegal and punishable) evasion, a "hidden action" or "hidden information" problem can arise between shareholders and tax departments; remuneration contracts based on what is observable to a corporate board, such as the effective corporate tax rate, may create incentives for tax directors to engage in tax fraud at shareholders' expense. Survey evidence of tax directors in Fortune 1000 companies indicates that the effective tax rate is the most important factor driving their department's overall objectives, substantially more likely to be cited than compliance (Slemrod 2004a). Applying penalties for corporate tax fraud to executives as well as shareholders may deter managers from engaging in fraud, but from the firm's perspective, the optimal remuneration contract will, in general, not eliminate evasion because doing so limits the willingness of employees to pursue legal avoidance opportunities. However, Crocker and Slemrod (2005) show that when penalties for evasion apply to the agent (i.e., the executive), the principal (i.e., the shareholders) can alter the ex ante compensation contract with the agent, possibly offsetting the intended consequences of the IRS policy.[8] The conclusion that enforcement strategies directed at the tax director and at the corporation itself may have different impacts on corporate behavior is especially pertinent in light of the Sarbanes–Oxley Act of 2002 that made important changes to the responsibility for misreporting, including requiring that the chief executive officer sign the company's federal income tax return.

3.1.4   Nonstandard Theories: Beyond Deterrence
Some social scientists have argued that the A-S deterrence framework misses important elements of the tax evasion decision, and question some of its central assumptions, including that (1) nothing per se about its illegality matters, and (2) everyone acts as a free rider, so that there is no issue of intrinsic willingness to pay, or "tax morale." Some have gone further to suggest that, in thinking about tax evasion, it is necessary to abandon the standard expected utility maximization model and incorporate "behavioral" considerations.

The models that abandon one or both of these assumptions take different tacks. One approach stresses that some people may fully comply with their legal obligation because of a sense of civic duty regardless of, or in addition to, the possible pecuniary gains and argue that the tendency to perform one's duty is susceptible to aspects of the enforcement process. Indeed, Frey (1997) argues that imposing more punitive enforcement policies may crowd out the "intrinsic" motivation to comply by making people feel that they pay taxes because they *have* to, rather than because they *want* to.

Another approach suggests that rather than behaving as free riders, some individuals' behavior depends on the process by which the tax and tax enforcement system are formulated and its features, holding constant the incentives the system provides. For example, they may be more willing to comply with a system whose formulation they had a part in through voting; compliance may be lowered by the imposition of an unpopular program, as investigated in a lab-experiment setting by Alm, Jackson, and McKee (1992).[9]

Taxpayer attitudes toward authority may also influence compliance behavior. Tyler (2006) argues that citizens are more likely to be law-abiding if they view legal authorities as legitimate. Interestingly, though, the degree of legitimacy may itself be a function of the level of enforcement. When explicit enforcement is weak (e.g., few audits), legitimacy may erode, undermining the intrinsic willingness of taxpayers to comply with the law. Separate from perceptions of legitimacy, Tyler (2006) highlights the role of personal morality in affecting compliance behavior. People may be willing to comply with a law because they perceive it to be just, quite aside from their beliefs about the authority government has to enforce it. Such individual judgments can be complex; for example, expenditures on warfare might contribute to a sense of fairness tolerated in a patriotic period, but rejected during another period characterized by anti-militarism.[10]

Levi (1998, p. 91) stresses the role of a form of reciprocal altruism in which some taxpayers' behavior depends on the behavior, motivations, and intentions not of any subset of particular individuals, but of the government itself: when citizens believe that the government will act in their interests, that its procedures are fair, and that their trust of the state and others is reciprocated, then people are more likely to become "contingent consenters" who cooperate in paying taxes even when their short-term material interest would make free riding the individual's best option.

Much of the evidence related to these nonstandard behaviors comes from how people react to other people, as in lab experiments. But the psychological attitudes of individuals toward government might be fundamentally different than their attitudes toward other people, or even other organizations. Individuals might feel more dutiful and even obedient toward government. Invocation of the word *obedience*, though, invokes a darker side of the relationship between individuals and government as an authority figure. Indeed, notorious experiments conducted by the Yale University psychologist Stanley Milgram (1963), showed that unwitting subjects were willing to deliver what they thought were substantial electric shocks when instructed to, and encouraged to, by authority figures. We return to this issue in chapter 10.

3.2   Empirical Analysis of Tax Evasion

The positive theories of tax evasion suggest what factors determine the extent and nature of evasion as well as its responsiveness to policy. Within the deterrence model only a small set of factors matter: (1) the (possibly endogenous) probability of getting caught and penalized for evading, conditional on taxpayer behavior; (2) the penalty for detected evasion, conditional on taxpayer behavior; (3) (in some models) the marginal tax rate; and (4) the risk aversion of the taxpayer. Nondeterrence models allow for a range of other factors to matter, such as tax morale, perceptions of fairness, altruism, and attitudes toward authority.

Neither type of model, though, pins down either the magnitude of evasion or, more important, how it depends on the policy environment, calling for empirical analysis. Alas, determining the extent of evasion—much less its responsiveness to policy—is not straightforward, for two perhaps obvious reasons. For one thing, the dividing line between illegal tax evasion and legal tax avoidance is blurry. Under US law, for example, tax evasion refers to a case where a person, through commission of fraud, unlawfully pays less tax than the law mandates. Tax evasion is a criminal offense under federal and state statutes, subjecting a person convicted to a prison sentence, a fine, or both. An overt act is necessary to give rise to the crime of income tax evasion; therefore the government must show willfulness and an affirmative act intended to mislead. The legal definitions vary across countries. Some tax understatement is, however, inadvertent error, due to ignorance of or confusion about the tax law (as is some overpayment of taxes).

Although the theoretical models of this issue generally refer to willful understatement of tax liability, the empirical analyses cannot precisely identify the taxpayers' intent and therefore cannot precisely separate the willful from the inadvertent. Nor can they, in complicated areas of the tax law, precisely distinguish the illegal from the legal. Although the term tax evasion generally refers to willful illegal behavior, the difficulty of identifying this behavior is reflected in the varying terms analyses refer to, such as evasion, noncompliance, misreporting, and the tax gap.

The biggest challenge for empirical analysis is measuring evasion. We turn to this issue next.

3.2.1   Methodological Approaches

Tax evaders' concealment activities make empirical analysis of evasion particularly challenging. The threat of punishment and perhaps social shame make taxpayers unwilling to respond accurately to surveys, so thorough investigations by tax authorities, which we discuss in the next chapter, are a promising approach to approximating the true extent of evasion. Because the data and results from randomized audits are typically unavailable to researchers, a range of indirect means have been followed in the literature. Slemrod and Weber (2012) argue that much can be learned from a combination of creative empirical methods and restrictions drawn from tax evasion theory.

What Slemrod and Weber (2012) dub the "traces-of-income" approach makes progress by looking for a variable correlated with true income, allowing the researcher to predict true income and back out the extent of evasion by comparing the prediction to taxpayers' reports. Pissarides and Weber (1989), who pioneered this approach, used UK Family Expenditure Survey data on food consumption to estimate the extent of evasion. Assuming that only the self-employed evade, and that the relationship between food consumption and true income is independent of employment status, they are able to predict true income—and therefore underreporting—for the self-employed survey respondents. Assuming income reports in the survey match those given to the tax authority, they estimate that self-employed people in the United Kingdom on average underreported their income by about one-third.

The same traces-of-evasion approach has been used by Gorod-nichenko et al. (2009) to estimate the effect of Russia's 2001 flat tax reform on the extent of evasion. Using household panel data containing reports on consumption, income, and a range of household character-istics, they estimate an observed consumption–income gap function (as a trace of evasion) for each household, and then use a difference-in-difference technique to estimate the effect of the tax reform on the consumption–income gap. Their treatment group consists of high-income households experiencing a decline in marginal tax rates from either 31 percent or 21 percent to the same 13 percent marginal tax rate faced by a low-income control group before and after the tax change. A nice feature of their identification technique involves running the reform in reverse: they group taxpayers into treatment and control groups using post- rather than pre-reform reported income, sidestep-ping the endogeneity between treatment–control group assignment and marginal tax rates because all taxpayers face the same constant marginal rate after 2001. To remove the influence of transitory income fluctuations—which the permanent income hypothesis implies will have little influence on current consumption—they use reported con-tractual earnings rather than reported current income in their analysis. Gorodnichenko et al. (2009) estimate a striking effect of lower marginal tax rates on voluntary compliance: the consumption–income gap fell by 10 to 11 percent more for the treatment group, whose tax rates declined, than the control group. This they interpret as a relative increase in reported income by those whose tax rate declined. Notably, the consumption–income gap fell by about 17 percent for the control group despite no change in marginal tax rates, suggesting an improve-ment in tax enforcement practices accompanying the change in tax rates, although the authors found no clear evidence that the decline was due to changes in tax administration. Separately estimating the impact of the tax change on consumption (rather than the consump-tion–income gap) Gorodnichenko et al. (2009) estimate a small −0.044 elasticity of labor income with respect to the marginal tax rate, com-pared to an evasion elasticity of 0.376. The welfare effects of the flat tax reform depend critically on the extent to which tax evasion has a real resource cost rather than being simply a transfer. The authors' pre-ferred calibration attributes half of the private marginal cost of evasion to transfer costs, and about half of the estimated total welfare gain from the tax reform to reduced evasion.

Traditionally income reports in household surveys have been treated as free of systematic misreporting, largely because underreporting income on a survey does not change tax liability. However, Hurst et al. (forthcoming) argue that the benefit to a noncompliant individual household of reporting accurately is so small that even a slight probability that their report is not confidential could result in underreporting. Using essentially the same methodology as Pissarides and Weber (1989), Hurst et al. (forthcoming) estimate that the self-employed underreport income in both the Consumer Expenditure Survey and the Panel Study of Income Dynamics by about 30 percent. They point out that failure to take account of income underreporting by the self-employed in household surveys can lead to bias in a wide range of situations, such as comparisons in income across municipalities that differ in the share of self-employed workers, in studies of life-cycle earnings because self-employment probabilities differ over the life cycle, or in comparisons of wealth holdings for wage earners and the self-employed.

Feldman and Slemrod (2007) follow a similar approach, but avoid the need to use survey data by instead using charitable giving as reported on income tax returns relative to reported income as the trace of evasion. They find that, other things equal, reported positive self-employment income of $1 is associated with the same level of contributions as $1.54 of wage and salary income, which implies—assuming a negligible wage and salary noncompliance rate and that the self-employed are not inherently more charitable than others—a self-employment noncompliance rate of 35 percent; for positive farm net income, the implied noncompliance rate is 74 percent. Intriguingly, negative reported values for self-employment income are also associated with more contributions than reported by taxpayers with no self-employment income, suggesting that on average these reported losses are associated with *higher* true incomes.[11]

Financial sector development is typically thought to facilitate tax compliance by generating a paper trail that can be accessed by the tax authority to enforce compliance. However, Artavanis et al. (2012) use household microdata from one of ten large banks in Greece to show that on average self-employed Greek workers spend 82 percent of their reported monthly income servicing debt, far exceeding the 30 percent rule-of-thumb maximum used by many banks in determining credit worthiness. Strikingly, they find a slight negative correlation between delinquency rates and the ratio of monthly debt repayments to reported income, providing compelling evidence of hidden income. Because financial sector formalization coexists with widespread underreporting of income, Artavanis et al. (2012) argue that southern European banks have had to become skilled at inferring true income from reported income in order to remain competitive. Using this insight, they employ econometric techniques to estimate the extent of underreported income for self-employed Greek workers by type of occupation. Based on the assumption that income is accurately reported for wage earners, they estimate a credit supply equation for wage earners using reported income, hard information (e.g., credit history, borrower characteristics), and soft information (e.g., local economic growth) available to the bank. Supposing this credit supply equation to be valid for self-employed workers, they infer the "multipliers" that the bank implicitly applies to reported self-employment income. For doctors, lawyers, engineers and scientists, and accountants and financial service agents, their estimated multipliers are greater than two, indicating that for these professions reported income is less than half of true income as inferred by the bank. This too may be an underestimate if the bank applies a discount for any additional income or collection risk assessed, or if the credit supply equation is biased because a multiplier is also applied to wage earners' reported income because of employee evasion.

Actions that only make sense for evaders may be used, under certain circumstances, to infer measures of noncompliance. Slemrod and Weber (2012) offer the nontax example of radar detectors used by speeding motorists to avoid detection: law-abiding motorists have no incentive to invest in a radar detector; however, not all speeders own a radar detector, so measuring the stock of radar detectors is unlikely to estimate the full extent of noncompliance. Indeed, if a "trace of evasion" is too good an indicator, it is likely to be subject to a presumptive tax or some form of deterrent, reducing its use in equilibrium and so its informativeness for measuring noncompliance.

In contrast to indirect means of inquiry, randomized field experiments can offer compelling evidence on the causal impact of particular policy interventions. In one of the first examples of applying this method to tax evasion research, Slemrod et al. (2001) conducted an experiment in Minnesota, sending a treatment group of taxpayers a letter warning them that their tax returns would be "closely examined." Kleven et al. (2011) have since conducted a similar, but more comprehensive, study in Denmark. They conclude that threat-of-audit letters (and prior audits) have a significant positive effect on self-reported (but not third-party-reported) income.

Despite the unrivaled internal validity of well-designed randomized control trials, it is not always clear that the results can be "scaled up." General equilibrium effects may matter, and without understanding the causal channels through which policy interventions affect taxpayers' behavior, it may not be possible to predict the effect of variations in the policy intervention without running repeated experiments. In addition some interventions that are credible in an experimental setting may not be credible in an economy-wide setting. For example, Kleven et al. (2011) sent treatment groups 50 percent probability and 100 percent probability audit threat letters, which taxpayers would know to be prohibitively expensive were either of these treatments expanded to the entire population. Lab experiments provide a less expensive means to evaluate a wide range of policy interventions and to control the environment more precisely, but suffer from the drawback that subjects—usually students—may not respond in the same way in the lab as they, or a more representative sample of taxpayers, would if the same interventions were implemented in reality.

3.2.2 Aggregate Evasion

The most careful and comprehensive estimates of the extent and nature of tax noncompliance anywhere in the world have been made for the federal taxes that the US Internal Revenue Service (IRS) oversees. Beginning in 1979, the IRS has periodically estimated what it calls the "tax gap," meaning how much tax should be remitted, but is not remitted voluntarily in a timely way. These studies provide separate estimates of the failure to remit the proper amount of tax due to underreporting of tax due on tax returns, nonfiling, and nonpayment or late payment of taxes owed. The IRS comes up with its estimates by combining information from a program of random intensive audits, originally known as the Taxpayer Compliance Measurement Program (TCMP) but now called the National Research Program (NRP), with information obtained from ongoing enforcement activities and special studies about sources of income such as tips and cash earnings of informal suppliers like nannies and housepainters that can be difficult to uncover even in an intensive audit. To correct for the errors potentially introduced by variability in auditor judgment, the recent tax gap studies make use of a correction procedure originally developed by Feinstein (1991).[12]

Table 3.1 presents the latest IRS tax gap figures, which apply to the 2006 tax year, based on the NRP study for the individual income tax and

Table 3.1
Tax gap components, tax year 2006 ($billion)

Estimated total tax liability	2,660
Gross tax gap	450
Nonfiling	28
Underpayment	46
Underreporting gap	376
Individual income	235
Nonbusiness income	68
Business income	122
Adjustments, deductions, exemptions	17
Credits	28
Corporation income tax	67
Small (less than $10m total assets)	19
Large (more than $10m total assets)	48
Employment tax	72
Estate tax	2
Enforcement and other late payments of tax	65
Net tax gap	385

Source: IRS (2012c)

estimates extrapolated from earlier studies for other taxes. The overall gross tax gap estimate is $450 billion, which amounts to 16.9 percent of estimated actual (paid plus unpaid) tax liability. Of the $450 billion estimate, the IRS expected to eventually recover $65 billion through its enforcement and collection activities, resulting in a "net tax gap"—that is the tax not collected—for tax year 2006 of $385 billion, which is 14.5 percent of the tax that should have been remitted (IRS, 2012c).

No other country has undertaken as broad-based an analysis of tax evasion as the US effort. Australia, Canada, Sweden, and the United Kingdom have in place small-scale random audit programs for selected taxes and taxpayer groups, but detailed results of these programs are generally not published (although they presumably inform their tax agencies' risk management assessments and resource allocation decisions). The Swedish Tax Agency (2004) estimated its total gap as a percentage of taxes to be 9 percent in 1997 and 8 percent in 2000. Although no official UK estimate has been released, an official document did speculate that "it is likely that the United Kingdom has a tax gap of a similar magnitude" to that of Sweden and the United States (O'Donnell 2004).

Although the TCMP-NRP analyses are certainly the world's most comprehensive and probably the most reliable, they are not immune from caveats. Some types of noncompliance are inherently difficult to measure, in particular business activity that is off the books and conducted in cash. Based on interviews of small business owners, accountants, and bankers, Morse et al. (2009) argue that many small businesses run parallel cash economies, collecting sales receipts in cash, paying for expenses in cash, and spending the cash profits rather than making a bank deposit. We discuss their findings in more detail in section 6.3.

Estimates of noncompliance with value-added tax are in the same ballpark. According to a confidential study made in 2005 by the Forum on Tax Administration, a subsidiary body of the OECD's Committee on Fiscal Affairs, noncompliance ranged from 4.0 to 17.5 percent of tax owed. These estimates are generally based on "top-down" exercises, which compare actual revenues from the value-added tax to a theoretical tax base and tax amount derived by examining consumption expenditure adjusted to account for factors that impact the base for the value-added tax (e.g., tax policy choices concerning goods that are exempt from the value-added tax, or that are subject to different rates). A recent report from the United Kingdom suggests a gap for its value-added tax in 2009 to 2010 of 13.8 percent, having averaged 13.7 percent over the period 2002–2003 to 2008–2009 (HM Revenue and Customs 2011). The UK reports claim to have validated their top-down estimates with "bottom-up" estimates based on examination of tax returns filed (and not filed), but the details of this procedure have not been published. Earlier studies across Europe found a wide range of estimated noncompliance rates for the value-added tax (Agha and Haughton 1996): from 2 to 4 percent for revenue forgone for the United Kingdom in 1986 (Tait 1988), 40 percent of revenue uncollected in Italy (Pedone 1981), 6 percent for the Netherlands in 1976, and 8 percent for Belgium in 1980 (Oldman and Woods 1983). Silvani and Brondolo (1993) report calculations of the net evasion rate for the value-added tax in 19 mostly developing countries and report a median evasion rate of 31.5 percent, with New Zealand the lowest at 5.1 percent and Peru the highest at 68.2 percent.

Finally, there are voluminous cross-country estimates of the extent of what is referred to alternatively as the shadow, irregular, underground, informal, or black economy. Although the definition of the shadow economy is often not precise, it typically entails the production and distribution of services that are not illegal per se but become unlawful either by tax evasion or the bypassing of regulations. The underground economy is generally measured as a fraction of GDP, not tax liability, and would include business activity that is not subject to regulations, but that does not generate taxable income. It also excludes some forms of tax evasion such as the overstatement of deductions and credits, and the use of sophisticated tax shelters. Despite these definitional differences, the underreporting of business income, particularly proprietor income, that is the focus of estimates of the underground economy, comprises a significant fraction of the estimated tax gap even in the United States.

The methodology for estimating the underground economy generally relies on inferring the level or trends in the underground economy from data on measurable quantities, such as currency demand, electricity consumption, or national income accounts. For example, Feige (1989) estimates the size of the underground economy by assuming that most unreported economic activity takes place in cash, and that there is a "base year" when the underground economy did not exist. Similarly Tanzi (1980, 1983) pioneered a methodology based on regressions explaining the ratio of currency to money more broadly defined as M2, and interpreting the portion of this ratio explained by changes in the tax level as an indication of changes in the size of the underground economy. It is very difficult to verify the accuracy of these estimates, and even Tanzi (1999, p. F340) has said that "as long as the estimates remain as divergent as they have been, they cannot provide much of a guidance for policy...." Schneider (2005) has compiled the most comprehensive set of estimates of the informal economy based on a methodology of which Breusch (2005) has presented a compelling critique. As elaborated on in Slemrod and Weber (2012), these studies may say more about the relative extent of the shadow economy, and even then only with limited reliability across time and countries, than about its magnitude.

3.2.3   Tax Evasion by Income Source

Table 3.1 breaks down the aggregate NRP estimate of the 2006 tax gap into its components. About two-thirds of all underreporting of income derives from the individual income tax. For the individual income tax, understated income—as opposed to overstating of exemptions, deductions, adjustments, and credits—accounts for over 80 percent of individual underreporting of tax. Business income, as opposed to wages or investment income, accounts for about half of the underreported individual income. Taxpayers who were required to file an individual tax return, but did not, accounted for slightly less than 10 percent of the individual income tax gap. While the individual income tax comprises about two-thirds of the estimated underreporting, the corporation income tax and the employment tax gap each make up about one-fifth of total underreporting.

A striking and important feature of the data is the huge variation in the rate of misreporting as a percentage of actual income by type of income (or offset). According to the IRS analysis, only 1 percent of wages and salaries are underreported, and 8 percent of income sources such as taxable interest and dividends are misreported. (These percentages exclude underreporting associated with nonfiling.) Of course, wages and salaries, interest, and dividends must all be reported to the IRS by those who pay them out; in addition, wages and salaries are subject to employer withholding. Self-employment business income is not subject to information reports or withholding, and its estimated noncompliance rate is sharply higher. An estimated 56 percent of nonfarm proprietor income, rents, royalties, and other income subject to little or no information reporting is not declared, comprising a total of $120 billion, which by itself accounts for about one-third of total estimated underreporting.

Together with indirect evidence on noncompliance discussed earlier, there is compelling evidence that the extent of evasion for sole proprietor income is very high compared to such income sources as wages, salaries, interest, and dividends, and may be more than half of true income. This variation provides, in our view, overwhelming evidence for the explanatory power of the deterrence model. It also shows convincingly the fallacy behind perhaps the most common justification for looking beyond deterrence—that it predicts a compliance rate much lower than what we actually observe. For example, Feld and Frey (2002, p. 5) assert that it is "impossible to account for tax compliance in terms of expected punishment." The dismissive argument goes something like the following: given the average probability of audit (in the United States recently less than 1 percent for individual returns with no business income), the penalties typically assessed for noncompliance (typically 20 percent of the amount underpaid in the United States), and what we know about the degree of risk aversion from other contexts, according to the A-S deterrence model noncompliance should be much higher than it apparently is. Thus the argument continues, something other than deterrence must be restraining people from evading taxes.

But this dismissive argument is not persuasive because the low overall audit coverage rate vastly understates the chances that evasion of the predominant kind of income would be detected. A wage or salary earner whose employer submits the employee's taxable income and Social Security number electronically to the IRS, but who does not report that income on his own personal return, will be flagged for further scrutiny with a probability close to 100 percent rather than close to 1 percent. These varying rates of the chance of detection are certainly broadly consistent with the evidence, discussed above, of very low noncompliance rates (about 1 percent) for wages and salaries and much higher rates (over 50 percent) for self-employment income. The central role of information reporting is reinforced by IRS data that shows that components of taxable income for which information reports are non-existent or of limited value, such as other nonwage income and tax credits, have relatively high estimated misreporting rates. IRS (2012c) reports that the net misreporting rate is 56, 11, and 8 percent for income types subject to "little or no," "some," and "substantial" information reporting, respectively, and is just 1 percent for those amounts subject to both withholding and substantial information reporting. These relative magnitudes are absolutely consistent with the deterrence model. Some (e.g., Andreoni et al. 1998, pp. 821–22, 850–52) suggest that, given the low chance of detection, a net misreporting rate of *only* 56 percent for income with little or no information reports suggests there are non-deterrence reasons for compliance. But recall that this noncompliance rate estimate is especially subject to error.

The reason to take nondeterrent theories seriously is thus *not* because the deterrence model grossly mis-predicts the magnitude of tax evasion. It is rather because there is considerable experimental (and anecdotal) evidence that there is more to tax evasion than the amoral cost–benefit calculation of the deterrence model. We will return to that issue later in this chapter.

3.2.4   Which Individuals Evade?

One intriguing question is how the level of noncompliance, and its proportion to income, varies by income class. Johns and Slemrod (2010) investigate this issue for the United States using data from the 2001 National Research Program (NRP), which contain the results of stratified random audits of about 45,000 tax returns conducted by the IRS. The net misreporting percentage—the sum of all income misreported, including possible overreporting, divided by true income as assessed by the IRS—rises steadily with true income, peaking at 21 percent for incomes in the range of one-half to one million dollars, and declines thereafter.

In contrast, the ratio of underreported tax to true tax liability declines sharply with true income, largely as a consequence of the progressivity of the tax code. As Johns and Slemrod (2010) explain, for multimillionaires the share of income understated and the share of tax understated will be roughly equal because the vast bulk of their income is subject to the top marginal tax rate, so that marginal and average tax rates are roughly equal. In contrast, low-income earners understating their true income by the same percentage may be pushed into a lower tax bracket and may benefit from additional credits, so their tax understatement rises more than proportionally with their income understatement. For example, a small amount of underreporting may result in a low-income taxpayer owing no tax on her reported income, in which case underreported tax is 100 percent of true tax liability even though the value of tax evaded is small.

The finding that noncompliance rises with true income raises the question whether this is due to high-income earners being more likely to receive income types that are, on average, more likely to be underreported or because high-income earners are more likely to misreport on the income types they receive. Breaking the NRP data down by tax return line item, Johns and Slemrod (2010) find that, although misreporting by line item is generally greater for high-income earners, the bulk of the variation in overall misreporting by income can be accounted for by high-earners receiving more of their income in forms that are understated by all income groups, such as business income on Schedule C and long-term capital gains.

Tax noncompliance also seems related to some other observable characteristics of taxpayers. According to Andreoni et al. (1998, pp. 821–22), married filers and taxpayers younger than 65 have significantly higher average levels of noncompliance than others, and econometric studies by Clotfelter (1983) and Feinstein (1991) that control for income and marginal tax rates come to similar conclusions. Baldry (1987) found evidence in an experimental setting that men evade more than women. Kleven et al. (2011) find that being employed in sectors prone to informal activity and working in a small firm are positively associated with noncompliance, but that these and other socioeconomic factors are much less important predictors of evasion than indicators proxying information flows between taxpayers and the tax authority, such as the presence of self-employment income.

There also seems to be substantial heterogeneity in tax evasion. The NRP studies concluded that within any group defined by income, age, or other demographic category, there are some who evade, some who do not, and even some who overstate tax liability. For example, for taxpayers with reported income between $50,000 and $100,000 in 1988, 60 percent understated tax, 26 percent reported correctly, and 14 percent overstated tax (Christian 1993–94, p. 39).

3.2.5 Business Tax Noncompliance

The evidence we have discussed points to substantial noncompliance among small businesses that are audited infrequently and whose income is subject to neither information reporting nor withholding. But what about big businesses? The IRS estimates a noncompliance rate of 17 percent for the corporate income tax and claims that the noncompliance rate is lower for larger companies (those with over $10 million of assets), 14 percent compared to 29 percent for corporations with less than $10 million of assets (Slemrod 2007).[13]

What should we make of this finding? First, note that the figures for the large corporations are for the most part based on operational, rather than randomized, audits, and because most big corporations are routinely audited, some caveats apply to the tax gap estimates they generate. The deficiencies proposed by the examination team are not a perfect measure of actual noncompliance. Due to the complexity of the tax law, exactly what is actual tax liability—and therefore what is actual tax noncompliance—is often not clear. Second, any given examination is not perfect. Some noncompliance may be missed, and there will also be mistakes in characterizing as noncompliance what is legitimate tax planning. For this reason the data reflect not only the reporting behavior of the companies but also the enforcement behavior of the tax authority. Knowing that the resolution of the ultimate tax liability is often a long process of negotiation that may or may not involve the judicial system, the tax liability per the originally filed return, as well as the initial deficiency assessed by the examination team, may be partly a tactical "opening bid" that is neither party's best estimate of the "true" tax liability. Indeed, IRS Commissioner Mark Everson testified to the President's Advisory Panel on Tax Reform that the IRS had "a reputation for trading [penalties] away," so that it was "always in the interest of the noncompliant taxpayer to take an aggressive position with the Service." (Everson 2005).

Based on an examination of previously undisclosed IRS operational audits and appeals data merged with confidential tax return data for corporations, Hanlon et al. (2007) calculated that 60 percent of the proposed deficiency was either agreed to by the taxpayer or upheld at a later stage. This 60 percent sustention rate is almost certainly an upper-bound estimate of the rate for all companies, however, because it excludes the (more contested) tax return filings that had not been settled when the data set was compiled. They also found that the largest companies (those with assets greater than $5 billion) had the greatest percentage of firms with a tax deficiency (74 percent) and the highest proposed deficiency rate (14.6 percent, versus a range of 9.9 percent to 13.4 percent for six other size groups). This finding is consistent with the larger firms with more complex operations having more opportunities for tax noncompliance (i.e., detected by the IRS). There was also some evidence suggesting that the noncompliance rate for corporations relative to their size is U-shaped, with medium-sized businesses among the set of large companies having the lowest rate of noncompliance.

On average, Hanlon et al. (2007) found that private companies have higher proposed deficiency rates than public companies (17.1 percent vs. 12.5 percent). Privately held firms may be more aggressive in angling for lower taxes because they have fewer capital market pressures and thus can sacrifice reporting high financial accounting earnings in an attempt to reduce taxes owed. They also found a positive relationship between the amount of intangible assets a firm holds (as proxied by research and development expenses and market-to-book ratio) and its tax deficiency rate, which is consistent with the idea that these firms have greater tax planning opportunities. Finally, the percentage of annual executive compensation that is bonus and the level of equity incentives from exercisable stock options are positively related to the proposed tax deficiency, suggesting that high-powered managerial incentives may generate more tax aggressiveness.

Rice (1992) uses data from the 1980 TCMP to study the noncompliance behavior of small corporations, defined as having assets between $1 million and $10 million in 1980. He finds support for three propositions: (1) characteristics that assure public disclosure of information (being publicly traded or in a highly regulated industry) about a corporation's operations are associated with higher tax compliance;[14] (2)

firm profitability has two opposing effects—poor performance may drive firms to noncomply, while relatively high profit may offer an attractive chance to understate profits without detection (evasion facilitation); and (3) a high marginal tax rate is associated negatively with compliance.

3.2.6 Analysis of What Determines Tax Evasion

Perhaps the most compelling empirical support for the A-S deterrence model is the cross-sectional variation in noncompliance rates across types of income and deductions. Line item by line item, there is a clear negative correlation between the noncompliance rate and the presence of enforcement mechanisms such as information reports and employer withholding. Klepper and Nagin (1989) showed convincingly that, across line items, noncompliance rates are related to proxies for the traceability, deniability, and ambiguity of items, which are in turn related to the probability that evasion will be detected and punished. They also find evidence of a substitution-like effect across line items, such that greater noncompliance on one item lowers the attractiveness of noncompliance on others, arguably because increasing the latter jeopardizes the expected return to the former by increasing the probability of detection. Another example of the link from deterrence to tax compliance involves US state use taxes, which are due on sales purchased from out-of-state vendors but consumed in the state of residence. These taxes are largely unenforceable (except for some expensive items like cars and boats that require registration in their state of use), and most experts believe that the noncompliance rates are in excess of 90 percent.

However, the effect on noncompliance of the penalty for detected evasion, as distinct from the probability that a given act of noncompliance will be subject to punishment, has not been compellingly established empirically. Using audit data from the 2001 National Research Program, Phillips (2010) concludes that the A-S model predicts well the observed patterns of evasion once one accounts for the fact that audits and detection are not purely random, but instead are targeted and depend on the taxpayer's endogenous choice of underreporting. In particular, audits and detection become significantly more likely when a taxpayer underreports the entirety of his unmatched income and begins to underreport income reported by a third party. Moreover, a marginal dollar of underreporting can increase the probability of audit and detection, reflecting the tax agency's ability to better identify larger, more conspicuous amounts of underreporting.

Attempts to verify and quantify the predictions of the deterrence model empirically have been plagued by the same measurement issues that arise in assessing the magnitude of tax noncompliance. Clotfelter (1983) examines the micro data from a single cross section of the Taxpayer Compliance Measurement Program studies and finds that noncompliance is strongly positively related to marginal tax rates. As with any cross-sectional study of the impact of taxes on behavior, their approach is made difficult by the fact that the marginal tax rate is a (complicated, nonlinear) function of income, making it difficult to separately identify the tax rate and income effects without making strong functional-form assumptions. Feinstein (1991) analyzes two years of data across which the tax schedule changed, which mitigates this problem to some degree, and finds a negative impact of marginal tax rates on noncompliance.

Beron et al. (1992) examined TCMP data aggregated to the 3-digit zip code level and concluded that increasing the odds of an audit significantly increased reported adjusted gross income and tax liability for some income groups, but not all. However, the district-level audit rate is not exogenous, perhaps reflecting something about the compliance characteristics of the population. The authors instrument for the audit rate with the level of IRS resources relative to the number of returns, arguing that the IRS has not been able to allocate its resources so as to achieve its goals, but this approach is invalid to the extent that the IRS succeeds in targeting its resources toward areas believed to be particularly noncompliant.

In more recent work Kleven et al. (2011) use a bunching methodology that is less susceptible to endogeneity concerns in order to estimate the effect of marginal tax rates on the extent of evasion. Based on data from a randomized tax audit experiment in Denmark, they infer the effect of marginal tax rates on evasion by comparing the extent of bunching in pre- and post-audit income for self-employed filers at the top kink in the income tax code, and at the bracket threshold in the stock income tax schedule.[15] There is substantial bunching in pre-audit taxable income at both kinks, with the extent of bunching reduced in post-audit assessments at the income tax schedule kink but less so at the stock income schedule kink. They suggest that bunching at the stock income kink is mostly due to legal timing response of dividend payments for nontraded stock, in contrast to bunching at the income tax schedule that audited reports reveal to be due to both legal income manipulation and illegal evasion. Taking the difference between pre- and post-audit taxable income elasticities—estimated at the kink in the income tax distribution for the self-employed—gives a compensated elasticity of the share of true income reported with respect to the marginal net-of-tax rate of 0.076. Notably the evasion response to higher marginal tax rates is much smaller than the avoidance response, although the magnitude of this difference could be biased by undiscovered evasion incorrectly attributed to legal avoidance behavior.

Randomized field experiments offer the promise of a compelling source of evidence about the effect of tax-system parameters. The researcher must overcome tax authorities' understandable reluctance to randomize tax rates or bases, so that randomized tax experiments have heretofore mostly concerned tax-system instruments such as communication with taxpayers. As discussed briefly in section 3.2.1, in one of the first examples Slemrod et al. (2001) analyzed the results of a randomized controlled experiment conducted by the State of Minnesota Department of Revenue. They found that low- and middle-income taxpayers who received a letter promising a certain audit reported slightly more, but statistically significantly more, income than those who did not receive such a letter, and the difference was larger for those with greater opportunities to evade. However, high-income taxpayers receiving an audit threat on average reported *lower* income. The authors speculate that sophisticated, high-income taxpayers (and their accountants) understand an audit to be a negotiation, and view reported taxable income as the opening (low) bid in a negotiation that does not necessarily result in the determination and penalization of all noncompliance.

In a field experiment in Austria, Fellner et al. (2013) use a randomized design to test the effect on compliance with Austrian television and radio licensing fees of various mailings to potential noncompliers. Austrian households owning a radio or television are required to remit a licensing fee, but because payment of the annual fee relies on self-reporting and access to public broadcasting is not dependent on whether or not fees have been remitted, evasion opportunities exist. Three types of mailing were randomly assigned to a subsample of individuals identified as potential evaders, with the remaining individuals in the sample sent no mailing and serving as the control group. All mailings asked recipients to clarify within 14 days why no payment had been received, with the letters differing in their emphasis of either the threat of detection and sanction, a moral appeal equating compliance with fairness, and a third variant providing social information on the overall high level of compliance. Those receiving any type of mailing were significantly more likely to make a payment within 50 days of receiving the letter, but only the variant emphasizing the threat of punishment induced an additional increase in compliance. Fellner et al. (2011) interpret the generic effect of the mailing as an "alert effect" signaling that nonpayment had been noticed, with the consequences of noncompliance amplified by the threat variant.

Field evidence on Chilean firms' compliance with the VAT highlights the connection between information reports received by the tax authority and levels of evasion. Because firms can only claim tax credits for inputs bought from tax-compliant suppliers, the invoice-credit VAT system has a built-in (albeit imperfect) self-enforcement mechanism. Firms purchasing inputs would like to overstate purchase costs to inflate tax rebates, but sellers need to understate sale proceeds to minimize VAT liability. Because these incentives conflict and—except for final sales to consumers—information reports are made by both parties to each transaction to the tax authority, the VAT system is believed to dramatically increase the probability of evasion being detected. Pomeranz (2011) tests this hypothesis by mailing increased audit threat letters to over 100,000 randomly selected Chilean firms, using a sample of over 300,000 firms receiving no letter as the control group. Consistent with theoretical predictions on the self-enforcement mechanism, the increase in VAT receipts (and therefore the level of inferred evasion) induced by the letters is concentrated at the level of sales from firms to final consumers, for which there is no paper trail, suggesting that for an individual firm, information reporting acts as a substitute for audit risk. In line with the findings of Fellner et al. (2011) and Blumenthal et al. (2001) from the Minnesota randomized tax experiment, Pomeranz (2011) found that a mailing appealing to tax morale but promising no increased enforcement had little effect on VAT remittances.

To combat sales and profit tax evasion by small firms and the self-employed, many developing countries have adopted "reverse withholding," where large firms remit to the tax authority a fixed share of their purchases from small firms and sellers can apply the withheld amount as a credit against their self-reported tax liability. Because cost–sales ratios differ across firms, true tax liability can fall short of or exceed the withheld amount, entitling firms to a tax refund or requiring additional tax payments. While withholding does not affect the firms' true tax liability, there is typically a discontinuity in the audit probability at the withholding rate; firms seeking tax refunds because self-reported tax liability is lower than the withheld amount are audited at a higher rate than firms making additional tax remittances. Examining data from Ecuador, Carrillo et al. (2012) find evidence of bunching in reported tax liability just above the 1 percent withholding threshold, suggesting firms manipulate their self-reported tax liability and possibly real economic choices to minimize tax payments subject to the discontinuity in the audit probability. The pattern of bunching changed dramatically in 2007 only for firms subject to a change in the required withholding rate, ruling out the possibility that the withholding rate had been chosen to match the distribution of true tax liabilities. Third-party data on sales and intermediate input costs filed by large firms as withholding agents indicate bunching is indeed associated with tax evasion: self-reported sales are smaller than third-party reports for at least 10 percent of firms.

Although subject to the caveats discussed in section 3.2.1, lab experiments can be useful in testing the impact on compliance of aspects of the environment that are not feasible to analyze in field and natural experiment settings, which is true both of critically important tax-system aspects such as tax rates and also of many of the hypothesized nondeterrence influences. While one cannot, in a field experiment, experimentally manipulate environmental aspects such as deep-seated trust in government, neither can a lab experiment. In a laboratory setting, subjects respond not only to the probabilities and stakes of a tax evasion game, but also to the context provided to them. Alm et al. (1993) found that experimental subjects are willing to pay more in taxes when they first choose the use of their taxes by voting than when the identical use is imposed upon them, that compliance is somewhat greater when the vote is decisive compared to when the vote is close, and that tax compliance is significantly lowered by the imposition of an unpopular program.

The difficulties of separating out whether people pay their taxes because they feel they "ought to" or whether they fear the penalties attendant to not doing so is well illustrated by some evidence from a survey sponsored by the Internal Revenue Service Oversight Board (2006). While 96 percent of those surveyed mostly or completely agreed that "It is every American's civic duty to pay their fair share of taxes," 62 percent said that "fear of an audit" had a great deal or somewhat of an influence on whether they report and pay their taxes "honestly."

Survey responses about individuals' attitudes toward tax evasion are also suggestive that factors not considered in the deterrence model may matter. Torgler (2003) and Slemrod (2003) show there is a positive relationship across countries between survey-based attitudes supporting tax compliance on the one hand and professed trust in government, and Slemrod (2003) finds that the same relationship holds across individuals within the United States and Germany. Of course attitudes and actions are not the same.[16] A 2002 poll in the Czech Republic indicated that a person would be more likely to evade taxes if that person believed government services were substandard (Hanousek and Palda 2004). Feldman and Slemrod (2009), using cross-country data on interstate conflicts from 1970 to the present and on attitudes toward tax evasion from the World Values Survey, find that positive attitudes toward tax compliance increase with the number and length of conflicts that a country faces, but decrease in the number of fatalities incurred in these conflicts. This suggests that patriotism, broadly interpreted, may affect compliance. Konrad and Qari (2012) find a positive cross-country and within-country correlation between professed patriotism and tax compliance attitudes, although it is difficult with their data to establish causality. None of these studies establishes definitively a causal connection between the two attitudes, and some of the observed correlation might be due to an ex post rationalization of tax noncompliant behavior. Moreover, establishing a causal relationship of some aspect of the environment to attitudes does not necessarily imply that changes in these aspects would also affect behavior in a given deterrence environment.

Indeed, it has been difficult to establish a connection between actual tax compliance behavior and, for example, appeals to conscience, although such appeals have a long history: Webber and Wildavsky (1986, p. 58) note that during Hammurabi's reign a taxpayer communication read "Why have you not sent to Babylon the 30 lambs as your tax? Are you not ashamed of such behavior?" Slightly more recently, in a randomized field experiment with Minnesota taxpayers in a modern, peacetime setting, Blumenthal et al. (2001) find no evidence that either of two written appeals to taxpayers' consciences had a significant effect on income tax compliance. One letter stressed the beneficial effects of tax-funded projects, while the other conveyed the message that most taxpayers were compliant. Torgler (2004), using a controlled field experiment in Switzerland, also found that moral suasion had hardly any effect on taxpayers' compliance behavior.

3.3 Avoidance

3.3.1 Definition

As we have noted, economists generally differentiate between illegal means of reducing tax liability, referred to as evasion, and legal means of reducing tax liability, referred to as avoidance. Of course in some contexts the law is unclear and either the taxpayer or the tax authority, or both, may not know for sure which is which.[17] But, more important, this definition of avoidance does not correspond to another common usage among economists, in which the term avoidance does not include "real" behavioral responses to changing tax rates such as reduced labor supply, altering the time path of consumption, or consuming less highly taxed cigarettes, but rather to a different class of behaviors.

If not all legal behavioral response to tax rates is avoidance, how can it be usefully defined and distinguished from real behavioral response? A good starting point is the definition of avoidance offered in Slemrod and Yitzhaki (2002): taxpayer efforts to reduce their tax liability that do not alter their consumption basket other than due to income effects. This definition covers a broad range of behaviors. It includes paying a tax professional to alert one to the tax deductibility of activities already undertaken. It covers changing the legal form of a given behavior, such as reorganizing a business from a C corporation to an S corporation, recharacterizing ordinary income as capital gain, or renaming a consumer loan as a home equity loan. It covers tax arbitrage, where economically equivalent, but differentially taxed, positions are held simultaneously long and short, producing tax savings. Finally, it covers (slightly) retiming a transaction to alter the tax year it falls under, or slightly re-engineering a vehicle to change its tax classification.

The distinction between real behavioral response and avoidance does not arise in, for example, the standard model of optimal commodity taxation, where consumption, and only consumption, triggers tax liability, so the model does not allow any other behavior that could reduce tax liability. The same is true of the standard optimal income tax model, where individuals' only decision is how much labor to supply, which affects tax liability by changing taxable income.

However, in many cases what triggers tax liability in actual tax systems is different than what triggers tax liability in stylized models.

Retail purchases rather than consumption trigger retail sales tax liability, receipt of labor income rather than the exertion of physical or mental labor itself generally determines the timing of tax liability. Sales of appreciated capital assets trigger tax liability rather than accrual of gain or consumption itself. Operational definitions of taxable income differ on many dimensions from the Haig–Simons definition of income: consumption plus the change in net worth. As an example, in the United States taxable income does not include employer contributions to employee health insurance, whereas Haig–Simons income would.

In what follows, we offer a formal framework for distinguishing avoidance from real behavioral response, and then provide some examples that illustrate the framework.

3.3.2 A Formal Model of Avoidance and the Excess Burden of Avoidance

One consequence of having tax liability determined by factors other than final consumption or, more generally, the arguments of individuals' utility functions, is that an additional efficiency cost arises, what we will call "excess burden of tax avoidance."[18] To formalize this argument, consider the following setting. A taxpayer chooses consumption $c = (c_1, \ldots, c_n)$ to maximize utility $u = u(c)$ subject to the budget constraint $\sum_{i=1}^{n} p_i c_i \equiv p \cdot c \leq A$, where $p = (p_1, \ldots, p_n)$ is the vector of prices for the consumption goods (of which leisure is a component), and A is exogenous income. Hence the taxpayer's maximized utility is

$$v(p, A) = \max_c u(c) \quad \text{s.t.} \quad p \cdot c \leq A. \tag{3.8}$$

Now introduce into the standard model a "transformation function" for the consumption goods that enter a taxpayer's utility function. We suppose that $c_i = h^i(x)$ for $i = 1, \ldots, n$, with $x = (x_1, \ldots, x_n)$ representing inputs to the generation of the consumption goods.[19] The set $H = \{h^1, \ldots, h^n\}$ collects the transformation functions for each consumption good.[20] We outline examples below in which the role and interpretation of these inputs differ. When the inputs, x, represent actions taken by a taxpayer, such as purchasing goods and seeking out tax deductions, the consumer chooses x such that

$$p \cdot c \equiv \min_x q \cdot x \quad \text{s.t.} \quad h^i(x) \geq c_i \quad \forall i = 1, \ldots, n, \tag{3.9}$$

where $q = (q_1, \ldots, q_n)$ are the per unit costs for the vector of inputs used to generate each good, x, which may depend on the amount of each input used. The taxpayer's problem can be reduced to choosing the vector of inputs x:

$$v(q,A) = \max_{x} u\left(h^1(x), \ldots, h^n(x)\right) \quad \text{s.t.} \quad q \cdot x \leq A. \tag{3.10}$$

If the tax authority were able to tax the fundamental determinants of utility, in this example c, we are back to the standard Ramsey optimal commodity tax problem, presented in section 2.3, where even at the second-best optimum an excess burden results due to a distorted consumption vector chosen by the taxpayer. But once we recognize that the tax authority often cannot base tax liability on the fundamental determinants of utility, c, but is instead restricted to taxing x, an additional excess burden arises.[21] The standard excess burden corresponds to substitution among $c = (c_1, \ldots, c_n)$ in response to a compensated change in effective tax rates, while the additional excess burden of tax avoidance corresponds to substitution among the vector x used to produce each of the consumption units c_i, other than would occur in a world with taxes on the determinants of utility c. As an analogy to Diamond and Mirrlees (1971), reliance on the tax base x corresponds to taxes on production inputs rather than the arguments of taxpayers' utility function, c. The socially inferior vector x chosen by the taxpayer can be thought of as a "utility production" distortion.

Formally, the equivalent variation measure of total excess burden, as defined in chapter 2, can be decomposed as follows:

$$EB_{ev} = \underbrace{\left[E(0, v(0,A)) - E(0, v(\theta(c), A)) - G\right]}_{a}$$
$$- \underbrace{\left[E(0, v(\theta(x), A)) - E(0, v(\theta(c), A))\right]}_{b}, \tag{3.11}$$

where $E(0, v)$ is the expenditure required to attain the utility level v in a world without taxes, $v(\theta(x), A)$ is the level of utility achieved when taxes levied on the inputs x are optimally chosen to raise G dollars, and $v(\theta(c), A)$ is the level of utility when taxes on the arguments of a taxpayer's utility function are optimally chosen to raise G dollars. Term a represents the standard excess burden of taxation—arising because consumption decisions are distorted—while term b represents the utility production distortion.

3.3.3 Consumption Good Characteristics
Barzel (1976) provides an example of tax-induced avoidance behavior that fits this framework nicely, where utility depends on characteristics

but only goods can be taxed. Suppose that a consumer purchases a consumption good, c_1, assembled by a competitive firm by combining two characteristics, $x = (x_1, x_2)$, in variable proportion. Assume that there is no interdependence between production of c_1 and all other goods in the taxpayers' consumption vector, which we denote by c_{-1}. Following the formulation of consumer preferences pioneered by Lancaster (1966) and Gorman (1980), utility is derived from characteristics, so the goods purchased by consumers themselves do not enter utility functions, other than through the particular characteristics they provide. Avoidance behavior may occur in this setting if taxes induce the production of goods with a socially inefficient mix of characteristics. Our avoidance framework embeds this example when the following functional forms are used:

$H = \{h^1, \ldots, h^n\}$,

$c = (c_1, \ldots, c_n)$, is the vector of consumption goods purchased,

$q = (q_1 (1 + t_1), q_2, \ldots, q_n)$, is the vector of input costs, with the first characteristic possibly subject to tax,

$c_1 = h^1(x_1, x_2)$,

$c_i = h^i(x_{-1})$ for $i > 1$,

$u_1 > 0$.

A competitive firm with a constant-returns-to-scale production technology assembles consumption good c_1 using the cost-minimizing combination of inputs (x_1, x_2):

$$p_1 = \min_{\{x_1, x_2\}} q_1 (1 + t_1) x_1 + q_2 x_2 \quad \text{s.t.} \quad h^1(x_1, x_2) \geq 1, \tag{3.12}$$

with p_1 the price to the consumer for a unit of c_1. Firms' cost minimization conditions yield the FOCs for each characteristic:

$$[\partial x_1] \quad q_1 (1 + t_1) = \mu \left[\frac{\partial h^1}{\partial x_1} \right], \tag{3.13}$$

$$[\partial x_2] \quad q_2 = \mu \left[\frac{\partial h^1}{\partial x_2} \right], \tag{3.14}$$

where μ is the Lagrange multiplier for a firm's cost-minimization problem. In the standard model, imposing a tax on the first good, c_1, reduces (compensated) demand for that good, and creates an excess burden, but when the tax falls on only a particular characteristic of the

good, in this case x_1, profit-maximizing firms will respond by econo-
mizing on the use of the first characteristic and substitute toward the
second, untaxed, characteristic. This additional distortion of a socially
inefficient mix of characteristics, ignored by the standard model, represents the excess burden of avoidance in this example.

To illustrate, consider, following Barzel (1976), that the consumption
good is a lightbulb, with the first characteristic being, for example,
strength and the second characteristic being durability. Assuming that
consumers value only the flow of light services, and that bulbs main-
tain perfect quality until some random failure time, consumers should
be willing to pay the same amount for a bulb that lasts one year, or two
bulbs that last six months each, where for simplicity the cost of changing the lightbulb is ignored. In the absence of taxes, the market will
supply a bulb that delivers light services at least cost. But if a per-bulb
excise tax is imposed that does not depend on the durability of the
bulb, producers will respond by increasing durability, because a longer-
lasting bulb requires fewer purchases and so delivers a given flow of
light services at a lower tax-inclusive cost to the consumer. Because
the quality of each bulb sold is higher—longer durability—the observed
market price of bulbs may rise by more than the excise tax imposed,
in contrast to what the standard model predicts if it ignores the tax-
induced change in the quality of the good. In a more modern context,
the substitutability of financial products and the incoherence of capital
income taxation implies that the same stream of financial flows can be
provided by a multiplicity of combinations of securities, and differential taxation can determine which exist. In chapter 11 we return to this
issue, and discuss at some length the model of Kleven and Slemrod
(2011), who take up the issue of how to set commodity taxes to avoid
the excess burden due to what they call tax-driven product innovation,
of which Barzel's (1976) example is a special case. This discussion raises
the issue of why tax systems ubiquitously rely on tax bases that generate an excess burden of tax avoidance. The answer is that they might
economize on other costs of the tax system, such as administration and
compliance costs, that are discussed in chapter 4.

3.3.4 Time Shifting

Within this framework we would regard a tax-induced change in the
timing of consumption as a real behavioral response. But much of the
intertemporal response to taxes is better thought of as tax avoidance.
This is because some taxes that strongly affect timing are not based on

the timing of consumption at all, a prominent example being realization-based capital gains taxes—changing the timing of the sale of an appreciated asset does not require changing the timing of consumption. Thus we observe timing responses of capital gains realizations that exceed by an order of magnitude what we would expect of the intertemporal substitution of consumption. A particularly striking example was the response of capital gains realizations to the capital gains tax-rate increase scheduled to occur on January 1, 1987, but fully anticipated by the fall of 1986. Aggregate realizations in 1986 were twice what they were in any previous year, or for several years thereafter. As Clausing et al. (1994) document, capital gains realizations on corporate stock in December of 1986 were *seven* times higher than in the previous December. Another striking example of timing response is provided by Goolsbee (2000), who documents that, in advance of the expected 1993 increase in the US top individual tax rate, corporate executives realized an extraordinary amount of income in 1992, primarily through exercising non-qualified stock options.[22]

Anticipated changes in the tax code have been shown to affect the short-term timing of births (Dickert-Conlin and Chandra 1999), marriage (Alm and Whittington 1999), and even death (Kopczuk and Slemrod 2003). Sophisticated econometric techniques using panel data have been developed for separately identifying the timing responses to tax-rate changes over time from the permanent behavioral response to a changed tax rate. These new techniques have been applied to capital gains realizations (Burman and Randolph 1994), to charitable contributions (Randolph 1995; Bakija and Heim 2011), and to housing transfer taxes (Slemrod, Weber, et al. 2012). In all of these cases the results suggest that the timing effect dominates the permanent effect.

3.3.5   Income Base Shifting and Re-characterizing Activities

In many tax systems a given flow of income may be taxed as part of alternative bases that are subject to different rates, providing an incentive to shift the income from the higher taxed base to the lower one. In other cases a given activity may be re-characterized for favorable tax treatment within a given tax base. The classic example of shifting is turning ordinary capital or labor income into preferentially taxed capital gains. Maki (1996) and Scholz (1994) have documented that, following the Tax Reform Act of 1986, there was a large shift from consumer loans, the interest on which was no longer deductible, into still-deductible mortgage or home equity loans. There is anecdotal evidence that, following the introduction of the R&D credit in the United States, much business activity was "discovered" to have a significant research component. MacKie-Mason and Gordon (1997) have investigated how, when the Tax Reform Act of 1986 lowered the top individual tax rate below that of the corporate tax rate, there was a large shift of business income from C corporations into S corporations, the latter of which are taxed like partnerships and therefore are not subject to the corporation income tax. Gordon and Slemrod (2000) discuss the shifting of income between the corporate and individual tax base via the method of compensation, and document evidence of such shifting in the United States. Pirttilä and Selin (2011) document that, in response to the introduction of a dual income tax in Finland, which levied significantly lower tax rates on capital versus labor income, self-employed people (but not employees) shifted reported income toward capital income. A paper by de Mooij and Nicodème (2008) examines to what extent income shifting from the personal to the corporate tax base can explain the fact that, in post-1980 Europe, declining corporate tax rates have been accompanied by rising corporate-tax-to-GDP ratios. Based on an analysis of a panel of European data on legal form of business, they find that this effect accounts for between 12 and 21 percent of corporate tax revenue, and that it has raised the corporate tax-to-GDP ratio by 0.25 percent points since the early 1990s. Sivadasan and Slemrod (2008) show that, when India eliminated a tax penalty on wages paid to partners in partnerships, firms subject to the change—but not other similar firms under different organizational form—effected an immediate and pervasive shift from profits to managerial wages.

Multinational corporations' (MNCs) shifting of taxable corporate profits from high-tax to low-tax countries is perhaps the most studied example of income shifting. It is well known that MNCs can shift profits through a variety of techniques. One method is the manipulation of transfer prices for international, intra-firm transactions overstating the prices of imports into a high-tax country and understating the prices of exports. Clausing (2003) reports some direct evidence that intra-firm trade prices deviate from "arm's-length" prices in ways that are consistent with income shifting. Second, the multinational can affect the international allocation of taxable profits through its financial structure, in particular by assigning (high-interest) debt to subsidiaries in high-tax countries. Finally, the multinational can assign common expenses, such as R&D expenses or headquarter services, to high-tax countries, thereby reducing accounting profits in these countries. Subsidiaries in low-tax countries are supposed to pay arm's-length prices for the use of these services, for example, via royalties for the use of intangible capital produced by R&D, but, in practice, there is substantial scope for manipulation.

Because these profit-shifting strategies are generally not directly observable, researchers have often resorted to looking for traces of such behavior: successful international profit shifting should reduce multinational company profits reported in high-tax countries. The first such study, by Grubert and Mutti (1991), showed that the observed pattern of reported profits of US multinational corporations in high- and low-tax-rate countries is consistent with income shifting behavior. Hines and Rice (1994) note that in 1982 US companies recorded extraordinarily high profit rates on both their real and financial investments in tax havens. This is the precise opposite of what theory, absent income shifting, would predict: that investment in high-tax countries would in equilibrium have to provide a higher before-tax return so as to generate a comparable after-tax return.

Instead, MNCs have the incentive to shift profits into the low-tax countries. Several other studies based on US data, some surveyed in Hines (1999), find that reported profits are higher in low-tax countries, and lower in high-tax countries, which is consistent with profit shifting through the manipulation of transfer prices, as well as other means of geographic income shifting. Demirgüc-Kunt and Huizinga (2001) find that the profitability reported by foreign-owned banks across 80 countries is negatively related to national top statutory tax rates, consistent with international profit shifting, and Bartelsman and Beetsma (2003) find that value added reported at the sector level in OECD countries is negatively related to statutory tax rates. Harris et al. (1993), using firm-level data, find that US manufacturing firms with subsidiaries in low-tax countries have, ceteris paribus, relatively low US tax payments per dollar of assets or sales, and that having a subsidiary in a high-tax region is associated with higher US tax payments, suggesting that US manufacturing companies do engage in income shifting. Grubert and Slemrod (1998) investigate income shifting in the context of Puerto Rican affiliates of US corporations, which until recently were essentially untaxed by either Puerto Rico or the United States, making it attractive to shift reported taxable income from a US parent corporation to its Puerto Rican affiliate. The analysis suggests that the income shifting advantages were the main reason for US firms' investment in Puerto Rico, as evidenced by the fact that the FDI was predominantly in industries with high capacity for income shifting: high-margin, intangible-intensive sectors.

3.3.6 Financial Transactions

Nowhere is the issue of tax avoidance more problematic, and _more_ ? economically important, than the taxation of financial products. As Weisbach (1994–1995) and others have noted, the tax law prescribes separate rules for stock, debt, options, forwards, futures, swaps, and other financial instruments, and the applicable tax rates are inconsistent. For example, debt and equity may in some cases be substantively indistinguishable, although taxed separately. Existing financial instruments can be combined into a single security, creating a hybrid instrument, combinations of instruments can produce tax instruments that are similar to the cash flows of another instrument, and cash flows can be divided into separate instruments and sold. At its extreme, the inconsistent tax treatment creates the possibility of pure tax arbitrage, in which a taxpayer can purchase and sell the same asset in different forms and gain from the differential tax treatment with no other financial consequences. In all cases the tax saving can be achieved with little or no change in real state-contingent consumption, and thus this behavior is avoidance according to our definition.

In part these inconsistencies arise because of the occasional use of the realization principle, under which certain transactions (e.g., sales of appreciated assets) trigger tax liability, which is often defended on grounds of administrability because an arm's-length price is available. An alternative, used in other instances, is "mark-to-market" taxation, which requires valuation of assets and liabilities even in the absence of a transaction. Thus an attempt to economize on collection costs leads to avoidance opportunities.

An early attempt to "taxonomize" tax avoidance, Stiglitz (1985), relies on tax arbitrage. Stiglitz (1985) distinguishes three basic principles of tax avoidance within an income tax: postponement of taxes, tax arbitrage across individuals facing different tax brackets (or the same individuals facing different marginal tax rates at different times), and, as we stress above, tax arbitrage across income streams facing different tax treatment. Many tax avoidance devices involve a combination of these three principles. In an example used by Stiglitz (1985), the basic feature of an individual retirement account (IRA) is the postponement of tax liability until retirement; if the individual faces a lower tax rate at retirement than at the time the income is earned, then the IRA also features tax arbitrage between different rates. Finally, if the individual can borrow to deposit funds in an IRA and the interest incurred to finance the deposit is tax deductible, then the IRA is a tax arbitrage between two forms of capital, one of which is taxed, and the other of which is not taxed.[23] Stiglitz (1985) argues that with perfect capital markets, these three principles can be exploited to eliminate all taxes while leaving the individual's consumption and bequests unchanged relative to the zero tax case, and facing no more risk than in the original situation. But capital markets are not perfect, and therefore all tax liability is not eliminated by tax avoidance,[24] and to reduce tax liabilities, distorting actions (e.g., investment in sectors where it is easier to convert ordinary income into capital gains) are utilized. There is considerable empirical evidence testifying to the extent and tax sensitivity of these kinds of avoidance behavior.

3.3.7 Consumption versus Purchases

As we have mentioned, standard theoretical models of consumption taxation do not distinguish between consumption and purchases. But in most consumption tax systems tax liability is triggered by purchases, retail purchases under a retail sales tax, plus business-to-business purchases under a VAT. This matters in a number of situations. When consumers anticipate tax rate changes, they have an incentive to accelerate purchases to beat the tax-rate rise (or decelerate purchases to take advantage of tax-rate cuts). When purchases are more substitutable over time than consumption, as they are certainly for durable goods and storable nondurable goods, this increases the distortion per dollar raised. Cashin (2012) and Cashin and Unayama (2011) document this phenomenon with respect to changes in value-added taxes in New Zealand and Japan, respectively, with the latter study finding that three-quarters of the tax-induced intertemporal substitution of purchases is attributable to durables and storable nondurable goods and services. Cole (2009) provides evidence of a large time-shifting elasticity of purchases around US states' sales tax holidays, under which for a few days sales tax is not levied on a set of goods, usually clothing, school supplies, and occasionally personal computers; no one suspects that the time pattern of *consumption* of these goods is much higher during the holiday. The distorted time pattern of purchases generates an excess burden of tax avoidance.

The distinction between consumption and purchases also arises in a geographic context. US states with a retail sales tax generally levy the same tax rate on purchases made out of state but consumed within the state; these days this is largely, but not only, purchases made over the Internet. The Supreme Court has ruled that out-of-state vendors need not remit tax to the state of the purchaser's residence in most circumstances, leaving the purchaser/consumer to submit a use tax declaration and payment. California estimated that $1 billion in use taxes owed annually is never remitted—a 1 percent compliance rate—despite the fact that the California income tax return "reminds" people of their use tax obligations (Legislative Analyst's Office 2011). Note that this is a telling example of a case where the location of remittance responsibility is hugely important, as we discuss in chapter 6.

The distinction between consumption and purchases is also the Achilles heel of proposals to implement personalized retail sales taxes via smart cards that encode personal information. Such a system could certainly trigger taxes at the cash register that depend on the purchaser's encoded characteristics but do not prevent transactions between the purchaser and the ultimate consumer that undermine the intended personalization of the tax burden. Teenagers below the legal drinking age are well aware of a similar loophole in such laws.

3.3.8 Aggregate Avoidance and Its Incidence

No one has attempted to calculate for avoidance a counterpart to the aggregate evasion "tax gap." There is, though, some indirect evidence that the avoidance tax gap is large. Gordon and Slemrod (1988) calculated that the US income tax system of 1983 raised approximately zero revenue from taxing capital income, due to the combination of legislated deviations from a pure income tax, income shifting, and tax arbitrage.[25] As to the incidence of the avoidance opportunities, Agell and Persson (2000) and Gordon and Slemrod (1988) argue that the availability of tax arbitrage opportunities will generally benefit those at the bottom and top of the tax-rate distribution, to the disadvantage of those in the middle. This generally corresponds to low- and high-income individuals, respectively, but there are exceptions to that rule; high-income individuals benefit through their ownership of tax-preferred pension assets.

3.3.9 The Relationships among Evasion, Avoidance, and Real Activity

To this point, we have focused on distinguishing among evasion, avoidance, and real activity. In this section we discuss the relationships among the three kinds of behavioral response. In doing so, we put aside differentiating between avoidance and evasion (the illegality of the latter) and stress their commonality. We do so in part to sidestep the difficulty and opacity of explicitly modeling uncertainty. We argue that some of the points we want to make about evasion can be made in a certainty-equivalent model, where part of the general cost of engaging in the activity is capturing the increased riskiness of a tax evasion gamble.

To illustrate this interrelationship, recall from section 3.3.5 the example studied in Grubert and Slemrod (1998), who provide empirical evidence of such an interaction for corporate income shifting to Puerto Rico. The fact that corporate income earned by US firms in Puerto Rico was essentially exempt from US corporate income taxation provided strong incentives for US corporations to use transfer pricing and other means of income shifting to declare as large a share as possible of their taxable corporate income in Puerto Rico. Grubert and Slemrod's (1998) key empirical finding is that the effective marginal cost of income shifting is declining in the amount of real activity conducted in Puerto Rico: more real activity makes it easier for the firm to claim legitimate income shifting.[26] Importantly, avoidance technology differs across firms, and as expected, Grubert and Slemrod (1998) found more evidence of tax-motivated production in Puerto Rico among firms for which arm's-length transfer prices are difficult to determine, such as manufacturers with intangible brand value or pharmaceutical companies with high R&D expenditure. This provides an implicit subsidy to real investment in Puerto Rico, what Slemrod (2001) calls "avoidance facilitation," but here we will generalize the concept to evasion. In the discussion that follows, for simplicity, we will use the term avoidance or sheltering, but we are thinking of the relationship between real activity, on the one hand, and avoidance and evasion, on the other hand.

The same facilitation role of real activity is likely to carry over to personal income taxation, where more actual income lowers the cost of effecting a given amount of avoidance activity. The tax authorities are aware of this association, and may condition examination attention on reported income. This has important implications for behavioral response to income taxes: if, for example, increased effort going toward earning income in response to lower marginal tax rates decreases the marginal cost of avoidance, this magnifies any observed behavioral response. To show this, we first demonstrate that a close variant of the seminal Mayshar (1991) model of income tax avoidance is a special case of our more general framework, and then we specialize the model as in Slemrod (2001) to incorporate an avoidance-facilitation role for labor income.

The standard income tax avoidance model assumes there is a single consumption good, and that labor income is subject to tax, but that the tax can be partially avoided by the taxpayer incurring some cost to shelter s dollars from taxes.[27] In terms of our general framework, the standard model has the following functional forms:

$$H = \{h^1, h^2, h^3\},$$

$$x = (C, l, s),$$

where H is the set of transformation functions, x represents the tax-payer's vector of choice variables, with C being the consumption good, l being labor supply, and s being the amount of income sheltered from income taxes in dollars,

$$c_1 = h^1(x) = C - \kappa (wl, s),$$

$$c_2 = h^2(x) = l,$$

$$c_3 = h^3(x) = 0,$$

$$u_1 > 0, u_2 < 0.$$

Here $\kappa (wl, s)$ is the taxpayer's income tax sheltering cost function, in dollars, depending on both the level of income earned, wl, and the extent of sheltering activity, s; its properties are crucial. The vector of input costs is $q = (1, -w(1 - t), -t)$, being the normalized price of consumption, the negative of the net-of-tax wage rate, and the tax saving from each dollar of income taxes avoided, respectively.

Substitution of these functional forms into equation (3.10) yields the taxpayer's maximization problem:

$$v(t, A) = \max_{\{C, l, s\}} u(C - \kappa(wl, s), l, 0) \quad \text{s.t.} \quad C \leq A + wl(1 - t) + ts. \tag{3.15}$$

As usual, the marginal utility of consumption is positive, $u_1 > 0$, and the marginal utility of labor supply is negative, $u_2 < 0$. The taxpayer's FOC for labor supply is

$$-\frac{u_2}{u_1} = w[(1 - t) - \kappa_1 (wl, s)]. \tag{3.16}$$

Equation (3.16) states that, at an interior optimum, the individual equates the marginal rate of substitution between labor supply and consumption to the net-of-tax wage rate plus a term that captures the avoidance (or evasion) facilitation effect. In the absence of sheltering activity, $\kappa = 0$, and the optimality condition is standard. The FOC for sheltering is

$$t = \kappa_2(wl, s), \tag{3.17}$$

indicating that sheltering activity is higher, the larger is the marginal tax rate, t, and the smaller is the marginal cost of avoidance activity, κ_2. The standard model assumes that the marginal cost of avoidance is positive and convex, so $\kappa_2 > 0$ and $\kappa_{22} > 0$.

In order to incorporate an interaction between real activity and the cost of avoidance, Slemrod (2001) makes a further assumption about the avoidance cost function, κ. Crucially, κ_{12} is assumed to be negative, so the marginal cost of avoidance activity is decreasing in the amount of true income earned. The idea is that a given absolute amount of avoidance is less likely to be detected when it is a smaller fraction of overall income.[28] In this case avoidance facilitation is an implicit subsidy to working. This captures the essence of the example about Puerto Rican investment discussed earlier: more real investment facilitates the shifting of taxable income to Puerto Rico.

Implicit differentiation of equations (3.16) and (3.17) yields a modified Slutsky expression for the response of labor supply to a marginal change in the tax rate t:

$$\frac{\partial l}{\partial t} = w\left(\frac{1 + (\kappa_{12}/\kappa_{22})}{S + X}\right) - (wl - s)\frac{\partial l}{\partial A}. \tag{3.18}$$

In equation (3.18) $X \equiv -w^2\left((\kappa_{11}\kappa_{22} - \kappa_{12}\kappa_{21})/\kappa_{22}\right)$ measures the change in the slope of the budget line as l increases, where $S < 0$ is the substitution effect (the rate of change of the slope of the indifference curve between consumption and leisure), and $\partial l/\partial A$ is the effect of exogenous income on labor supply. The second-order conditions for a maximum ensure that $S + X$ is negative, while $X < 0$ corresponds to the assumption that κ is a convex function. Together with the assumption that $\kappa_{12} < 0$, equation (3.18) implies that the compensated decline in labor supply that would occur when t increases is somewhat mitigated when labor income has an avoidance-facilitation role.

If κ_1 is zero (i.e., sheltering is infra-marginal), substantial sheltering can exist without lowering the effective marginal tax rate on the real activity. This issue came up in the recent US policy debate about the estate tax, during which opponents argued that (1) it was largely avoided, and (2) it deterred wealth accumulation. How, a supporter of the tax asked, could it do both? We now see that it is possible, in principle, for avoidance to exist without much reducing the effective tax rate on wealth accumulation. This is, though, an empirical question, because it depends on the nature of the κ function.

The notion of avoidance facilitation allows us to reinterpret the fascinating study of Rosen (1976) that, in a regression analysis of female labor supply, splits apart as explanatory variables the before-tax wage rate, w, and the net-of-tax $(1 - t)$ terms, interpreting any difference in estimated coefficients (which Rosen did not ultimately find) as evidence of "tax illusion"—lack of salience in more modern language. But we can now say that, in the presence of avoidance and evasion, no appeal to tax illusion is needed to explain a differential effect of the w and $(1 - t)$ terms, because the effective relative price of the real decision depends on the avoidance or evasion technology—the tax can be "finessed," but the before-tax wage rate cannot be. *In general, one should not expect a homologous response to a before-tax price and a net-of-tax term.*

4 Multiple Sources of Costs

Standard tax analysis focuses on the efficiency costs due to the distorted real behavior caused by tax-induced relative price changes. Chapter 3 focused on classes of behavioral response—evasion and avoidance—that are often ignored in positive and normative models of taxation. But social costs due to distorted private decisions are not the only resource cost of tax systems. Administrative costs are costs incurred directly by the tax authority in establishing and operating tax systems. Compliance costs are, in the first instance, borne by taxpayers in following the rules and procedures set out by a tax authority, and in planning to reduce tax liabilities. It is often in an effort to reduce these costs that tax systems feature aspects that cause excess burdens due to real behavioral response, evasion, and avoidance. Governments that are inappropriately focused on the explicit costs of administration may be tempted to reduce these costs even if the other "hidden" costs increase by more than the administrative cost savings.

4.1 Administrative Costs

Even if all taxpayers were scrupulously honest, any tax system requires an administrative system with a bureaucracy to calculate tax liabilities and to record and check remittance.[1] But, as we noted in the previous chapter, not all taxpayers are honest, nor are taxpayers obliged to arrange their affairs in a way that suits the tax authority. As a result some taxpayers go to considerable lengths to reduce the size of their tax bill. In response to avoidance and evasion, all tax authorities judge it worthwhile to expend resources to limit revenue loss as well as any undesirable efficiency, horizontal, or vertical equity consequences. Moreover, it will always be relatively cheap to collect taxes in a capricious way—without measurement or verification—so capriciousness must be balanced by the value of horizontal equity or legitimacy.[2]

Scholars of the historical evolution of tax structure, notably Hinrichs (1966) and Musgrave (1969), have stressed the importance of tax administration issues and the identification of "tax handles," tax bases for which administration cost is low relative to revenue collected. They note that modern tax structure development has generally been characterized by a shift from excise, customs, and property taxes to corporate income and progressive individual income taxes, made possible by the expansion of the market sector and the relative decline of the rural sector, the concentration of employment in larger establishments, and the growing literacy of the population. Hinrichs (1966, p. 117) notes portentously that "taxes that are easiest to collect tend to be collected from the wrong sources, in terms of promoting economic development."

Until recently, quantitative evidence on tax administrative costs and procedures was scattershot and not readily comparable across countries. However, since 2004, the OECD has collected and produced such data for OECD member countries, and since 2006 for a number of non-OECD countries. Table 4.1 contains cross-country data from their 2011 report on administrative costs for national revenue bodies as a percent of net revenue collected. The first point to note is that they are significantly lower than standard efficiency costs, at least as measured by Ballard et al. (1985). Note also that a number of caveats limit the comparability of these data across countries, and through time. For example, administrative costs tend to have a large fixed-cost component, so differences in the level of taxes can make low-tax countries appear to run high-cost systems. Similarly business-cycle fluctuations in revenue are typically greater than for administrative costs, making comparability dependent on the state of the business cycle when measured. Temporary expenses, such as those due to tax-system reform, and changes in the scope of taxes collected by revenue authorities, can also potentially distort comparisons. Nevertheless, the data in table 4.1 provide some quantitative grounding to the costs of tax administration through time and across countries.

Looking only at total administrative costs can also obscure the multidimensional nature of tax administration, with tax systems differing on a wide range of important non-rate dimensions that affect revenue collection. Important procedural differences between tax systems include the degree of self-assessment, the extent to which income withholding at source is used, and the amount of arm's-length information reporting on tax liabilities to the tax authority. Similarly, important

Table 4.1
Administrative cost as a percentage of net revenue for OECD countries

	2001	2002	2003	2004	2005	2006	2007	2008	2009
Australia	1.06	1.07	1.05	1.05	1.03	0.99	0.93	0.96	1.02
Austria	0.71	0.72	0.91	0.78	0.66	0.65	0.64	0.79	0.85
Belgium				1.89	1.42	1.35	1.40	1.27	1.40
Canada	1.08	1.20	1.33	1.17	1.31	1.35	1.22	1.14	1.33
Chile			0.89	0.88	0.69	0.63	0.60	0.66	0.90
Czech Republic		2.08			1.29	1.38	1.25	1.18	1.46
Denmark		0.73	0.87	0.83	0.74	0.63	0.62	0.64	0.67
Estonia					1.03	0.88	0.86	0.38	0.40
Finland	0.77	0.82	0.82	0.80	0.79	0.78	0.77	0.80	0.87
France	1.41	1.44	1.41	1.35	1.07	1.23	1.20	1.17	1.31
Germany					0.86	0.83	0.78	0.75	0.79
Greece			1.65	1.69					
Hungary	1.23	1.35		1.14	0.99	1.11	1.15	1.17	1.20
Iceland		1.12	1.06	1.02				0.28	0.32
Ireland	0.90	0.95	0.91	0.86	0.82	0.78	0.79	0.95	1.08
Israel								0.75	0.79
Italy					1.36	1.24	1.16	1.08	1.20
Japan	1.42	1.54	1.66	1.67	1.58	1.45	1.43	1.49	1.71
Korea	0.85	0.85	0.82	0.86	0.81	0.79	0.71	0.79	0.84
Luxembourg				1.59	1.42	1.25	1.18	1.01	1.13
Mexico		1.44	1.41	1.29	1.18	1.06	0.95	0.43	0.58
Netherlands	1.74	1.76	1.39	1.30	1.35	1.15	1.11	0.99	1.11
New Zealand	0.90	0.87	0.83	0.81	0.76	0.71	0.75	0.76	0.88
Norway	0.56	0.59	0.59	0.56	0.72	0.71	0.67	0.54	0.50
Poland	1.50	1.78	1.95	2.62	1.93	1.75	1.42	1.59	1.72
Portugal	1.61	1.68	1.51	1.49	1.59	1.43	1.41	1.17	1.44
Slovak Republic	1.43	1.46	1.45	1.26	2.43	2.49	2.41		
Slovenia	1.14	1.13	1.17	1.05	0.93	0.98	0.83	0.81	0.90
Spain	0.81	0.78	0.83	0.82	0.74	0.68	0.65	0.82	0.97
Sweden	0.55	0.56	0.57	0.59	0.38	0.39	0.41	0.39	0.40
Switzerland			0.66	0.62	0.30	0.29	0.28	0.31	0.31
Turkey	0.81	0.72	0.74	0.83	0.87	0.84	0.83	0.85	0.93
United Kingdom	1.06	1.11	1.04	0.97	1.10	1.12	1.10	1.12	1.14
United States	0.46	0.52	0.57	0.56	0.52	0.47	0.45	0.49	0.61

Source: OECD (2011, pp. 126–27). General caveats are described in the text, with country-specific caveats available in the source document.

differences in enforcement include the breadth of audit coverage, the ability of the tax authority to access bank records, the size of fines that can be levied, and the powers available to enforce compliance with audit findings.

The qualitative nature of some of these administrative dimensions complicates cross-country comparisons. Recently, though, using OECD data sourced primarily from national revenue authorities, Robinson and Slemrod (2012) developed numerical codings for 10 important non-rate tax-system aspects. Interestingly, high-tax countries feature less self-assessment and expend more resources on tax administration than low-tax countries, measured by the ratio of administrators to the working-age population. Assuming complexity rises with the tax burden, Robinson and Slemrod (2012) suggest that shifting the cost of acquiring the expertise necessary to comply with tax laws onto taxpayers may not be efficient in high-tax countries, potentially explaining the lower levels of self-reporting in high-tax countries. The positive cross-country relationship between the amount of resources spent on administration and tax rates is consistent with the optimal tax prescription we discuss later that an optimum equates the marginal cost of funds across all available means to raise revenue.

For any given objective, there are more and less effective ways for a tax administration to operate. For example, what is the optimal use of computers and information technology? Should a tax administration be organized by tax levy (e.g., corporate tax vs. value-added tax), or by taxpayer segment (e.g., corporations vs. high-income individuals)? How should it be organized to minimize corruption? These questions have been addressed extensively, but informally, especially in a developing-country context in, for example, Bird (1983), and are certainly context-specific.[3]

As we have stressed, information is central to tax systems, especially when minimizing the capriciousness of the tax burden is an objective. This central role is clear in the modern theory of taxation, although often this is not emphasized. In the seminal optimal income tax model of Mirrlees (1971), it is assumed that income can be measured perfectly and costlessly, but ability cannot be measured at any cost. Proceeding with these extreme assumptions provides much insight, but these models are caricatures of a world in which income is often extremely difficult to ascertain accurately, and some indicators of ability can be obtained.

In practice, information gathering is a central task of all tax administrations, and the cost of gathering information depends on how accessible the information is, from whom it can be obtained, and whether it can be easily hidden. This raises several intriguing questions. As we discuss further in chapter 6, there are several advantages to taxing a market transaction relative to taxing an activity such as consumption. First, in any market transaction there are two parties with conflicting interests—to one party it represents revenue, and to the other it represents a cost. Hence any transaction has the potential of being reported to the authorities by one unsatisfied party. A second property is that the more documented the transaction, the lower is the cost of the tax authority to gather information on it. For this reason it is easier to tax a transaction that involves a large company, which needs the documentation for its own purposes, than to tax a small business, which may not require the same level of documentation. In addition market transactions establish arm's-length prices, which greatly facilitate valuing the transaction.

Administrative costs also have implications for the optimal boundary between firms. Coase (1937) argued that (in the absence of externalities) the equilibrium boundary is optimal because firms consider all relevant costs and benefits of expanding their size. But Dharmapala et al. (2011) show that administrative costs are akin to an externality, because firm size, and industrial organization more generally, will affect the cost of administering a tax system at a given effectiveness, in part because they affect the availability of more easily observable arm's-length transactions. They show that when administrative costs are fixed per firm, then a taxed firm should face a fixed fee—a Pigouvian tax—equal to the administrative cost of taxing it. The set of taxed firms is endogenous in their model, and it may be optimal to exclude firms below a certain size threshold from taxation if the ratio of administrative costs to tax collected is sufficiently high. This results in a "missing middle" of firm size, as some firms reduce their size to be below the taxing threshold. Such a phenomenon is commonly observed in developing economies. We discuss the model further in chapter 6.

The administrative cost of obtaining information will also be a function of the physical size, tangibility/visibility, and the mobility of the tax base (e.g., it is harder to tax diamonds than windows); whether there is a registration of the tax base (e.g., owners of cars, holders of drivers' licenses); the number of taxpayer units; and the extent of information sharing with other agencies, both non-tax agencies within a jurisdiction and tax authorities in other jurisdictions. Administrative cost is also an increasing function of the complexity and lack of clarity of the tax law, ceteris paribus.

Administrative costs possess two additional properties that compli-
cate the formal modeling of tax-system issues: they tend to be discontinuous and to have decreasing average costs with respect to the tax
rate. To see the first property, consider two commodity tax rates,
denoted by t_1 and t_2. If $t_1 = t_2$, then only the total sales of the two commodities need be reported and monitored. If, however, the two rates
differ even slightly, then the sales of the two commodities must be
reported separately, approximately doubling the required flow of information. This undoubtedly explains why, in contrast to optimal commodity tax theory that suggests different tax rates on each commodity,
real tax systems feature a very small number of tax rates. Second, there
are decreasing average costs because the cost of inspecting a tax base
does not depend on the tax rate (except to the extent that people may
be more inclined to cheat with a higher tax rate). Hence a higher tax
rate reduces the administrative cost per dollar of revenue collected
(Sandford 1973). Administrative cost may also be a function of the
combination of the taxes employed and their rates, because the collection of information concerning one tax may facilitate the collection of
another tax (e.g., inspection of VAT receipts may facilitate the collection
of income tax). Note, finally, that in cases of negative marginal and
average tax rates, such as arise under the earned income tax credit, the
administrative problem is of a different nature, as the evading taxpayer's incentive is to overstate, rather than understate, income.

4.2 Compliance Costs

Compliance costs, in contrast to administrative costs, are incurred in
the tax remittance and collection process directly by taxpayers and by
third parties (e.g., employers who are required to remit tax on behalf
of their employees and provide information to the tax authority). We
say "directly" for two reasons: (1) the burden of the compliance costs
may be shifted away from the party that expends the resources to
comply, just as an explicit tax may be shifted, due to changes in relative
prices, and (2) administrative costs also ultimately burden taxpayers
but show up, in the first instance, as government expenditures, not as
monetary or time costs to taxpayers even though ultimately taxpayers
bear these costs.

Measuring the extent and nature of compliance costs is not, as in the
case of administrative costs, as straightforward as culling the relevant
data from government budgets. Surveys are the most commonly used

method to measure compliance costs, although low response rates can impair the reliability of their findings. While re-weighting survey results based on observable demographics is often helpful, unobserved heterogeneity between respondents and nonrespondents is likely to be important. The direction of nonrandom underreporting bias is generally unclear, so survey results may not even accurately bound compliance costs. Pitt and Slemrod (1989) estimate the size of taxpayer compliance costs by inferring the value of tax deductions forgone by taxpayers who chose not to itemize their deductions and instead claim the simpler standard deduction. Some taxpayer characteristics, such as state income tax rates, are assumed to affect the tax saving from itemizing but not the cost of itemizing deductions, and so can be used to separately estimate equations for the tax saving and cost of compliance of itemizing deductions. Only taxpayers whose compliance cost is less than the tax saving from itemizing their deductions will do so. Using a stratified random sample of 1982 Treasury Tax File microdata, they estimate compliance costs to be $43 per itemizing taxpayer, or about $104 in current dollars.

While respondents may see compliance as a "vexatious cost" (Tait 1988, p. 352) and overstate their costs in an attempt to influence policy, it is also possible that those who find responding to surveys most burdensome also find tax-system compliance particularly costly (Sandford 1995).

Another tricky issue arises because much of compliance cost is composed of time spent by taxpayers. Even if an unbiased measure of hours spent to comply with the tax system was available, converting the cost into dollars is not straightforward. For example, should time be valued at the before or after-tax wage rate, should "psychological" cost be included if tax-related tasks are more onerous than the taxpayer's regular job, or should a self-reported measure of time cost be used instead? Regardless of the choice made, simply measuring the time cost of tax compliance will overstate the marginal cost imposed by the tax system if valuable recordkeeping and information reporting—needed, for example, by mortgage lenders and college financial aid officers—is facilitated by tax-compliance related activities. These problems make it especially difficult to meaningfully compare estimates across countries, although see Sandford (1995) for estimates of compliance costs for a variety of taxes in several countries.

Regardless of these methodological difficulties, one fact stands out among all studies of all taxes in all countries: compliance costs dwarf

Table 4.2
Compliance costs of the US income tax system: Individuals

Tax year 2004	
Hours (bn)	3.5
Average value of hours ($/hour)	20.0
Total value of hours ($bn)	70.0
Out-of-pocket expenditures ($bn)	15.0
Total compliance cost ($bn)	85.0
Total compliance cost as a percent of receipts	11.1

Source: Slemrod (2004b).

administrative costs. For example, Slemrod (1996) estimates that for the US income tax, the private compliance cost is about 10 cents per dollar of revenue collected, compared to an administrative cost of about 0.6 cents per dollar collected for all the taxes the IRS administers. Using updated data and assumptions, Slemrod (2004b) estimates total compliance costs to have risen to be 11.1 cents per dollar of income tax receipts in tax year 2004. Table 4.2 breaks down the estimated compliance cost for individuals, highlighting that the value of time spent greatly exceeds taxpayers' out-of-pocket expenditures in complying with the US income tax system. Based on a survey of Minnesota taxpayers for the 1982 tax year, Slemrod and Sorum (1984) estimate that a majority of time spent by taxpayers complying with the income tax system is due to recordkeeping, followed by return preparation, research, and interacting with a tax advisor. The relative magnitudes were found to be broadly similar across income levels, although total hours spent on compliance had a U-shaped pattern in income.

For corporations, Slemrod (2004b) estimated total collection costs at $40 billion for the 2004 tax year, representing a much larger 23.7 percent share of corporate income tax receipts. One suspects that, compared to individuals, a larger proportion of these costs is devoted to tax planning, as opposed to conforming to the tax filing requirements. Among the 1,500 largest US corporations, Slemrod and Blumenthal (1996) found that about two-thirds of compliance cost was due to within-firm personnel, about one-sixth due to outside assistance, and the remaining one-sixth due to within-firm nonpersonnel costs such as computers. Medium-sized businesses have a proportionately larger compliance burden than large businesses, and small businesses have the highest ratio, making corporate income tax compliance costs highly regressive in the sense that the ratio of costs to sales, or to assets, falls with firm size.

Some of what is measured as compliance cost is an unavoidable cost of complying with the law, and some of it is voluntarily undertaken in an effort to reduce tax liability. In either case it approximately represents resource costs to society because otherwise-productive resources are diverted to compliance activity. That taxpayers will voluntarily spend time on compliance in an effort to reduce their tax liability does not make it any less of a social cost; efficiency cost arises because taxpayers are encouraged by the tax system to engage in avoidance activity they would not engage in were it not for taxes.

To some extent administrative costs and compliance costs are substitutes, in the sense that either the government or the taxpayer may have the lead role in collecting key information. As an example, consider when is it optimal to delegate to employers the authority to remit taxes on behalf of, and convey information about, employees, thus allowing the administration to audit both the taxpayer agent and the taxpayer himself, and when it is optimal to deal only with the employee. Clearly, given that the employer already has the necessary information, it would save administrative costs to require him to pass it along to the tax administrator. This might also reduce total social costs if the cost of gathering information by the administration is higher than the increase in cost caused by imposing a two-stage gathering system. Note that a withholding system requires two information-gathering systems and might generate incentives for the withholding agent to evade the taxes it collects, or to collaborate with withholdees in withholding less than required (Yaniv 1988, 1992).

However, the potential efficiency of involving taxpayers in the administrative process must be tempered with a practical consideration. Administrative costs must pass through a budgeting process, while compliance costs are hidden. Hence there may be a tendency to view a policy that reduces administrative cost at the expense of an equal (or greater) increase in compliance costs as a decrease in social cost, because it results in a decrease in government expenditures. Moreover, administrative costs should be weighted higher than compliance costs because they are funded by tax revenue raised through distortionary taxes, for which the marginal cost of funds exceeds unity; we return to this issue in chapter 7.

5   Tax Base Elasticity

5.1   Elasticity of Taxable Income

Because it holds the promise of summarizing the welfare cost of all behavioral responses undertaken to reduce tax liability, the elasticity of taxable income (ETI) has assumed a central role in measuring the marginal excess burden of income taxation (Feldstein 1999; Usher 1986).[1] The larger is the elasticity of response, the higher is the marginal excess burden per dollar raised. In most standard models, hours of work is the only dimension of behavioral response to changes in marginal tax rates, but the ETI concept generalizes the set of behavioral responses to all the margins of adjustment affecting taxable income discussed in chapter 3. In addition to hours of work, higher marginal tax rates may affect taxpayer's choices over intensity of work, quantity of income-tax-deductible consumption (e.g., charitable giving), career choice, form and timing of compensation, tax avoidance, and tax evasion (Saez et al. 2012).

These behavioral responses matter because, provided that the private and social costs of sheltering one dollar of income from taxation are equal, the ETI is a sufficient statistic for welfare analysis. At the margin a taxpayer will incur cost equal to one dollar, or sacrifice utility valued at one dollar, to save one dollar in taxes. Taxpayers adjust all means available to reduce taxes by one dollar up to the point that the marginal cost of doing so rises to one dollar. The anatomy of behavioral response does not, in principle, matter because at an optimum for the taxpayer the marginal cost of saving a dollar in taxes is equal across all margins of behavioral response. We discuss exceptions to this general principle in section 5.2.

To show this argument more formally, we use the tax avoidance model outlined in chapter 3, but following Chetty (2009), we simplify the model by assuming that the utility function has a quasi-linear form. The taxpayer's utility maximization problem is now

$$\max_{\{C,l,s\}} C - \psi(l) \quad \text{s.t.} \quad C = A + (1-t)wl + ts - \kappa(wl,s), \tag{5.1}$$

where C is consumption, l is labor supply, $\psi(l)$ is a convex function capturing the disutility of labor supply, A is a demogrant or exogenous income, w is the wage rate, t is the tax rate on taxable income, and s is tax avoidance, which has a real resource cost to the taxpayer equal to $\kappa(wl, s)$, where $\kappa_2 > 0$, $\kappa_{22} > 0$, $\kappa_1 < 0$, and κ_{12} may be positive or negative.[2] We assume that revenue raised by the government is returned to taxpayers in a lump-sum manner, so that social welfare with quasi-linear utility has the following simple form:

$$\begin{aligned} W(t) &= [C - \psi(l)] + R(t) \\ &= [A + (1-t)(wl-s) + s - \kappa(wl,s) - \psi(l)] + t(wl - s). \end{aligned} \tag{5.2}$$

We can also assume that l and s have been chosen by the taxpayer to maximize utility, so the behavioral response to a small change in the tax rate t does not affect the maximized value of utility (the term in square brackets); the envelope theorem implies that taxpayer utility is only affected by the mechanical revenue consequences of the tax-rate change. Hence the welfare effect of a marginal increase in the tax rate t is

$$\begin{aligned} \frac{\partial W(t)}{\partial t} &= [-(wl-s)] + (wl-s) + t\frac{\partial[wl-s]}{\partial t} \\ &= t\frac{\partial[wl-s]}{\partial t} \\ &= t\frac{\partial z}{\partial t}, \end{aligned} \tag{5.3}$$

where $z \equiv wl - s$ is taxable income. Equation (5.3) illustrates that, provided the taxpayer's sheltering activity involves a real resource cost, we need only know how taxable income responds to changes in the marginal tax rate, and the larger the response, the bigger is the welfare cost. Whether the response of taxable income is due to reduced labor supply or increased sheltering effort does not matter. While this model has only two margins of adjustment (labor supply and sheltering), this sufficiency proposition generalizes to all margins of adjustment provided that the private and social marginal costs of behavioral response to taxes are equal. When utility is not quasi-linear, the uncompensated and compensated elasticity of taxable income are no longer equal, so for welfare analysis the uncompensated response of taxable income in equation (5.3) should be replaced with a compensated response.

The higher is the ETI, the larger is the marginal welfare cost of taxation per dollar raised, which we can conveniently express in terms of the marginal efficiency cost of funds. Recalling equation (2.7) from chapter 2, we can write the general MECF formula for tax instrument θ_i as

$$MECF(\theta_i) = \frac{1}{1 - (B_{\theta_i}/T_{\theta_i})}. \tag{5.4}$$

For the taxpayer's problem here, an increase in the marginal tax rate t causes a marginal mechanical burden of $T_t = wl - s = z$, while the revenue consequence of the taxpayer's behavioral response to a higher marginal tax rate is $B_t = -t\{\partial[wl-s]/\partial t\} = -t(\partial z/\partial t)$. Substituting these expressions into equation (5.4) yields

$$MECF(t) = \frac{1}{1 + \dfrac{t}{z}\dfrac{\partial z}{\partial t}} = \frac{1}{1 - \left(\dfrac{t}{1-t}\right)\left(\dfrac{1-t}{z}\dfrac{\partial z}{\partial(1-t)}\right)} = \frac{1}{1 - \left(\dfrac{t}{1-t}\right)\varepsilon}, \tag{5.5}$$

where ε is the elasticity of taxable income with respect to the net-of-tax rate, which is generally a positive number.

From now on, we will let $y \equiv wl$, and refer to y as earned income, recognizing that changes in earned income depend on choices made by taxpayers that affect both their labor supply and the rate of compensation for their time.

Rather than assume that there are exogenous differences in taxpayers' wage rates, we will now assume that people differ in their disutility of producing income, denoted by the parameter n. Hence taxpayers of type n choose some (c_n, z_n) given their budget constraint. This is not a substantive change: we can measure a taxpayer's ability by her market income for a given quantity of labor supplied or, equivalently, by her disutility of producing a given amount of income. This latter formulation is analytically convenient when there are multiple margins of behavioral response to taxes.

Importantly, the validity of equation (5.5) does not depend on there being a representative taxpayer or a linear tax system. To show this, we follow Saez et al. (2012) by considering a marginal increase in the top marginal income tax rate applying to taxpayers with taxable incomes above $\bar{z}$. Having assumed away income effects, taxpayers' choices depend only on the marginal tax rate, and not on A as well. Assuming no behavioral response to the increase in the top marginal tax rate, we write the marginal mechanical increase in tax paid as

$$\frac{\partial T}{\partial t} \equiv T_t = \sum_{i=1}^{N}(z_i - \bar{z}) = N(z_m - \bar{z}), \tag{5.6}$$

where N is the number of top-bracket taxpayers and $z_m = \sum_{i=1}^{N} z_i / N$ is their mean taxable income. But behavioral response, B_t, reduces the amount of revenue collected, with

$$\frac{\partial B}{\partial t} \equiv B_t = -\sum_{i=1}^{N} t \frac{\partial z_i}{\partial(1-t)} \frac{d(1-t)}{dt}$$

$$= N z_m \frac{t}{1-t} \sum_{i=1}^{N} \frac{z_i}{N z_m} \frac{(1-t)}{z_i} \frac{\partial z_i}{\partial(1-t)} \tag{5.7}$$

$$= N z_m \frac{t}{1-t} \varepsilon,$$

where ε is now the *average* ETI with respect to the net-of-tax rate, weighted using individual taxable incomes. Recalling again the expression for the marginal efficiency cost of funds, we write the welfare cost in dollars of a marginal increase in the top marginal tax rate as

$$MECF(t) = \frac{1}{1 - \frac{B_t}{T_t}}$$

$$= \frac{1}{1 - \varepsilon \left(\frac{t}{1-t}\right)\left(\frac{z_m}{z_m - \bar{z}}\right)} \tag{5.8}$$

$$= \frac{1}{1 - \varepsilon a \left(\frac{t}{1-t}\right)},$$

where $a = z_m/(z_m - \bar{z})$. Saez (2001) shows that the upper tails of actual income distributions are well approximated by a Pareto distribution, in which case a is almost constant. Given an estimate for the Pareto parameter a, the average elasticity of taxable income with respect to the net-of-tax rate is thus a sufficient statistic for the marginal efficiency cost of funds in a world with heterogeneous taxpayers. As the value of a rises, the marginal mechanical revenue gain declines because the tax-rate increase applies only to incomes above $\bar{z}$. But the magnitude of the substitution effect is unchanged, so the MECF is increasing in a. For a linear income tax, a change in *the* marginal tax rate, by definition, applies to all income, in which case $a = 1$ and equations (5.5) and (5.8) are identical, except for the use of an income-weighted average elasticity of taxable income in the latter case with heterogeneous taxpayers.

In contrast to typically low estimates of short-term labor supply elasticities—economists know little about long-term elasticities—there is ample evidence that taxpayers respond more elastically along other dimensions. But despite the promise and apparent simplicity of the ETI concept—in principle, eliminating the need to separately estimate each margin of behavioral response—its application comes with several limitations and some of the required assumptions are violated in practice. In what follows, we discuss the main issues in applying the ETI concept and empirically estimating its magnitude.

5.2 Issues in Applying the Elasticity of Taxable Income

Two main issues come up in applying an estimated ETI to welfare analysis: (1) fiscal externalities and income shifting, and (2) changes in the definition of the tax base. Fiscal externalities arise if a change in marginal income tax rates induces taxpayers to shift income to another tax base, be it, for example, from the individual to the corporate income tax base, or to any base at a different date. When fiscal externalities arise, the ETI overstates efficiency cost because the observed reduction in taxable income is, to some extent, offset by socially valued revenue that is collected in another base or period. Hence, when constructing an ETI suitable for welfare analysis, it is necessary to determine for each tax change under consideration the extent to which revenue reductions in the applicable base lead to increased revenue elsewhere, and to know the relevant tax rate applying to that income.

There are several prominent cases of income shifting across tax bases. For example, the Tax Reform Act of 1986 reduced the top-bracket marginal personal income tax rate to below the corporate income tax rate, increasing the attractiveness of partnerships and S corporations, for which distributions are taxed as personal income, compared to C corporations where income is first subject to the corporate tax rate. Thus revenue shifted into the personal tax base from the corporate tax base. Similarly, anticipated increases in top-bracket marginal income tax rates for 1993 led some taxpayers to re-time income realization to the 1992 tax year (Feldstein and Feenberg 1996). On the one hand, the ability of many high-income earners to re-time income suggests fiscal externalities across time periods are likely to be larger for temporary than permanent tax changes (Goolsbee 2000). On the other hand, adjustment frictions and longer-run considerations, such as bequest planning, point to potentially larger fiscal externalities for permanent tax changes. A complete accounting of fiscal externalities would also take general equilibrium effects into account. For example, lower marginal income tax rates may increase labor supply and raise the before-tax return on complementary factors, such as capital, that are taxed via other bases. Section 3.3.5 discusses cross-border income shifting, which could be relevant to a welfare analysis from a global perspective that must recognize that revenue lost to one country will, in general, be accompanied by revenue gained by other countries.

Some changes in the definition of the tax base also affect the magnitude of the ETI, and its policy implications. A narrow tax base is likely to have a higher ETI than a broad base with few exemptions because avoidance schemes are facilitated by loopholes in the tax code. Because the ETI is a function of the breadth of the tax base, it is not an immutable structural parameter, instead being partially under policy makers' control. As we discuss in chapter 9, Slemrod and Kopczuk (2002) outline a model in which a social planner optimally chooses the breadth of the tax base, and effectively the ETI, to balance higher administrative costs against efficiency gains from a broader tax base.

5.2.1 Does Tax Evasion Fit This Framework?

Changes in revenue collected through audits and fines on evaded income represent another fiscal externality, but when risk is an element in taxpayers' evasion decision, there are additional welfare consequences.[3] Chetty (2009) argues that some tax-reducing activities, the most prominent being tax evasion, represent a transfer between agents, in which case the private costs differ from social costs. The fines levied on discovered evasion represent a cost to a tax evader but not a social cost because the evader's loss is everyone else's gain. As an alternative to the ETI, Chetty (2009) proposes a welfare measure based on a weighted average of taxable income and earned income elasticities, with the weights depending on the marginal social resource cost of sheltering income. While Chetty's (2009) formulation is robust to all margins in which private and social costs of sheltering differ, we show next that the welfare consequences of tax evasion can be handled in an arguably more intuitive fashion by directly adjusting the standard formula for the marginal efficiency cost of funds.

Following Chetty (2009), suppose that taxpayers simultaneously choose earned income, y, and evaded income, e, given exogenous, untaxed income, A, to solve the following Allingham–Sandmo style expected utility maximization problem:

$$v(A,t,p,F) = \max_{\{y,e\}}(1-p(e))u(A+(1-t)y+te)$$
$$+ p(e)u(A+(1-t)y - F(e)) - \psi(y), \tag{5.9}$$

where utility, u, is concave in consumption, ψ represents the disutility of work, p is the audit probability, t is the marginal tax rate faced by the taxpayer, and F is the fine for tax evasion. To simplify notation, let $c_h = A + (1 - t)y + te$ and $c_l = A + (1 - t)y - F(e)$ denote consumption in the nonaudited and audited states, respectively. The separability of consumption and disutility of work is made for analytical convenience but does not constrain the distortionary effects of taxation on labor supply and evasion to be independent (Yitzhaki 1987). The FOCs for the taxpayer are

$$[\partial e] \quad (1-p(e))tu'(c_h) - p(e)F'(e)u'(c_l) = p'(e)[u(c_h) - u(c_l)] \tag{5.10}$$

and

$$[\partial y] \quad (1-p(e))(1-t)u'(c_h) + p(e)(1-t)u'(c_l) = \psi'(y). \tag{5.11}$$

We assume that p is convex in e, which is standard in the tax evasion literature, and is intended to capture, in a reduced-form representation, the assumption that the tax authority has some ability to ascertain the taxpayer's true tax liability and that this is more likely the larger is evasion. We also assume that ψ is convex in y.

Recall now from chapter 2 that, when the social planner optimally chooses the marginal tax rate t, an optimum satisfies

$$[\partial t] \quad R_t = [T_t - B_t] = \frac{\alpha}{\lambda}T_t$$
$$= -\frac{1}{\lambda}\frac{\partial v}{\partial t}, \tag{5.12}$$

where the second equality makes use of Roy's identity, λ is the Lagrange multiplier on the social planner's budget constraint, $v = v(A, t, p, F)$ is the taxpayer's indirect utility function, R_t is marginal net revenue collected, T_t is the mechanical burden, and B_t is the behavioral response to a change in the marginal tax rate, t.[4] Each of these terms needs further interpretation in the presence of tax evasion. Net tax revenue,

R, is equal to tax receipts on reported income, plus revenue from detected evasion and fines, less the administrative costs from tax audits, as follows:

$$R(t) = t(y - e) + p(e)[te + F(e)] - D(e), \qquad (5.13)$$

so that the marginal change in net revenue from an increase in the income tax rate, t, is equal to

$$R_t = \underbrace{[y - e(1 - p(e))]}_{T_t}$$

$$+ \underbrace{\left[t\frac{\partial[y - e]}{\partial t} + t\frac{\partial e}{\partial t}[p'(e)e + p(e)] + \frac{\partial e}{\partial t}(p'(e)F(e) + p(e)F'(e) - D'(e)) \right]}_{-B_t}.$$

$$(5.14)$$

The marginal mechanical revenue effect, T_t, considers the revenue consequences on both reported revenue and detected evasion, while the behavioral response captures all the adjustments that taxpayers make in response to an increase in the marginal tax rate, t. Recognizing that p and F are functions of e, which depends on t, we can further simplify the behavioral response term, B_t, and decompose it, as follows:

$$B_t = -t\left[\frac{\partial[y - e]}{\partial t} \right] - \left[t\frac{\partial[ep]}{\partial t} + \frac{\partial[pF - D]}{\partial t} \right]. \qquad (5.15)$$

The first term is the response of initially reported taxable income to a change in the marginal tax rate, which numerous empirical studies have attempted to estimate (see section 5.4 and Saez et al. 2012 for a review). The second term reflects the fact that when the tax rate changes, evasion choices of taxpayers may change, which can impact the amount of revenue collected via audits and fines, and the administrative cost of the tax authority (which has been modeled as a function of the amount of evasion, e).[5] This term illustrates the broader point that, for the elasticity of taxable income to be a sufficient statistic for marginal efficiency cost, one must consider income shifted across tax bases (in this case between revenue remitted "voluntarily," revenue collected from fines, and administrative costs) and time, as discussed in Slemrod (1998) and Saez et al. (2012). To empirically estimate this term, one would need data on the tax responsiveness of discovered evasion, ep, revenue from fines, pF, and administrative cost, D, even though the enforcement-induced revenue and fines may be collected years after the tax-rate change.

Focusing now on the welfare implications for taxpayers, recall that in the absence of risk aversion, $\partial v/\partial t = -u_c T_t$. But, in the presence of evasion with risk-averse taxpayers, there is an additional loss to the taxpayer, due to an increase in the risk-bearing cost of tax evasion. Making use of the envelope theorem, we have

$$-\frac{\partial v}{\partial t} = (1-p(e))(y-e)u'(c_h) + p(e)yu'(c_l)$$

$$= y[(1-p(e))u'(c_h) + p(e)u'(c_l)] - e(1-p(e))u'(c_h)$$

$$= \mathbf{E}u'(c)\left(y - e(1-p(e))\frac{u'(c_h)}{\mathbf{E}u'(c)}\right) \qquad (5.16)$$

$$= \mathbf{E}u'(c)\left(T_t - e(1-p(e))p(e)\left(\frac{u'(c_h)-u'(c_l)}{\mathbf{E}u'(c)}\right)\right),$$

where $\mathbf{E}u'(c) = (1-p(e))u'(c_h) + p(e)u'(c_l)$ is the marginal expected utility of exogenous income, using $\mathbf{E}$ to represent an expectation taken over utility in the audited and nonaudited states. Combining equations (5.12) and (5.16) yields the following expression:

$$MECF = \frac{\lambda}{\mathbf{E}u'(c)} = \frac{1 - \frac{1}{T_t}\left[e(1-p(e))p(e)\left(\frac{u'(c_h)-u'(c_l)}{\mathbf{E}u'(c)}\right)\right]}{1 - \frac{B_t}{T_t}}. \qquad (5.17)$$

This marginal efficiency cost of funds representation differs from the standard case presented in chapter 2. The additional term in the numerator captures the marginal increase in the risk-bearing cost of tax evasion, first discussed in Yitzhaki (1987). This is the loss in expected utility compared to a revenue-equivalent tax system in which taxpayers agree not to evade taxes. A marginal increase in the tax rate increases the amount of risk the taxpayer bears because the size of the evasion gamble mechanically increases with the tax rate. Further intuition can be gained by assuming constant-relative–risk-aversion utility and taking a Taylor series approximation around $\bar{c} = \mathbf{E}c = (1-p)c_h + pc_l$, as follows:

$$e(1-p)p\left(\frac{u'(c_h)-u'(c_l)}{\mathbf{E}u'(c)}\right) \approx -ep(1-p)\gamma\left(\frac{\Delta c}{\bar{c}}\right), \qquad (5.18)$$

where γ is the coefficient of relative risk aversion, and $\Delta c = te + F$. For a given amount of evasion, e, the excess burden is larger the more risk averse is the taxpayer, the greater is the variance of returns between the audited and nonaudited states, $p\,(1-p)$, and the larger is the difference in consumption between the two states, as a share of mean consumption. This term can be estimated for any given audit class using an estimate of risk aversion and data on evasion rates, audit probabilities, and penalties for evasion. Note that if taxpayers are risk neutral, there is no excess burden from tax evasion and this term disappears.

In sum, taking account of the welfare effects of tax evasion requires:

1. Adding in changes in revenue from discovered evasion and accompanying fines as well as changes in administration cost, as shown in equation (5.14);
2. Adding the change in the private risk-bearing cost of tax evasion to the numerator of the marginal efficiency cost of funds expression.

While our formal analysis here closely parallels Chetty (2009), we reach a somewhat different conclusion about the value of the ETI in measuring the marginal welfare cost of taxation. Rather than adopting the general framework developed by Chetty (2009)—which requires separately estimating both an elasticity of taxable and labor income, and the marginal social cost of sheltering with which to weight these elasticities—we argue for retaining the centrality of the ETI in welfare analysis and making the two modifications described here to ensure that evasion is appropriately addressed. Unlike Chetty's (2009) more general approach, we make no attempt to account for optimization errors due to misperceived prices or costs; while Chetty's (2009) critique is important, the implications of allowing for optimization errors extend well beyond the ETI literature. Our approach does, however, address one important source of divergence between the private and social costs of sheltering—tax evasion.

5.3   Empirical Estimation and Identification Issues

Empirically identifying the ETI boils down to estimating what taxpayers' taxable income would have been absent any change in marginal tax rates. The main approaches followed in the literature fall under three broad categories, (1) before and after tax-reform comparisons, (2) analysis of income shares, and (3) difference-in-difference (DD) methods, using panel data.

A taxpayer's income before a tax reform is unlikely to be a good estimate of their income, absent the tax change, because incomes vary through time for many reasons unrelated to taxes, such as a change in fortune, real economic growth, and business-cycle dynamics. Provided that the group affected by a tax reform is relatively small, secular trends in income may be controlled for by using changes in the *share* of income accruing to the affected subpopulation to estimate the ETI, which effectively normalizes the incomes of the affected group by average incomes in the population. However, share analysis only provides an unbiased estimate of the ETI if changes in the income distribution are uncorrelated with marginal tax rates, which is unlikely to be true given the substantial increase in wage inequality over recent decades. For these reasons most recent empirical work has been based on more sophisticated DD methods.

Difference-in-difference estimates—for which share analysis is a particular example—identify some "control" group to measure the change in income that would have occurred to the "treatment" group absent the tax reform. Unlike experimental studies, treatment and control groups are not randomly chosen, but are selected into by taxpayers according to income. This makes estimates biased if there is any systematic variation across income groups correlated with, but not caused by, the tax reform under investigation. In addition, for tax reforms in which both the treatment and control groups experience a change in tax rate, but by a differential amount, DD analysis will only consistently estimate the ETI if members of both the treatment and control groups have the same ETI. The greater access to and use of tax avoidance opportunities by high-income earners is just one reason why the ETI is likely to differ by income.

When an individual's pre-reform income is a good indicator of their income absent the reform, panel data can be potentially informative. However, the presence of mean reversion in incomes is a particular concern for panel data estimates. To see this, suppose that we are using panel data to estimate an ETI based on the 1993 increase in top-bracket marginal income tax rates. Even absent any behavioral response to taxes, we would expect members of the top bracket, based on 1992 incomes, to see their average 1993 incomes decline relative to other taxpayers through mean reversion alone, upwardly biasing our ETI estimate. For a cut in marginal tax rates, mean reversion and any behavioral response partially cancel out, downwardly biasing any estimate of the ETI. With sufficiently long data panels, flexible time trends may be able to control for the presence of mean reversion. These issues are discussed at much greater length in Saez et al. (2012).

5.4   Lessons from Empirical Work

In a pioneering contribution, Feldstein (1995) used panel data to estimate the ETI from the differential marginal tax-rate changes in the Tax Reform Act of 1986. Employing a tabulated difference-in-difference methodology, he estimated the ETI at between 1 and 3, suggesting that the United States was on the wrong side of the Laffer curve, so that tax cuts would raise revenue. However, adopting a regression framework enabling the inclusion of variables intended to control for changes in income inequality and mean reversion, Auten and Carroll (1999) estimate a much lower ETI of 0.55 for the same tax change. Because non–tax-related variation in income alters taxpayers' marginal tax rates, a spurious correlation arises between changes in incomes and observed changes in tax rates for each individual, which Auten and Carroll (1999) attempt to deal with in a two-stage least squares framework. In the first-stage, they used the tax rate that applied in 1989 to 1985 incomes grossed up by CPI inflation as an instrument for the 1989 net-of-tax rate (i.e., the net-of-tax rate absent behavioral response); in the second stage, they regressed the change in adjusted gross income (AGI) on the change in the instrumented net-of-tax rate, and other controls. Notably, Auten and Carroll (1999) were able to make use of a large data panel that oversamples high-income earners, providing a degree of precision to their estimates not possible in Feldstein's analysis given the small sample of high-income earners in his public-use data.

Making use of a tax panel spanning the period 1979 to 1990, Gruber and Saez (2002) examine the tax changes in both 1981 and 1986, for which they investigated the response of both taxable and broad income (income before deductions). Unlike the previous studies, their data panel includes state income taxes, providing variation in tax rates in both the cross-sectional and time dimensions. Data for each individual in their panel is grouped into three-year periods, and they use an instrument for the change in the net-of-tax rate very similar to Auten and Carroll (1999). Because their data span multiple periods, they were able to richly control for changes in income inequality and mean reversion in incomes. For broad income (total income less capital gains and Social Security benefits), Gruber and Saez (2002) estimate an elasticity of only 0.12, with an estimate for upper-income earners not much larger at 0.17. However, they report larger estimates for the elasticity of taxable income, suggesting that most of the behavioral response for taxable income is via deductions, exemptions, and exclusions; for itemizers, the ETI estimate is 0.65, but negative (although statistically insignificant) for non-itemizers. Their data do not allow precise conclusions about variation by income levels, although there is some evidence that the ETI rises with income.

Consistent with the finding by Gruber and Saez (2002) that the behavioral response is much larger for taxable income than broad income, Kopczuk (2005) finds that the ETI is larger the narrower is the tax base (defined to be taxable income as a share of total income). Intuitively, the more deductions that are available, the less costly it is for taxpayers to shift income out of the tax base in response to higher marginal tax rates. Formally, Kopczuk (2005) augments the Gruber and Saez (2002) framework by including an interaction between tax base breadth and the change in the net-of-tax rate, instrumenting for this term using the predicted change absent any behavioral response to taxes. Of particular note, Kopczuk (2005) estimates that, for a taxpayer without access to deductions, there would be *no* behavioral response to taxes within a three-year period. Chapter 9 lays out the framework developed by Slemrod and Kopczuk (2002) for the optimal setting of the ETI achieved by varying the broadness of the tax base.

Based on a comprehensive reading of the literature, Saez et al. (2012) suggest a longer term ETI between 0.12 and 0.40. The increased sophistication of more recent studies on a variety of dimensions, such as the use of datasets with larger samples of top-income earners, the availability of panel data spanning long-enough time periods to allow non–tax-related trends in income to be more carefully controlled for, and the opportunity to study not just tax-cutting episodes but also the tax increases of the early 1990s, has generally been associated with a downward trend in estimates of the ETI. *(A puzzling one)*

The overwhelming evidence of fiscal externalities in the empirical ETI literature highlights the need to carefully adjust raw ETI estimates to arrive at an accurate measure of marginal welfare cost. Despite the attraction of the ETI as a sufficient statistic—in principle, eliminating the need to identify the anatomy of behavioral response—accurately accounting for fiscal externalities will require an improved understanding of individual margins of taxpayer response to tax changes.

6   Multiple Tax-System Instruments

In the standard model taxes magically collect themselves, but in the real world no government can expect taxpayers to comply with a tax code without devoting resources to administration and enforcement. Procedures for ensuring compliance, audit rates, penalties, and reporting requirements all represent important tax-system instruments absent from our standard models.

6.1   Withholding, Remittance Responsibility, and the Role of Firms

Withholding refers to a situation where some or all of a tax liability must be remitted by someone other than the statutory bearer of the liability. It facilitates administration by allowing the tax authority to take advantage of economies of scale that exist in dealing with a smaller number of larger remitters who have relatively sophisticated record-keeping and accounting systems. It also acts as a revenue safeguard, ensuring that some tax is remitted even when the statutory bearer fails to file a return or otherwise disregards the tax obligations.[1]

Withholding remittance responsibility is usually restricted to businesses and government agencies. Individuals in their capacity as employees and consumers are usually excluded—they are too numerous and not sufficiently capable in general to be suitable withholding agents. In order to be able to withhold an appropriate amount of tax, the withholding agent must have an ongoing relationship with the statutory bearer of the tax or, alternatively, the withholding scheme must be sufficiently simple to avoid the need for such a relationship.

Withholding is about which individuals or entities remit a given tax liability, not about what triggers tax liability. The tax remittance (or, alternatively, tax collection) structure is, however, a more general concept than what is called withholding. For example, a retail sales tax is a consumption tax under which all tax liability is remitted by retail businesses, while a value-added tax is a consumption tax under which the tax liability is remitted by firms all along the importing, producing, and distributing chain. Although a VAT is generally not referred to as a withholding tax arrangement for a retail sales tax, the relationship between the two taxes is very similar, and is especially clear in an invoice-credit method VAT, where each business purchaser can credit against its own tax liability the tax remitted on the transaction by the seller. Schemes of corporate taxation, and in particular integrated corporate and individual tax systems, can be considered as the collection of tax levied on corporate income from a convenient tax handle—the corporation—and which may be credited back to the individual shareholders. The main apparent difference between a VAT and the Hall–Rabushka flat tax is that in the latter, but not the former, payments by businesses to workers are deductible from business taxable income but taxable at the individual level.[2] Nevertheless, given the reality of firm withholding for labor income tax, the collection and remittance system would be very similar. After all, labor income taxes could be re-labeled labor usage taxes.

Withholding and remittance play a prominent role in tax history. The first modern income tax, introduced in the United Kingdom in 1799 by William Pitt the Younger, was deemed a failure because it raised much less revenue than anticipated. The income tax introduced in 1803 by Prime Minister Henry Addington was successful largely because it introduced the concept of withholding (and, using our terminology, remittance) at source. Although the rate of tax under Addington's system was half that of Pitt's, revenue to the Exchequer rose by half and the number of taxpayers doubled (Farnsworth 1951). The introduction of income tax withholding in the United States during World War II helped facilitate its change from a "class tax" faced by only the wealthy to a "mass tax" faced by most Americans. Peacock and Wiseman's (1961) ratchet theory of taxation argued that such wartime innovations in the infrastructure of tax collection, once in place, lowered the marginal cost of taxation thereafter and made possible—and optimal—higher tax collections after the war. Some less historically important episodes are instructive about the central role of the remittance structure. Douglas (1999, p. 62) recounts that in the early 1800s Catholic and other Irish farmers were refusing to remit tithes meant for the Protestant church—over half were not collected. An act passed in 1838 switched the remittance responsibility to the landlords rather than the tenants, making the tithe less visible to the tenants and, more important, making their unwillingness to comply less of an issue. The notorious US Immigration Act of 1882 imposed a 50-cent head tax on all immigrants, remittable by the ship captain, to facilitate collection. For less clear reasons, the Roman emperor Nero ordered that the 4 percent tax on slave purchases be remitted by the seller rather than the buyer (McCulloch 1975, p. 156n1).[3]

Withholding for income tax is now widespread. It is required for wages and salaries in all but two of the 30 OECD countries, and for interest in 21 of these countries.[4] The use of withholding for other sources of income varies across the OECD. In the United States and eight other OECD countries, the withholding is approximate, so that tax returns must be filed and liability reconciled with the amount withheld (or remitted as estimated tax payments during the tax year). In the United States the default withholding schedules imply that over three-quarters of taxpayers over-remit and are entitled to a refund with no interest. Some taxpayers may acquiesce to zero-interest loans plus refunds as a kind of forced saving. Others may be acting conservatively to avoid under-withholding penalties. Jones (2012) suggests a third reason—inertia—based on his finding that tax filers only partially adjust tax prepayments in response to changes in default withholdings or tax liability. He finds that generally individuals offset less than 30 percent of a change to their expected refund after one year, and about 60 percent of this shock after three years. But adjustments in tax prepayments by EITC recipients offset no more than 2 percent of the reduction in tax liability caused by the expansion of the EITC program over the past 25 years.

Of the 30 OECD countries, 15 feature exact cumulative withholding for most taxpayers, allowing a return-free system.[5] Four countries use information reports to produce pre-populated returns that are mailed to taxpayers who need only make additions and corrections before signing and posting their return. Only two countries, Switzerland and France, have no withholding, requiring taxpayers to both complete an annual return and remit regular installments on tax owed. As of 2009 six revenue bodies (Chile, Denmark, Finland, Norway, Slovenia, and Sweden) provide a capability that is able to generate at year-end a fully completed tax return (or its equivalent) in electronic and/or paper form for the majority of taxpayers required to file tax returns, while three tax authorities (New Zealand, Singapore, and

Spain) achieved this outcome for between 30 and 50 percent of their personal taxpayers.

Our attention to withholding might seem strange to someone who knows only what textbooks say, and do not say, about taxation. This is because almost all of modern tax theory is about what *triggers* tax liability, be it receiving wages, consuming a particular good or service, or owning a piece of property with a certain value. Who or what entity must *remit* the tax triggered is unspecified, and presumed irrelevant. Indeed, there is an invariance, or irrelevance, proposition emphasized in most, if not all, public finance textbooks: it doesn't matter which side of a taxed transaction must remit tax (or which has the statutory liability), the incidence is the same, and indeed *all* of the consequences (other than what the before- and after-tax prices are called) are the same. To convince yourself temporarily of the irrelevance, consider the following cup-at-the-counter image, at a retail establishment in a state with a 5 percent sales tax. You buy an item for one dollar before tax, and approach the cashier, noting a small jar next to the cash register with the words "for the tax collector" scrawled on it. Now imagine two different remittance schemes. Under the first, you hand a dollar bill and a nickel to the cashier, who puts the bill in the register and the nickel in the jar. Under scenario number two, you hand the cashier a dollar and put the nickel in the jar. In this example it is clear that whether the cashier handles the nickel for a moment matters not at all—the remittance scheme is irrelevant.

The invariance theorem is a folk theorem, in that the assumptions are not made explicit. The theorem suggests that it doesn't matter if a retail business or a consumer remits a retail sales tax: the outcome is exactly the same. It doesn't matter whether only the retail businesses remit based on their sales, as under a RST, or whether all businesses remit based on their value added, as in a VAT. Current and historical practice suggests that the remittance structure does in fact matter. Over 30 countries levy a value-added tax at a rate of 25 percent or above, and more than 70 countries levy a value-added tax at a rate of 15 percent or above (KPMG 2012), and none levy a retail sales tax at a rate over 10 percent; we can infer that these textbook-equivalent systems are not practice-equivalent.[6] The widespread existence of withholding and remittance at the source of payment demonstrates the importance given to it by tax administrators.

In the spirit of Walter Heller's famous definition of an economist as someone who, when he finds something that works in practice, wonders if it works in theory, we turn now to see how this invariance result can break down, in theory. Consider first a standard partial equilibrium commodity tax incidence analysis. When suppliers have the legal liability to remit taxes, equilibrium requires that the price of the good paid by the consumer to the supplier, p_c, clears the market in the presence of a specific tax at rate t:

$$S(p_c - t) = D(p_c),$$ (6.1)

and conversely, when consumers are legally required to remit the tax,

$$S(p_s) = D(p_s + t),$$ (6.2)

where p_s is the price received by the supplier. Recognizing that $p_s \equiv p_c - t$, both parties are in an identical economic position regardless of who remits the tax.

But when consumers and suppliers have different evasion and/or avoidance technologies, the demand function when the consumer remits the tax is

$$D = D(p, \tau, \omega_c),$$ (6.3)

and the supply function when the supplier remits the tax is

$$S = S(p, t, \omega_s),$$ (6.4)

where τ and t are the tax rates remitted by consumers and suppliers when they bear the legal incidence, respectively, and ω_c and ω_s are parameters describing their respective avoidance/evasion technologies. Only in the special case when

$$\frac{\partial D}{\partial p} - \frac{\partial D}{\partial \tau} = \frac{\partial S}{\partial p} + \frac{\partial S}{\partial t}$$ (6.5)

are the economic incidence and other consequences independent of the party remitting the taxes, as in the standard model where $\partial D/\partial p = \partial D/\partial \tau$ and $\partial S/\partial p = -\partial S/\partial t$. In general, the evasion and avoidance opportunities will differ between buyers and sellers—due, for example, to different reporting requirements, observability, and ease of auditing transactions.

In some instances the assignment of remittance responsibility constrains the type of taxes that can be implemented. For example, the retail sales tax is well known to impose a "regressive" burden on small firms given the fixed per-firm costs of compliance, but if sales taxes were remitted by consumers and could not be adjusted according to the size of the retail firm, the two remittance arrangements have a different economic impact even abstracting from evasion and avoidance behavior. In general, the facility with which a tax can be personalized depends on the assignment of remittance responsibility.

Given the paramount importance of withholding, and remittance more generally, in modern tax systems, it is striking how little empirical analysis of its impact exists. One exception is Dušek (2006), who exploits the variation in the timing of the adoption of income tax withholding by state governments in the United States during the 1940s through 1970s to investigate whether more efficient taxes, proxied by the presence of withholding, lead to bigger government. He finds that the introduction of withholding immediately and permanently increased income tax collections by 24 percent at given tax rates and increased states' reliance on the income tax. Withholding increased total (i.e., including non-income taxes) tax revenues by 7.7 percent, but Dušek (2006) argues that the causal relationship from more efficient taxes to a bigger government accounts for at most 3.9 percent of that figure, while at least 3.8 percent should be attributed to a higher demand for spending that stimulated the adoption of withholding.

Acknowledging that remittance arrangements can have important efficiency consequences, optimality requires allocating responsibility between buyers and sellers—or between workers and firms in the case of employment relationships—to minimize a weighted sum of administrative and compliance costs. While taxpayers ultimately bear—directly and indirectly—all the costs imposed by a tax system, administrative costs are funded by income raised through taxation, and so need to be weighted by the marginal efficiency cost of funds, which exceeds one when taxes are anything but lump-sum. Chapter 7 develops a general model that addresses this issue more formally.

Logue and Slemrod (2010) show that the economics underlying the optimal assignment of tax remittance responsibility closely parallels Coasean insights on the optimal assignment of tort liability. Beginning with a costless negotiation benchmark, the Coase theorem establishes that economic efficiency is unaffected by the assignment of legal rights: for example, whether a smoker is given the right to smoke or a non-smoker the right to clean air, the same socially efficient amount of smoking will result from negotiation. Of course, the relative wealth of the two parties is affected by the assignment of legal rights. However, in real-world situations where negotiation is costly the assignment of legal rights does matter for efficiency. Calabresi (1970) argues that tort liability should be assigned to minimize social cost, which in his automobile example comprises the cost of accidents, the cost of avoiding accidents, and the administrative cost of the tort system.

Moving from a situation where one neighbor causes harm to another to a world where buyers' and sellers' interaction results in harm to a third nontransacting party—as in the case of tax evasion, with the third party being the population as a whole—requires a generalization of the benchmark Coasean framework. When the third party is unable to negotiate with the parties causing harm, or take any action to avoid that harm, a classic externality arises. Coasean insight tells us that when neither the buyers nor sellers are a "cheapest cost harm avoider," the legal assignment of tort costs to buyers or sellers does not matter. Precisely paralleling the textbook tax remittance invariance proposition, the incidence depends only on the relative demand and supply elasticities for buyers and sellers, not on who writes the check to the government.

Drawing on Calabresi's insight, Logue and Slemrod (2010) show that when buyers and sellers differ in ways that affect the private and social costs of operating a tax system, remittance responsibilities should be assigned to the party that minimizes the overall social cost of the tax system. As a consequence remittance responsibility need not be assigned to the party with the lowest private compliance cost if they are also innately dishonest or can more easily disguise their activities to avoid tax, requiring higher administrative expenditures to collect a given amount of revenue.

In practice, firms are responsible for the bulk of remittance, which is powerfully illustrated by two recent studies finding that over 80 percent of all taxes are remitted by firms in both the United States and the United Kingdom.[7] Anecdotal evidence suggests that collection of taxes from businesses is even more prevalent in developing countries. It is important to recognize that the role of business we are discussing is in the *implementation* of tax systems—the remittance of tax revenue and information reporting. This must be distinguished both from the taxes for which businesses have statutory liability, and from the incidence of taxes.

The impetus behind the role of business has been elegantly stated by Richard Bird (2002, p. 199), who wrote: "The key to effective taxation is information, and the key to information in the modern economy is the corporation . . . The corporation is thus the modern fiscal state's equivalent of the customs barrier at the border." Collecting taxes from businesses saves on administrative and compliance costs because of the economies of scale inherent in tax remittance (it is cheaper dealing with a smaller number of larger businesses than it is dealing with each individual—customer or employee—separately) and because businesses often already have recordkeeping and accounting systems in place that simplify the process of tax remittance and information reporting.

Notably, though, dealing with *small* businesses is not generally cost efficient, and many tax systems either entirely exempt small businesses from remittance responsibility, or else feature special tax regimes for small businesses that simplify the tax compliance process, and thereby change the base on which tax liability is based. In many countries the exemption of small firms is de facto, due to lax enforcement.[8] One implication of these policies is that the collection of taxes is highly concentrated among relatively large firms. A recent report asserts that the typical distribution of tax collections by firm size for African and Middle Eastern countries features less than 1 percent of taxpayers remitting over 70 percent of revenues, and the report gives specific examples of highly concentrated patterns: in Argentina, 0.1 percent of enterprise taxpayers remit 49 percent of revenues; and in Kenya, 0.4 percent remit 61 percent.[9] In chapter 11 we discuss in detail the optimal treatment of small firms in the presence of collection costs.

6.2 Information Reports

Information is central to the operation of non-capricious tax systems that are based on observable, verifiable quantities. In self-assessment systems, much information is provided to the tax authority by the taxpayer, subject to verification by the former, which can be obtained via audit, as discussed below, or third-party information reports. Third-party information reporting refers to a mandatory requirement on certain third parties (e.g., businesses, financial institutions, and non–tax-related government agencies) to report payments of money (and other tax-related transactions) and payee details (generally with a taxpayer identifying number) to the tax authority. This information can then be compared against tax actually remitted, allowing suspect returns to be identified and for enforcement actions to follow. Successful evasion now requires coordination between the party providing the information report and the party responsible for remittance, but—and here is the key—their incentives and willingness to falsify the data are

unlikely to be the same (incentives can even work in opposite directions). Thus a working system of information reporting discourages
noncompliance by increasing the risk of detection for a given amount
of tax authority resources. In practice, for such arrangements to be sufficiently efficient to make them attractive to revenue bodies, there must
be electronic reporting by third parties of information reports and the
use of a high-integrity taxpayer identifier to facilitate the matching of
information reports with tax authority records.

Most developed countries require the mandatory reporting of payments of salaries and wages, dividend, and interest income (much of
which is also subject to withholding). However, beyond these categories of payments, use of mandatory third-party reporting varies substantially across countries. Under the requirements of the US tax code,
an extremely wide variety of transactions must be reported to the IRS,
generally in electronic format, for matching with tax records. In addition to wages and investment incomes, these transactions include
agricultural payments, allocated tips, barter exchange income, brokers'
transactions, capital gains distributions, nonemployee compensation
and fees, fishing boat crew member proceeds, fish purchases for cash,
prescribed gambling winnings, real estate transactions, rents, and sales
of securities (OECD 2009).

A particularly striking example of the impact of information reporting on evasion is the introduction in 1987 of the requirement for taxpayers to report a Social Security number (SSN) for each child over the age
of five claimed as a dependent. The IRS had long suspected that many
dependents claimed either did not exist or qualify under tax law for a
deduction, and implemented the SSN reporting requirement on the
suggestion of an IRS official named John Szilagyi. To the surprise of
many, 5.2 million fewer dependents were claimed in 1987 than in 1986
(LaLumia and Sallee 2013). Some of the disappearing claims may have
represented legitimate dependents for whom parents had not obtained
a SSN, or dependents claimed in error by both parents following a
divorce, but LaLumia and Sallee (2013) estimate that 4.2 million dependents had been improperly claimed.

Gillitzer and Skov (2013) study the introduction of information-
reporting and pre-population of charitable tax deductions in Denmark
in 2008. They find that the reform coincided with a doubling in
the number of returns claiming a deduction, but only a 15 percent
increase in the value of such claims. They attribute the bulk of this
change to inattentive taxpayers who did not bother to claim charitable

deductions for which they were eligible under the previous self-reporting regime.

A rather different requirement to report information to the tax authority is the obligation (introduced in the United Kingdom) to disclose tax avoidance schemes shortly after they are first marketed. This policy is designed to improve the tax authority's ability to combat what is seen as unacceptable planning: the tax authority has the chance to initiate early legislative action and gets to understand who is promulgating and using such schemes. Importantly, when evasion and real economic decisions are jointly determined, information-reporting requirements have effects beyond evasion.

Of course, a tax authority need not just sit back and wait for information reports to come in; it can actively seek out information that would help verify tax obligations. This can come from, for example, publicly available professional license registers. Some have suggested clever ways to obtain information. An estimate of the imputed rental value of owner-occupied housing might be obtained by a law under which a stated value would be considered to be an offer to sell the property to the government at, say, 30 times the reported rental value. Of course, the viability of such an arrangement depends on government being able to credibly commit to meeting all potential offers.

Internationally, tax havens can play a key role in facilitating tax evasion for high-net-wealth individuals. At an April 2009 summit, the G20 group of nations initiated a coordinated effort to reduce the extent of tax-haven-facilitated evasion, pressuring haven countries to each sign at least 12 treaties containing information-exchange agreements (Johannesen and Zucman, forthcoming). By the end of 2009, over 300 such treaties had been signed. Using confidential data from the Bank of International Settlements (BIS) on bilateral deposits, Johannesen and Zucman find that havens signing a new treaty experienced a modest decline in deposits. However, total haven deposits were little affected, so rather than inducing remittance to non-havens, the wave of new treaties appears to have induced a shift in deposits to noncompliant havens that have resisted pressure to engage in information sharing. Before the modest decline in deposits for complying havens is interpreted as evidence that information-sharing agreements are ineffective, it is worth noting that the agreements only required information sharing on request—a relatively weak threat of enforcement compared to automatic, universal information sharing.

6.3   Relying on Market Transactions

Basing tax liability on market transactions—those between a willing buyer and an unconnected willing seller—has several advantages. First, in a market transaction information can potentially be obtained from either party, which provides a natural check on its accuracy. A second property is that market transactions tend to be better documented, and the more documented a transaction, the lower is the cost of gathering information on it. Finally, market transactions between unrelated parties establish arm's-length prices, the availability of which greatly facilitates valuing the transaction. VAT, for example, relies almost entirely on market transactions, while taxing capital gains on a realization basis rather than the theoretically preferable accrual basis takes advantage of the measurement advantage of market transactions. In contrast, estate and wealth taxation cannot, in general, take advantage of market transactions to reliably value wealth.[10]

Where no suitable market transaction exists, implementing a tax can become quite costly. An example of this involves subsidiaries of a multinational corporation that deal with one another and are based in different countries. Without appropriate safeguards, there is considerable scope for taxable income to be shifted to relatively low-tax jurisdictions through the manipulation of prices used for transactions between subsidiaries (transfer prices). To avoid this happening, the tax authority tries to ensure that arm's-length prices are used; this can be extremely complicated if the subsidiaries do not deal with outsiders (where prices won't be artificially manipulated), especially when the priced transactions are intangible, such as leasing of a patent.

Not all market transactions facilitate monitoring of the tax base. Market transactions carried out in cash are particularly difficult for a tax authority to monitor. A fascinating glimpse into the cash economy in the United States is provided by the description in Morse et al. (2009) of their interviews with individuals associated with cash businesses, including cash business owners, bankers, and tax preparers. One pattern that emerges is that evasion of multiple taxes is common. For example, "a storekeeper who underreports cash income and uses that cash to pay employees underreported wages and/or pay herself underreported self-employment income evades income, payroll, and self-employment taxes" as well as, if relevant, retail sales taxes (p. 48).[11] Many evading cash businesses do so by constructing a parallel cash economy in which they collect cash revenue, pay some expenses in cash, and then use the unreported cash they receive for cash purposes. A cash business might also pay for inventory and other expenses in cash, and not report the expenditure, thus reducing any suspicious discrepancy between revenues and costs that should be nearly proportional to sales.

One problem that arises for cash businesses is that when the time comes to apply for a bank loan, their tax return understates their profitability and therefore their credit-worthiness; Morse et al. (2009) report that some cash businesses submit fictional tax returns.[12] Another problem is that cash transactions are susceptible to employee whistle-blowing, a possibility relied upon by Kleven et al. (2009) to explain why the private cost of evasion is convex in size. Morse et al. (2009) suggest that employee pilfering, facilitated by the presence of cash, is a bigger problem and note that hiring family members is one strategy to address this. Kopczuk and Slemrod (2011) offer a stylized model of family firms in which the benefit of a trusted employee is balanced against the cost of hiring an otherwise ill-suited employee, while the optimal choice of some inputs (i.e., cash vs. bank deposits) reflects their observability for tax purposes.

6.4 Other Information-Based Tax-System Instruments

Another information-based tax-system instrument is public disclosure of tax details. As discussed in Lenter et al. (2003), supporters of public disclosure cite the gains to the transparency of tax policy, but also note that it may contribute to tax compliance because egregiously low-income declarations might elicit private information that contradicts a noncompliant taxpayer's claim; thus it is a way for the tax authority to collect relevant information. The small empirical literature on the effects of public disclosure has so far provided mixed evidence about its effect on tax compliance. Hasegawa et al. (2013) examine the Japanese disclosure system, which ended in tax year 2004, and required disclosure of corporate and individual taxable income only over a threshold amount. They find evidence that many corporations and individuals manipulated their reported income to be below the disclosure threshold, but do not find evidence supporting an overall positive effect on compliance for either tax. Slemrod, Thoresen, et al. (2012) study the Norwegian disclosure system, making use of the fact that from 2001 the Norwegian tax data were made available on the Internet, whereas prior to that date they were easily available only in a select number of communities. They find a small average increase in reported business incomes after 2001 in communities that previously had limited disclosure, consistent with public disclosure deterring tax evasion.

Another class of policy instruments is the provision and availability of information about the tax law to taxpayers. To the extent that some noncompliance is due to lack of information about the tax law, as is often argued, educating taxpayers will be beneficial: information booklets are published and distributed, toll-free numbers are set up to answer questions, websites are populated with FAQs, and seminars for tax preparers are organized. To tax authorities, the choice between adding enforcement resources or offering taxpayers more information is a common and often contentious carrot-versus-stick choice.[13] The Australian approach to tax compliance, in particular, takes this seriously, accepting that maintaining trust and respect for the tax authority is key to encouraging voluntary compliance (Braithwaite 2003; Leviner 2008). As our discussion in chapter 3 suggests, the reduction in aggregate evasion from adopting such an approach is likely to be relatively modest given the overwhelming evidence in support of the deterrence model. Note also that better information does not necessarily contribute to more tax remittances, but rather more accurate tax remittance. In our discussion of horizontal equity in chapter 7, we discuss how formally incorporating the social value of accurate tax assessments has proved to be elusive. Aside from its effect on tax remittances, better information may be socially beneficial if it reduces compliance costs and administrative costs.

There is mixed evidence that providing information can affect taxpayer choices. Chetty and Saez (2013) conducted a large randomized experiment among H&R Block clients to test the impact on earnings of eligible EITC recipients of receiving information tailored to convey their marginal incentives—the effective marginal tax rate, or subsidy, to earning (or reporting) more income. Survey evidence indicates a low level of baseline knowledge about the EITC among potential recipients, suggesting that better information may help taxpayers make more informed income-earning choices. To test this hypothesis, Chetty and Saez (2013) randomly assigned half of 43,000 individuals who had both received EITC payments at an H&R Block office in 2007 and had one or more dependents to a treatment group receiving simple, personalized information about the incentives created for them by the EITC. For example, those in the phase-in region of the EITC were told "It pays to work more." Constructing a panel with the 72 percent of filers returning to H&R Block the following year, they found that on average there was no significant effect on earnings of information provision. However, there was significant heterogeneity among tax preparers. Among a subset classified as compliers (defined to be those with a high share of returning clients with incomes above $7,000 but below the beginning of the phase-out region), information provision led to a statistically significant 3 percent increase in EITC income. Chetty and Saez (2013) conclude that while information provision alone appears ineffective at changing earnings, information may be influential when coupled with advice from tax professionals.

Not only do many taxpayers appear to not internalize the incentives designed into the EITC, the participation, or take-up, rate among eligible taxpayers is only about 75 percent (Plueger 2009). To assess the role of lack of information, transaction costs, and complexity in suppressing EITC take-up, Bhargava and Manoli (2011) randomly assigned a variety of program mailings—differing in their information content and complexity—to about 35,000 taxpayers in California who had filed a tax return for the 2009 tax year but did not claim EITC benefits for which they appeared to be eligible. Despite the fact that all tax filers in their sample had already failed to respond to a standard mailing indicating likely eligibility, the receipt of a further standard IRS reminder (the experimental control treatment) induced EITC take-up by 14 percent of the sample group. Experimental mailings with a simplified layout and less repetition induced a further statistically significant 6 percentage point increase in response rate compared to the control group filers receiving the standard second reminder notice. Consistent with evidence that households often underestimate the size of EITC benefits for which they are eligible, providing benefit information further boosts take-up. Intriguingly, providing information on the expected time to complete the application process, and mailings with information designed to de-stigmatize claimants—for example, by describing the EITC as a bonus for hard work—did not increase take-up. As discussed earlier in the context of tax compliance, appeals to social conscience do not seem to affect behavior.

6.5   Audits and Penalties

The tax-system instruments discussed so far deal largely with how a tax authority can make efficient use of information to ascertain tax liability. Ultimately, though, some taxpayers provide deliberately inaccurate information or none at all, and the tax authority must investigate further and, perhaps, impose penalties for tax noncompliance. As shown in table 6.1, the total share of individual tax returns audited is only 1.11 percent, but there is significant variation by type and size of reported income. For individuals, the probability of audit is generally rising in reported income:[14] 3.42 percent of returns reporting no or negative adjusted gross income (AGI) were audited by the IRS in fiscal year 2011, with the audit rate falling to 0.73 percent for returns with

Table 6.1
US audit coverage by type and size of return

Returns examined in fiscal year 2011	
Type of return	Percent covered
Individual income tax	1.11
No adjusted gross income	3.42
More than $1 and under $25,000	1.22
More than $25,000 and under $50,000	0.73
More than $50,000 and under $75,000	0.83
More than $75,000 and under $100,000	0.82
More than $100,000 and under $200,000	1.00
More than $200,000 and under $500,000	2.66
More than $500,000 and under $1m	5.38
More than $1m and under $5m	11.80
More than $5m and under $10m	20.75
More than $10m	29.93
Returns with total positive income under $200,000	
Nonbusiness returns without EITC	0.6
Business returns without EITC	1.8
Returns with EITC	2.1
Returns with total positive incomes above $200,000 and below $1m	
Nonbusiness returns	3.2
Business returns	3.6
Corporation income tax returns	1.5
Small corporations (less than $10m in total assets)	1.0
Large corporations (more than $10m in total assets)	17.6
Employment tax returns	0.2
Estate tax returns	18.2

Source: IRS (2012b, tabs. 9a and 9b) and authors' calculations.

reported AGI between $25,000 and $50,000, rising to a 29.93 percent rate for returns with over $10 million in reported AGI (IRS 2012b, tab. 9b). High audit rates apply to only a small fraction of returns filed: more than three-quarters of all returns filed have a positive AGI less than $75,000 and are audited at a rate of about 1 percent (IRS 2012b, tab. 9b). Individuals with business income—which is subject to little third-party information reporting—face a higher audit probability than do those not reporting business income. Similarly for corporations the share of returns audited rises dramatically with the amount of total assets: all but 20 of the 450 corporate income tax returns reporting $20 billion or more in total assets in 2010 were subject to examination in 2011 (IRS 2012b, tab. 9a). Audits of corporate income tax returns are almost entirely conducted face-to-face, but for individuals over 80 percent of audited returns are subject to examination by correspondence.

As a result of audit operations in fiscal year 2011, the IRS recommended payment of an additional $14.6 billion in individual income tax, and an additional $25.6 billion in corporate income tax (IRS 2012b, tab. 9a). For individuals, more than a third of the assessed underpayment of income taxes was among tax returns with reported AGI over $1 million, while another $2.5 billion in underpayment was assessed on returns reporting EITC income and gross receipts under $25,000. Reflecting in part the high rates of audit for large corporations, over 90 percent of assessed corporate income tax underpayment was for corporations with $1 billion or more in total assets. Not all audits result in recommendations for additional payments: almost $1.1 billion in refunds was recommended for individuals as a result of audit operations (with more than half of the total due to returns reporting AGI above $1 million), and another $4.5 billion in refunds for primarily large corporations (IRS 2012b, tab. 12). Partly offsetting this, audit operations prevented the payment of over $5 billion in refunds, with $4.2 billion of this total accounted for by corporate income tax filings (IRS 2012b, tab. 11).

The IRS imposes a standard 20 percent penalty on underpayment that "lacks economic substance"—meaning underpayment that does not, apart from federal tax effects, meaningfully change a taxpayer's material circumstances—with underpayment due to fraud penalized at a higher 75 percent rate, plus interest (IRS 2012a). This compares with the common feature in administrative penalties on underreporting tax liabilities across countries: the penalty varies according to the seriousness of offense, based on the failure to exercise reasonable care, deliberate underreporting, or whether it is a fraud or criminal case. While practices vary, a common approach sees penalties for minor offenses in the region of 10 to 30 percent of the tax evaded while more serious offenses involving deliberate evasion are in the region of 40 to 100 percent of the tax evaded (OECD 2011, p. 255).

Faced with an audit probability of 1.1 percent and the standard 20 percent penalty rate on underpayment, the A-S model predicts that a taxpayer would have to be extremely risk averse to declare a non-negligible share of their income to the tax authority. Supposing the taxpayer has utility with constant relative risk aversion γ, and a tax rate of 30 percent, the A-S model, assuming the Yitzhaki penalty form (see equation 3.5), implies that even with $\gamma = 20$ they will only report about one-third of their income. Even at the 75 percent penalty rate the A-S model predicts an evasion rate above 30 percent for $\gamma = 20$. Survey-based methods used to impute risk tolerance imply *much* smaller estimates of γ for most people (see Kimball et al. 2008), suggesting that the detection probability for most people is substantially higher than reported audit rates—for example, due to third-party information reporting.[15]

6.6   The Econometrics of Multiple Instruments

One immediate and important implication of multiple tax instruments is the potential bias that arises in econometric analyses that ignore them. To the extent that the non-rate instruments have behavioral effects and are correlated with the tax rate, the effects of the non-rate instruments will be inappropriately attributed to the tax rates. Empirical investigation of this issue has been hampered by the relative dearth of data on non-rate tax instruments, but this is changing due to the newly available OECD-provided country-level data about tax administration, which in its latest 2010 edition covers 49 countries (34 OECD countries plus 15 others). In addition Kawano and Slemrod (2012) have constructed a new database of corporate tax-system changes for OECD countries from 1980 to 2004 based on narrative accounts of tax changes in the annual reports of the International Bureau of Fiscal Documentation. For each of a dozen tax base measures, such as thin-capitalization rules, loss carryback and carryforward provisions, accelerated depreciation allowances, investment tax credits, foreign tax credits, and R&D allowances, the database records the timing of base changes and codes each change according to whether it broadened or narrowed the tax base. They note that tax base changes were more likely to occur when there were tax-rate changes than when there were no statutory rate changes, with tax-rate decreases more likely to be associated with tax base broadening than tax base narrowing measures.

Augmenting previous empirical studies with their new data on tax base changes, Kawano and Slemrod (2012) overturn the apparent statistically significant negative cross-sectional relationship between corporate tax revenues and statutory tax rates. This is important because typical studies regressing corporate tax revenue as a share of GDP on the corporate tax rate, the corporate tax rate squared, and year fixed effects to proxy for worldwide macroeconomics conditions, had implied revenue-maximizing corporate tax rates in the 20 to 30 percent range, indicating that countries such as the United States are on the wrong side of the Laffer curve. Correcting for the omitted-variables bias caused by simultaneous changes in corporate tax rates and tax base definitions and provisions, no statistically significant relationship between statutory rates and tax revenues is evident. Interestingly, Kawano and Slemrod (2012) find that some tax base changes that broaden the base appear to be associated with increases in corporate tax revenue, with R&D credits and the taxation of foreign corporations appearing to have a large influence on corporate tax revenues.

6.7   Can Tax-System Variation Explain the Striking Positive Cross-country Correlation between Tax Levels and Real Per Capita Income?

Slemrod and Kopczuk (2002), discussed at length in chapter 9, suggest that variation in the cost of collecting taxes (and social tastes for redistribution) can explain cross-country variation in tax systems. This variation may also explain how much in taxes are raised and one of the most striking (and to some advocates of limited government, most troubling) statistical regularities in the study of taxation—richer countries levy more taxes, as a fraction of income, than do poor countries, both across countries and within a country over time. Although the existence of this empirical relationship is not controversial, its interpretation is. At first blush one steeped in the consequences of taxation might imagine the causation running from tax levels to prosperity: higher taxes *cause* more prosperity and higher real incomes. Given that taxes are presumed to dampen incentives to produce income and to generate deadweight losses, this is unlikely. However, it is certainly possible that some of the services that governments provide with the tax money it collects, such as education, health care, and infrastructure, are indeed conducive to prosperity, so it is plausible that the positive correlation between tax level and income could in part be picking up the causal effect of (certain) government activities on prosperity. Another explanation, dubbed Wagner's law, is that the positive correlation reflects a demand phenomenon: more affluent citizens value, demand, and obtain through the political process a greater fraction of their income in government services; Wagner (1911) associated the increased demand for these services over time with growing urbanization.

Another, not mutually exclusive, possibility is that in richer countries the cost of collecting revenue is lower, so that other things equal it is appropriate for governments of affluent nations to provide more of the relatively cheaper services. As Slemrod (1995) has discussed, sorting out these explanations with only cross-sectional data is difficult, if not impossible, given the identification issues that arise. This is not for lack of trying. Goode (1968) examined cross-country variation in tax levels and suggested that, rather than income being the driving factor, this association results from the positive correlation between per capita income and other social and economic conditions that make direct taxes acceptable and effective, such as a high level of literacy, wide use of standard accounting methods, effective public administration, and political stability. Tanzi (1992) studied the determinants of the tax ratio in 83 developing countries from 1978 to 1988 and concluded that, although by itself the log of per capita income is positively associated with the tax ratio, the share of agricultural output to GDP—a proxy for the costs of collecting tax revenue—explains more of the variation in tax shares than does per capita income (with a negative sign); when both variables are included as explanatory variables, per capita income no longer has a statistically significant positive effect, although the negative effect of the agricultural share survives.[16]

Noting the systematic relationship between per capita income and non-rate aspects of tax systems, Robinson and Slemrod (2012) go on to examine whether the strong positive correlation between tax levels and per capita income survives as a partial relationship when one holds constant tax-system measures. They conclude that variations in administrative effort affect tax levels, and these variations are correlated with a country's level of development. They interpret this as tentative evidence that the famous relationship between tax levels and GDP per capita is in part picking up the fact that administrative procedures, and in particular administrative effort, happen to vary by the level of development, so that high-income countries are more successful at raising taxes than other countries.

Part III Optimal Tax Systems

Having laid out the building blocks of tax systems, we turn now to what a tax-systems perspective implies about the appropriate design of tax policy. We take a fresh look at some standard optimal tax questions, and also examine what insights can be gained from applying the standard optimal tax analysis to nonstandard aspects of tax systems.

7   General Model

Analysis of tax systems must—and can—address a wide variety of tax instruments that extend well beyond the usual optimal tax concerns—tax-rate schedules and the choice of base. In this chapter we show how optimal tax analysis can naturally be extended to cover other instruments.

7.1   Multiple Tax Instruments

We begin this task by developing a normative model of income tax policy that allows for both multiple tax instruments and multiple kinds of cost. As in section 3.3, here we refer to sheltering income as short-hand for avoidance and evasion. The model is inspired by Mayshar (1991), but differs in a number of ways. The representative taxpayer chooses earned income, y, and the amount of income to shelter, s, knowing their tax liability is $T(y, s, \theta)$, with $T_y > 0, T_s < 0, T_{\theta_i} > 0$, where θ is an n-dimensional vector of tax instruments, with $\theta_i \in [0, \infty)$ if instrument i is continuous, and $\theta_i \in \{0, 1\}$ if instrument i is binary. When tax instrument i is not used, $\theta_i = 0$ and there is no distortion caused or revenue raised by tax instrument i. Taxpayers face a monetary cost of sheltering income—here interpreted as avoidance or evasion—$\kappa(y, s, \theta)$, with $\kappa_s > 0$. In addition they face a compliance cost of $m(\theta)$ dollars with a fixed cost component f_i^m for each $\theta_i > 0$. In most cases $\partial m / \partial \theta_i \geq 0$, but there are certainly interesting examples when $\partial m / \partial \theta_i < 0$, such as when cracking down on tax shelters raises revenue but reduces compliance costs by eliminating the private incentive to engage in and camouflage complicated transactions.

The social planner's problem is to choose $\{\theta_i\}_{i=1}^n$ to maximize the representative taxpayer's utility $u(c, y)$ subject to the aggregate budget constraint $T(y, s, \theta) = D(\theta) + G$ and the constraints on θ, where $D(\theta)$ is the administrative cost of tax policy θ, with a fixed cost component f_i^d, and G is an exogenous revenue requirement. Marginal utility of consumption is positive, $u_1 > 0$, while $u_2 < 0$ because, for given consumption, it is costly to earn income by, notably but not only, sacrificing leisure to increase labor supply. For continuous tax policy instruments, $\partial D/\partial \theta_i$ is often positive, but as in the case of $\partial m/\partial \theta_i$, this is not always true. For example, it may be less costly to administer a commodity tax base with no exceptions than one with a small number of exceptions.

The taxpayer takes $\{\theta_i\}_{i=1}^n$ as given and chooses $\{y, s\}$ to maximize utility subject to their budget constraint $c = y - \kappa(y, s, \theta) - m(\theta) - T(y, s, \theta)$. We assume that there are interior solutions for $\{y, s\}$.

The FOCs for the taxpayer's optimization problem are

$$[\partial y] \quad u_1\left[(1-T_y)-\kappa_y\right]+u_2 = 0 \tag{7.1}$$

and

$$[\partial s] \quad T_s + \kappa_s = 0. \tag{7.2}$$

With a representative taxpayer, the social welfare function coincides with the taxpayer's utility function, in which case, the Lagrangian for the social planner's problem is just

$$L = v(\theta) + \lambda\left[T\left(y(\theta), s(\theta), \theta\right) - D(\theta) - G\right], \tag{7.3}$$

where $v(\theta)$ is the taxpayer's indirect utility function. The fixed-cost components are implicitly incorporated into the function $m(\theta)$ for the taxpayer and $D(\theta)$ for the tax authority. If $\theta_i > 0$ is continuous, making use of the envelope theorem, the FOC for any tax instrument not at a corner solution is

$$[\partial \theta_i] \quad u_1\left[T_{\theta_i}+\kappa_{\theta_i}+m_{\theta_i}\right] = \lambda\left[T_y\frac{\partial y}{\partial \theta_i}+T_s\frac{\partial s}{\partial \theta_i}+T_{\theta_i}-D_{\theta_i}\right] \quad \forall i. \tag{7.4}$$

The term $\left[T_{\theta_i}+\kappa_{\theta_i}+m_{\theta_i}\right]$ represents the marginal cost of instrument θ_i to the representative taxpayer (in dollars), while

$$\left[T_y\frac{\partial y}{\partial \theta_i}+T_s\frac{\partial s}{\partial \theta_i}+T_{\theta_i}-D_{\theta_i}\right] = \left[T_{\theta_i}-B_{\theta_i}-D_{\theta_i}\right] \tag{7.5}$$

is the marginal net revenue raised by instrument θ_i. The ratio of these two terms is the marginal efficiency cost of funds for tax instrument θ_i:

$$MECF(\theta_i) = \frac{T_{\theta_i}+\kappa_{\theta_i}+m_{\theta_i}}{T_{\theta_i}-B_{\theta_i}-D_{\theta_i}} = \frac{1+\left[(\kappa_{\theta_i}+m_{\theta_i})/T_{\theta_i}\right]}{1-\left[(B_{\theta_i}+D_{\theta_i})/T_{\theta_i}\right]}. \tag{7.6}$$

This expression is simply a generalization of equation (2.7), incorporating the welfare consequences of administrative and compliance costs. The effect of a marginal increase in tax instrument θ_i on marginal taxpayer compliance costs, m_{θ_i}, appears in the numerator of equation (7.6) because it is a cost borne directly by taxpayers. In contrast, administrative costs are funded by *after* tax revenue, and so appear in the denominator of equation (7.6).

As long as the *MECF* is weakly increasing in each θ_i, for each continuous instrument the *MECF* at an optimum θ^* will be described by either of the following cases:

1. If $\theta_i^* = 0$, then $MECF(\theta_i) \geq \lambda/u_1$.
2. If $\theta_i^* > 0$, then $MECF(\theta_i) = \lambda/u_1$.

Case 1 applies when tax instrument θ_i is not used as part of an optimal tax system because the variable cost or fixed cost components—due to compliance or administrative costs—are prohibitively costly, while case 2 describes an interior optimum.

Thus, at an optimum, for instruments not constrained by a corner solution, *the marginal welfare loss per dollar of net revenue raised is the same across all tax instruments*. This is an implicit characteristic of all optimal tax problems (that ignore redistributional goals) where the focus is tax rates, but here we extend the intuition to all varieties of tax instruments, from information provision, to adding audits, to broadening the tax base. Thus the standard optimal tax approach naturally generalizes to the analysis of optimal tax systems.

7.2 Heterogeneous Taxpayers

This model can be extended to a world with a continuum of taxpayers who differ in their abilities, where ability is defined as the return per unit of time or, equivalently, the disutility of producing earned income: a more able person must give up less disutility (because it takes less time) to acquire a unit of goods. The notation used is the same, except for the following change: $u = u(c, y/n)$, where n differs across taxpayers, capturing differing disutility of producing earned income. With taxpayers now differing in income-earning ability, the social planner's problem depends on how individual utilities are weighted in the social objective function. As is standard, we assume an individualistic social welfare function, $W(u_1, u_2, \ldots)$, that is strictly increasing and strictly concave in each of its arguments. The more concave is the social welfare function, the greater is the social planner's preference for equality.

Given these changes, a taxpayer of type n has the following FOCs for y and s:

$$[\partial y] \quad n u_1 [(1 - T_y) - \kappa_y] + u_2 = 0, \tag{7.7}$$

$$[\partial s] \quad \kappa_s + T_s = 0. \tag{7.8}$$

A taxpayer of type n will choose $y^* = y(\theta, n)$ and $s^* = s(\theta, n)$.

Suppressing the (θ, n) arguments for y and s for notational simplicity, the Lagrangian for the social planner's problem is

$$L = \int W(v(\theta, n)) dF(n) + \lambda \left[\int T(y, s, \theta) dF(n) - D(\theta) - G \right], \tag{7.9}$$

where $v(\theta, n)$ is indirect utility for a taxpayer of type n.

If $\theta_i > 0$ is continuous, the FOC, making use of the envelope theorem, for each tax-system instrument not at a corner solution is:

$$\int (W'u_1 [T_{\theta_i} + \kappa_{\theta_i} + m_{\theta_i}]) dF(n) = \lambda \int \left(\left[T_{\theta_i} + T_y \frac{\partial y}{\partial \theta_i} + T_s \frac{\partial s}{\partial \theta_i} - D_{\theta_i} \right] \right) dF(n)$$

$$= \lambda \int [T_{\theta_i} - B_{\theta_i}] dF(n) - \lambda D_{\theta_i}. \tag{7.10}$$

Re-arrangement and normalization of equation (7.10) yields an expression for the marginal cost of funds (MCF):

$$MCF(\theta_i) = \frac{\left(\int W'u_1 [T_{\theta_i} + \kappa_{\theta_i} + m_{\theta_i}] dF(n) \right) \left[1 / \left(\int W'u_1 dF(n) \right) \right]}{\int [T_{\theta_i} - B_{\theta_i}] dF(n) - D_{\theta_i}}$$

$$= \frac{\int MSWC(\theta_i, n) dF(n)}{\int MR(\theta_i, n) dF(n)}, \tag{7.11}$$

where $MSWC(\theta_i, n)$ is the marginal social welfare cost, and $MR(\theta_i, n)$ is the marginal net revenue raised for tax instrument θ_i and a taxpayer of type n. Unlike the $MECF$, the MCF takes into account the distributional implications of tax instrument θ_i in a many-person economy with heterogeneous income-earning abilities. Following Feldstein (1972), we can decompose the MCF for any tax instrument into two components: the $MECF$, and a distribution component, DC, that sums the cost to taxpayers according to their social welfare weight. Formally,

$$MCF(\theta_i) = \left(\frac{\int [T_{\theta_i} + \kappa_{\theta_i} + m_{\theta_i}] dF(n)}{\int MR(\theta_i, n) dF(n)} \right) \left(\frac{\int MSWC(\theta_i, n) dF(n)}{\int [T_{\theta_i} + \kappa_{\theta_i} + m_{\theta_i}] dF(n)} \right) \tag{7.12}$$

$$= MECF(\theta_i) DC(\theta_i).$$

For instruments whose optimal setting is not at a corner solution, the social planner chooses θ_i to equate the marginal cost of funds across all tax instruments.

7.3 Horizontal Equity

Horizontal equity (HE)—the equal treatment of equals—is widely held to be a desirable feature of any tax system. Although the notion has widespread popular appeal, it has not proved easy to integrate into formal optimal tax analysis. In evaluating tax reform proposals, Feldstein's (1976) definition of HE requires leaving individuals with equal pre-reform utility with equal post-reform utility. In contrast to HE, the social welfare function we introduced in chapter 2 describes a society's preference for vertical equity (VE), being differentiation in welfare among taxpayers who differ in an important way, such as income-earning ability.

The apparent simplicity of HE as a concept masks the difficulty involved in coming up with an economically meaningful measure. Early attempts focused on evaluating tax reform proposals based on the number of rank reversals in the pre- and post-reform distributions of income. But as Kaplow (1989) points out, such measures are insensitive to the magnitude of differences in income: two reforms, one which results in large differences in post-reform income for taxpayers with identical pre-reform income will be judged as severely as another reform leaving post-reform income infinitesimally different among pre-reform equals. Distance-sensitive measures, such as proposed by King (1983), remain problematic because reforms resulting in large changes in relative incomes but no rank reversals are accorded no penalty on HE grounds, but a reform resulting in rank reversals due to tiny changes in income may be assigned a high social cost.

An alternative measure developed by Auerbach and Hassett (2002) addresses the issue of classifying pre-reform equals by employing a weighting function to define overlapping groups of individuals with similar characteristics. Their measure nests concern for HE within a standard social welfare function, enabling reforms to be evaluated on both HE and VE grounds but, in doing so, drawing into sharper focus the question of whether HE should be accorded normative significance beyond its implications already encompassed by concern for VE. Under this approach most tax reforms that result in equals receiving dissimilar tax liabilities will be penalized on VE grounds, in which case concern for HE is redundant, but in other instances preference for HE may overrule reforms that would raise social welfare. Because Auerbach and Hassett's (2002) measure assigns weight to information other than individual utilities—differences in income compared to a pre-reform income distribution—their measure can come into conflict with the Pareto principle, long held to be a weak but necessary feature of any welfare measure (see Kaplow 2001; Kaplow and Shavell 2001). For example, a tax reform that raises everyone's income but results in arbitrary gains for pre-reform equals may be judged inferior to the status quo if the concern for HE is sufficiently strong.

Unlike policy evaluation on a social welfare basis, HE considerations can make the desirability of a reform dependent on the initial distribution used to define equals. If the reference distribution of income used to assess HE is itself the product of previous reforms featuring some arbitrariness in treatment of equals—as is almost certainly the case— the normative significance of HE is further weakened. As Kaplow (1989) points out, basing evaluation on an ideal rather than a pre-reform distribution of income removes dependence on the status quo, but this is a stark departure from standard interpretations of HE.

8 Standard Instruments with New Costs

In this chapter we consider some examples of how introducing administrative and compliance costs modifies and enriches the normative analysis of the standard set of tax instruments.

8.1 Commodity Taxation with Compliance Costs

The key insight of the classic optimal commodity tax problem, laid out in chapter 2, is that at an optimum, the marginal excess burden per dollar raised is equated across all taxed commodities. This is a special case of the proposition in chapter 7: for all tax-system instruments at an interior solution the marginal efficiency cost of funds should be equalized. Assuming perfectly elastic supply of commodities, we need know "only" the matrix of compensated own and cross-price demand elasticities to determine the optimal set of relative commodity tax rates, and in the special case where all cross-price elasticities of demand are equal to zero, optimal commodity taxes follow an "inverse elasticity" rule, in which at an optimum the least price-elastic commodities face the highest tax rates.

Crucially, in this model the tax base—which commodities can be taxed—is held fixed. However, because collection costs—administrative and compliance costs—can vary substantially by commodity, the breadth of the commodity tax base is also an important real-world choice variable. In general, a broad commodity tax base distorts purchasing decisions less than a narrow tax base, but *if* breadth comes with additional collection cost, optimality requires trading off reduced excess burden from distorted consumption choice against higher collection cost.

8.1.1 The Optimal Tax Base

Yitzhaki (1979) studies this problem in a model with a representative consumer and a set of commodities arranged in increasing order of fixed administrative cost per dollar of consumer expenditure, with untaxed items imposing no direct cost on the tax authority. The representative consumer is assumed to have Cobb–Douglas preferences, which greatly simplifies the choice of tax rates for each commodity, because the homotheticity and separability properties of these preferences together imply that excess burden is minimized with an equal tax rate on all taxed commodities. This highlights the trade-off between the tax rate and tax base breadth and sidesteps the question of the optimal pattern of taxes on the taxed commodities—it is always uniform at a rate high enough to raise the fixed required revenue.

Formally, the tax authority's problem is to jointly choose the uniform commodity tax rate, t, and the breadth of the tax base, defined as the sum of expenditure shares for the taxed commodities, b, subject to a revenue constraint. This formalizes a ubiquitous tax policy issue—to what extent to broaden the tax base and "use" the revenue raised thereby to lower tax rates or, in this model, to lower *the* tax rate. For the retail sales tax the recurring issue is whether to include services in the tax base; services are a growing fraction of consumer expenditures but are arguably more costly to collect per dollar raised. To be sure, there are other justifications—real and imagined—for special treatment of some consumption goods, such as externalities or redistribution, but this model captures the essence of the policy trade-off.

Broadening the tax base is also a perennial issue in income taxation where, for example, eliminating the deduction for charitable contributions would allow a lower tax rate(s) without sacrificing revenue. Although the formal model we outline next is expressed in terms of the optimal breadth of the consumption tax base, because we use a single-period framework and the tax rate on all taxed goods is the same, the model can be equivalently expressed in terms of the share of goods whose expenditure is deductible from taxable income in a linear income tax. Permitting a large share of goods to be deducted from taxable income is equivalent to a narrow commodity tax base. But putting it this way highlights that it is not always true, as in the Yitzhaki model, that broadening the base raises collection costs: a comprehensive income tax base may be less costly to collect than one with exceptions.

We can express the tax authority's problem as follows:

$$\max_{\{t,b\}} v(A, \theta, p) \quad \text{s.t.} \quad T(\theta) - D(b) \geq G, \tag{8.1}$$

where v is the representative consumer's indirect utility function, $\theta = \{t, b\}$, $p_i = q_i(1 + t)$ for $i \in [0, I]$, $p_i = q_i$ for $i \in (I, 1]$, with q_i being exogenous producer prices, b is the breadth of the tax base, and A here represents exogenous income, with the remaining notation as defined earlier. Hence, goods $i \leq T$ are taxed. The representative consumer has Cobb–Douglas utility with an expenditure share on good i equal to α_i, so the breadth of the tax base, b, of expenditure shares for the taxed goods is the sum $b = \int_0^I \alpha_i di$. Note that, for convenience, this model treats commodities as a continuum rather than as discrete, to avoid integer problems that are not important for the issue at hand.

Using the properties of the Cobb–Douglas utility function, we can write the Lagrangian as follows:

$$L = v^R (1+t)^{-b} + \lambda \left[bA\left(\frac{t}{1+t}\right) - D(b) - G \right], \tag{8.2}$$

where v^R is the representative consumer's indirect utility in the absence of commodity taxes.[1] Assuming that $D(b)$ is a smoothly increasing function, we have as the relevant FOCs

$$[\partial t] \quad v^R (1+t)^{-b} - \lambda\left(\frac{A}{1+t}\right) = 0 \tag{8.3}$$

and

$$[\partial b] \quad -(1+t)^{-b} v^R log(1+t) + \lambda\left[A\left(\frac{t}{1+t}\right) - D'(b) \right] = 0. \tag{8.4}$$

Combining these terms yields an expression describing the optimal combination of tax rate and tax-system breadth:

$$\frac{t - log(1+t)}{1+t} = \frac{D'(b)}{A}. \tag{8.5}$$

A narrow tax base creates a relatively large excess burden but has low administrative cost, while a broad tax base has small excess burden, but requires more resources to administer. Unlike the Ramsey tax problem, a lump-sum tax is a special case of this model, corresponding to a comprehensive tax base, $b = 1$. While a lump-sum tax does not distort consumer purchases, it is only an optimal choice in the context of this model if its administration cost is less than the combined efficiency and administrative cost of a narrower tax base raising the same amount of revenue. Moreover, a lump-sum tax could be administered directly on people rather than via taxing all goods. As our discussion in chapter 7 suggests, at an optimum the marginal efficiency cost of funds must be equal whether it is raised from a broader tax base (the RHS of equation 8.5) or a higher commodity tax rate (the LHS of equation 8.5). As mentioned above, the assumption of smoothly increasing administrative costs overlooks some important real-world practicalities. For example, it may in some settings be less costly to tax *all* commodities than all but one, in which case administrative costs are discontinuous, as we discuss in chapter 4, and the optimally taxed set of commodities no longer varies smoothly with revenue required.

The intuition gleaned from this model survives relaxing the assumption of Cobb–Douglas utility to the more flexible constant-elasticity-of-substitution form, in which case Wilson (1989) finds that the higher is the elasticity of substitution between taxed and untaxed commodities, the broader is the optimal tax base. Intuitively, a high elasticity of substitution between taxed and untaxed commodities raises the excess burden of differential taxation because consumers can easily switch to untaxed commodities, thus raising the value to the social planner of a broad commodity tax base.

8.1.2 Optimal Commodity Tax Enforcement

In the model just outlined, compliance is perfect once administrative cost has been incurred. Of course, in reality some taxpayers find ways to evade taxes, including commodity taxes. The tax authority may be able to increase compliance at some cost, but what then is the optimal mix of enforcement effort and tax-rate choice? This is another ubiquitous issue in tax policy naturally addressed by the theory of optimal tax systems, because it poses the choice between a standard instrument, such as a tax rate, and an enforcement variable.

In contrast to the model analyzed in the previous section, we now hold the set of taxed goods fixed, but allow the share of consumers able to evade taxes to be controlled by the tax authority at some resource cost. Revenue can be raised by either taxing a small share of the population at a high rate, or by incurring administrative cost to observe a greater share of purchasers, by taxing a large share of the population at a low rate. At first it may seem that higher tax rates are always preferable to enforcement effort because greater enforcement generally (i.e., aside from increasing fines for detected evasion) has a direct resource cost, while higher legislated tax rates do not. However, as Kaplow (1990) explains, this logic is likely to be faulty: because the excess burden of taxation is convex in the tax rate for compliant taxpayers, a revenue-neutral increase in enforcement and reduction in statutory tax rates may reduce the excess burden of the tax system as a whole. This is another example, with the model of section 8.1.1, in which a broader base may come at a cost but enable lower tax rates with a concomitantly reduced distortion. Here the breadth of the tax base refers to the fraction of taxpayers covered, whereas in section 8.1.1 breadth referred to the fraction of commodities covered.[2]

We can formalize this intuition in a three-good commodity tax model based on Kaplow (1990), in which revenue is raised to fund an exogenous level of government purchases, G. A fraction $(1 - \alpha)$ of taxpayers are able to costlessly, and with certainty, evade the commodity tax on the first good, but compliance is perfect for the second good, while labor supply is untaxed.[3] The tax authority chooses the tax rate on each commodity, and can increase compliance for the first good by incurring an observation cost, φ, with its choices summarized by the tax-system policy vector, $\theta = \{t_1, t_2, \varphi\}$. All consumers have the same quasi-linear and separable utility function, which simplifies the problem by eliminating income effects on consumer demands for the taxed goods and cross-price substitution effects. Formally, each taxpayer has an identical utility function of the form

$$U = \sum_{i=1}^{2} u_i(x_i) - \frac{y}{n}, \tag{8.6}$$

where u_i is utility from consumption of good x_i, and y is earned income, with the parameter n setting the ability/disutility of producing income. Taxpayers choose x_1, x_2, and y to maximize utility, subject to the budget constraint

$$y = \sum_{i=1}^{2} (q_i + t_i) x_i \tag{8.7}$$

for compliant taxpayers, and

$$y = q_1 x_1 + (q_2 + t_2) x_2 \tag{8.8}$$

for noncompliant taxpayers, where q_i is the exogenous producer price for good i, and t_i is the tax rate on good i faced by a compliant taxpayer. Because compliance is complete for the second good, both types of taxpayers face the tax rate t_2, but only the fraction α of taxpayers face the tax rate t_1 on the first good, with noncompliers able to purchase the good tax-free. Letting variables marked with a tilde denote choices of noncompliant taxpayers, and those without a tilde choices made by compliant taxpayers, note that as a consequence of the quasi-linear and separable specification of utility $x_2 = \tilde{x}_2$. Revenue raised net of administrative costs is equal to

$$R(\theta) - D(\theta) = \alpha(\varphi)x_1 t_1 + x_2 t_2 - D(\theta), \qquad (8.9)$$

where φ is the level of resources devoted by the tax authority to observing purchases of good one. D represents administrative cost, with $\partial D/\partial \varphi > 0$, and $\alpha' > 0$, $\alpha'' < 0$. Assuming for simplicity a utilitarian social welfare function, the Lagrangian for the social planner's problem is

$$L = \alpha(\varphi)v + (1 - \alpha(\varphi))\tilde{v} + \lambda[\alpha(\varphi)x_1 t_1 + x_2 t_2 - D(\theta) - G], \qquad (8.10)$$

where v represents indirect utility for compliers, $\tilde{v}$ represents utility for noncompliers, and λ is the social marginal cost of funds. As a consequence of consumers' preferences being quasi-linear and separable, and assuming interior solutions, the FOCs for the social planner's tax rate and enforcement choices simplify to

$$[\partial t_1] \quad \frac{\partial v}{\partial t_1} + \lambda \left[x_1 + t_1 \frac{\partial x_1}{\partial t_1} - \frac{1}{\alpha(\varphi)} \frac{\partial D}{\partial t_1} \right] = 0, \qquad (8.11)$$

$$[\partial t_2] \quad \frac{\partial v}{\partial t_2} + \lambda \left[x_2 + t_2 \frac{\partial x_2}{\partial t_2} - \frac{\partial D}{\partial t_2} \right] = 0, \qquad (8.12)$$

$$[\partial \varphi] \quad x_1 t_1 - \left(\frac{\tilde{v} - v}{\lambda} \right) = \frac{1}{\alpha'(\varphi)} \frac{\partial D}{\partial \varphi}, \qquad (8.13)$$

where equation (8.12) uses the fact that $\partial v/\partial t_2 = \partial \tilde{v}/\partial t_2$. Imperfect compliance for the first good reduces the amount of revenue raised for any pair of tax rates t_1 and t_2, necessitating higher tax rates than in the complete-compliance alternative. But without further restrictions on consumers' demand functions and the administrative cost function D, the optimal tax rates do not need to be uniform, in contrast to the model analyzed by Yitzhaki (1979), in which tax rates are uniform as a consequence of the Cobb–Douglas specification of consumer preferences.

Of particular interest here is the social planner's optimal enforcement choice, described by equation (8.13). Incurring administrative cost to observe additional purchasers of the first good allows the distortionary tax rates t_1 and t_2 to be lowered, yet still raise the same amount of net revenue. But exposing additional consumers to tax on the first good reduces their welfare by distorting their consumption of that good. These effects are shown by the terms on the LHS of equation (8.13): $x_1 t_1$ is revenue raised from observing additional purchases of the first good, and $(\tilde{v} - v)/\lambda$ is the utility loss in dollar terms for consumers now subject to tax on the first good. Supposing an interior solution for compliance expenditure, the sum of these terms is positive, and at an optimum is equated with the marginal cost to observe—and thereby tax—the purchases of an additional consumer, as shown by the expression on the RHS of equation (8.13).

Note that the optimal level of enforcement is *below* the revenue-maximizing level, which as we explain in the next section, is true in general. This general result can be seen for the special case here by noting that at an optimum $(\tilde{v} - v) > 0$, in which case a revenue-maximizing rather than a welfare-maximizing planner would choose a higher than socially optimal level of enforcement effort. The revenue maximizer raises no net revenue at the margin because the marginal dollar spent on enforcement yields only one dollar in revenue. But the social cost exceeds one dollar at the margin: the revenue maximizer ignores the dollar of income lost to taxpayers, and the efficiency cost of raising revenue to pay for enforcement.

8.2   Optimal Income Tax Enforcement

8.2.1   The Optimal Size of a Tax Collection Agency

How many resources should government devote to tax enforcement? Intuitively, not as much as would be needed to eradicate evasion completely, just as it does not make sense to station a police officer at every street corner to eradicate street crime. One needs to distinguish economically recoverable tax evasion just as one distinguishes economically recoverable oil reserves from total oil on the planet.

Because one measure of output of a tax agency—extra tax revenue received through direct collection efforts as well as deterrence—is denominated in dollars and in principle measurable, some people have been tempted to assert a simple rule for the optimal extent of tax enforcement: maximize net revenue. It is often heard, in particular from IRS commissioners seeking a higher budget appropriation and in public finance textbooks of a certain vintage, that increasing the audit budget for the IRS is appropriate because it would raise net revenue, implicitly presuming that at an optimum marginal audit revenue and the marginal cost of obtaining that revenue, say via additional audits, should be equated. But, as Slemrod and Yitzhaki (1987) show, this apparently intuitive argument leads to a socially excessive level of enforcement because it ignores the fact that real resources are being consumed to implement what is simply a transfer of funds between households and the tax authority; thus the implied optimality condition compares (marginal) apples and oranges.

To formalize this intuition, recall from chapter 2 that at an optimum for an arbitrary tax instrument θ_i with an interior optimal solution, the social planner's FOC for a representative taxpayer satisfies

$$[\partial\theta_i] \quad \frac{\partial v(\theta,A)}{\partial\theta_i} + \lambda[R_{\theta_i} - D_{\theta_i}] = 0, \tag{8.14}$$

where the Lagrange multiplier λ is equal to the social marginal utility cost of funds. The set of instruments for this model is $\theta = \{t, p, F\}$, where t is the tax rate on labor income, p is the audit probability, and $F \equiv 1 + \tilde{\pi}$ is the gross penalty rate for tax understatement. Hence equation (8.14) implies the following expressions for the optimal labor income tax rate, t, and audit probability choice, p:

$$[\partial t] \quad \frac{\partial v(t,p,F,A)}{\partial t} = -\lambda[R_t - D_t], \tag{8.15}$$

$$[\partial p] \quad \frac{\partial v(t,p,F,A)}{\partial p} = -\lambda[R_p - D_p]. \tag{8.16}$$

As described in chapter 5, the utility cost to taxpayers of an increase in audit probability is not equal to the expected mechanical burden alone because changes in the audit probability affect the risk-bearing cost of taxpayers' evasion gamble. To gain further insight, note first that the excess burden of this tax system is

$$EB = v(0,p',F',A-G) - v(t,p,F,A). \tag{8.17}$$

In this expression $v(0, p', F', A - G)$ is utility under a lump-sum tax system that raises G dollars in revenue, with enforcement parameters p' and F' chosen to deter all evasion. The expression $v(t, p, F, A)$ is utility under a labor income tax system with $pF < 1$, so the penalty rate for evasion is not large enough to deter evasion at feasible audit rates. There is an excess burden arising from the distortion caused by proportional labor income taxation, and from evasion because it involves paying taxes in the form of a gamble rather than with certainty. Holding revenue raised, R, constant at G generates an expression for the marginal excess burden:

$$\frac{\partial EB}{\partial p} = -\frac{\partial v(t,p,F,A)}{\partial p} - \frac{\partial v(t,p,F,A)}{\partial t}\frac{\partial t}{\partial p}\Big|_{R=G}$$

$$= -\frac{\partial v(t,p,F,A)}{\partial p} + \frac{\partial v(t,p,F,A)}{\partial t}\frac{R_p}{R_t} \tag{8.18}$$

$$= -\frac{\partial v(t,p,F,A)}{\partial p} - \lambda R_p,$$

where the last equality makes use of equation (8.15). We assume for simplicity that $D_t = 0$; that is, there are no administrative costs associated with the collection of additional income taxes via tax-rate increases. Substituting equation (8.16) into equation (8.18) gives an intuitive expression for optimal law enforcement:

$$-\frac{\partial EB}{\partial p} = \lambda D_p. \tag{8.19}$$

Equation (8.19) says that the optimal audit probability is set such that the marginal social cost of conducting audits, λD_p, equals the marginal reduction in the representative taxpayer's excess burden. Using equation (8.16), we can see that equating marginal audit revenue and marginal administrative cost—as IRS commissioners and certain textbooks suggest—always results in a socially excessive level of enforcement; the term $-(\partial v/\partial p)/\lambda$, which measures the marginal social cost of revenue raised via tighter enforcement, is necessarily positive, implying $R_p > D_p$ at an optimum. Intuitively, a revenue maximizer, who sets $R_p = D_p$, raises no net revenue on the margin but takes a full dollar from taxpayers. Spending a dollar in administrative costs to take a dollar from taxpayers can never be optimal.

This line of reasoning, and its emphasis—ceteris paribus—on the excess burden of tax evasion attributed to increasing the riskiness of tax liability, is apparently at odds with the surprising result of Stiglitz (1982) and Weiss (1976), who argue that even when taxpayers are risk averse it may be optimal to induce a certain amount of randomness in tax liabilities. Weiss (1976) identified a large and positive second derivative of marginal utility (i.e., third derivative of utility) with respect to consumption as the necessary condition for randomness to be desirable. Intuitively, the additional risk-bearing cost imposed on taxpayers by inducing randomness in ex post tax liability may be more than compensated by increased labor supply (if $u_{ccc} > 0$), reducing the dead-weight cost of non–lump-sum income taxation. However, Yitzhaki (1987) shows that the special cases examined by Weiss (1976) feature an optimum on the wrong side of the Laffer curve (i.e., a tax-rate increase would decrease revenue collected), making any reduction in tax liability socially optimal. Baldry (1979) and Pencavel (1979) demonstrate the difficulty of reaching any clear-cut comparative statics conclusions from such a model; the response of reported income to changes in tax rates, penalties, and fines becomes ambiguous (see the discussion in section 3.1.2). Thus the strong conclusions of Stiglitz (1982) and Weiss (1976) are derived from a very restrictive setup.

Although conducting audits consumes real resources, <u>revenue obtained from fines imposed on detected evaders represents a transfer of resources between taxpayers, making it apparently appealing to deter evasion via high penalty rates rather than broad audit coverage</u> (see Becker 1968). Even with a tiny audit probability, the A-S model predicts that all evasion can be deterred if the penalty rate is set high enough to make the expected value of evasion negative. Because there is no evasion in equilibrium, this policy has been described as "hanging with zero probability." A commonly heard objection to such a policy is its violation of the requirement that "the punishment fit the crime," implying a regime with a low penalty rate and substantial audit coverage, although Becker (1968) argues that this is not a useful guide for policy because it ignores the resource cost of enforcement. There is a large literature in law and economics, surveyed in Polinsky and Shavell (2000, 2007), that explores this logic and elaborates on exceptions to this stark policy implication.

The possibility of accidental evasion provides one justification for non-maximal penalties, the implications of which Boadway and Sato (2000) study in a model where high-income taxpayers face uncertainty over their true taxable income. In their two-type model—featuring rewards for low-income taxpayers who are discovered upon an audit to have reported honestly—an optimal audit and penalty scheme eliminates all intentional evasion. Even though the tax authority knows that all discovered evasion is unintentional, it must punish the discovered evasion to deter intentional evasion. Crucially, maximal penalties are no longer optimal given that only unintentional evaders pay fines. In addition to consuming real resources, raising the audit probability also increases the chance that an unintentional evader is punished, although with a preference for redistribution this cost is partly offset by an increased probability that an honestly reporting low-income taxpayer receives a reward. An important element is the tax authority's ability to commit to punishing discovered evaders: if the tax authority is unable to fine innocent tax evaders, then it is no longer feasible to collect more tax from high-income earners. In practice, the ability of a tax authority to commit to punishing innocent evaders is likely to be greater the lower is the penalty rate. Similar conclusions are reached in a version of the model where taxpayers face no uncertainty about their true taxable income, but administrative errors made by the tax authority mistakenly identify some truly low-income taxpayers as having high income.

8.2.2 Optimal Audit Rules

In the previous section we examined the optimal audit probability in an economy with a large number of identical agents each earning and misreporting the same level of income. We now ask who the tax authority should audit when taxpayers differ in their true and reported level of income, and when the only information received by the tax authority is reported income. Sanchez and Sobel (1993) characterize the solution for an expected-revenue-maximizing tax authority with a fixed budget and no control over the tax function. They show that in a world with risk-neutral taxpayers, fixed labor supply, a continuous distribution of true income, and an exogenously bounded penalty for evasion, the optimal audit rule requires randomly auditing taxpayers reporting incomes below some threshold level of income. The audit probability is set just high enough so that all taxpayers with true incomes below the threshold choose to report truthfully. Knowing the form of the audit rule, taxpayers with true incomes above the threshold report just above the threshold and are never audited.[4]

Clearly, this type of audit rule is not time-consistent.[5] Knowing that those reporting below the threshold are reporting truthfully, once reports have been received the tax authority has an incentive to audit only those untruthfully reporting at the threshold. Melumad and Mookherjee (1989) suggest the commitment problem might be solved by contracting an independent agency to follow the ex ante optimal audit policy. Alternatively, introducing into the model some taxpayers who report truthfully at all income levels—regardless of the audit policy followed and regardless of their apparent self-interest—may lessen the tax authority's commitment problem (see Graetz et al. 1986).

Of course, tax authorities observe information beyond reported income that can be used to generate more sophisticated audit rules. For example, Scotchmer (1987) supposes that taxpayers are assigned to different audit classes based on characteristics (e.g., occupation) known to the tax authority. In any given audit class, a similar threshold policy is optimal, but because low-income taxpayers are audited with greater frequency in any class than high-income earners, the post-audit distribution of income becomes more regressive.

Bigio and Zilberman (2011) suppose that in addition to reported income, the tax authority can condition its audit strategy for self-employed entrepreneurs on the number of their employees. Unlike income reports for the self-employed, wage and salary income is reported accurately because there is information reporting to the tax authority by both employees and employers, for which collusion to evade taxes is difficult to sustain. In their model, entrepreneurs differ in managerial ability, but because an entrepreneur's number of employees is assumed to be information costlessly available to the tax authority, an estimate of the true business income can be made.

When audit policy is based solely on an entrepreneur's number of employees, optimal policy calls for random audits of only those entrepreneurs reporting above some employment threshold. In contrast to audit policy based on income reports alone, large firms report truthfully, small firms report no income and go unaudited, and firms close to the audit-threshold level of employment produce using an inefficiently low level of employees to evade taxes by avoiding audits. This policy endogenously generates features consistent with empirical regularities: an informal sector consisting of small firms that are not subject to audits and a "missing middle" of firm sizes. The model developed by Dharmapala et al. (2011), discussed in chapter 11, endogenously generates a similar firm size distribution, but in their model it is optimal to exempt small firms from taxes because including them in the tax base does not warrant the associated administrative cost; in contrast, in the Bigio and Zilberman (2011) model small firms are exempted because audits are costly.

Characterizing optimal audit strategies when both income reports and employee information are used is complex, but supposing that the tax authority either audits an entrepreneur with a fixed probability or not at all produces features consistent with real-world audit policy in several countries. The observed number of employees is used to impute income, with entrepreneurs reporting below their imputed level subject to a random audit.

One policy question the literature has not addressed is how forth-coming the tax authority ought to be about its audit rules. In models of the Sanchez and Sobel (1993) tradition, the audit cutoff is publicly announced (although not credible).[6] In practice, what affects audit probability is a closely guarded secret, as is the discriminant formula (DIF) in the United States, which is a scalar derived from reported items that affects, among other factors, the probability of audit. Whether, and under what conditions, it makes sense to advertise what triggers an audit, has not been rigorously analyzed, and is an issue that warrants further analysis. Another important research priority is to characterize optimal audit rules that are credible.

8.3   Redistribution When Avoidance Behavior Is Heterogeneous

So far we have assumed taxpayers' proclivity and opportunity to avoid income taxes is uniform or correlated only with true income. In this case the implications for optimal progressivity are no different than those of real behavioral response, except that the former is often endog-enous. In reality, some taxpayers view the pursuit of legal "loopholes" as unethical, while others see tax minimization by all legal means as common sense. Opportunities for tax avoidance also differ greatly by employment status, with wage and salary earners likely to face few opportunities for avoidance compared to the self-employed who often have substantial freedom over the form and timing of income receipts. What are the implications of such heterogeneity?

To investigate this, we consider the model in Kopczuk (2001), who introduces heterogeneous avoidance behavior into an otherwise stan-dard linear income tax problem, studying the desirability of avoidance behavior as a means for redistribution and its impact on the optimal progressivity of the tax system. Adding to the standard setup, Kopczuk (2001) allows for taxpayers to differ in two unobservable dimensions: their disutility of work and their cost of income tax avoidance. Taxpay-ers' indirect utility depends on their disutility of work n; their cost of avoidance, ϕ, with higher values of ϕ corresponding to lower levels of avoidance behavior; and the linear income tax rate and demogrant chosen by the social planner, $\theta = \{t, A\}$. That is, $v = v(n, \phi, t, A)$. The Lagrangian for the social planner's problem is

$$L = \int [v(n,\phi,t,A) + \lambda (T(y,s,\theta) - G)] dF(n,\phi), \qquad (8.20)$$

where $F(n, \phi)$ is the joint cdf of the disutility of work and avoidance cost among taxpayers, $T(y, s, \theta) = t(y - s) - A$, and a utilitarian social welfare function has been assumed for simplicity. The remaining notation is as defined earlier. The FOCs for the social planner's choices are

$$[\partial A] \quad \int \frac{\partial v}{\partial A} + \lambda \left(t \frac{\partial z}{\partial A} - 1 \right) dF(n,\phi) = 0 \qquad (8.21)$$

and

$$[\partial t] \quad \int \frac{\partial v}{\partial t} + \lambda \left(z + t \frac{\partial z}{\partial t} \right) dF(n,\phi) = 0, \qquad (8.22)$$

where $z = y - s$ is taxable income. Using the Slutsky formula, Roy's identity, and combining these two FOCs gives an expression for the optimal tax rate t:

$$t = \frac{\int z(b-1) dF(n,\phi)}{\int (\partial z^c / \partial t) dF(n,\phi)}, \qquad (8.23)$$

where $b \equiv [(\partial v / \partial A)/\lambda] + t(\partial z / \partial A)$ is the social marginal valuation of income for an (n, ϕ) individual and z^c is compensated taxable income. This formula is very similar to the Atkinson and Stiglitz (1980) representation for the optimal linear income tax rate shown in equation (2.20), the only difference being explicit recognition of heterogeneity in taxpayers' avoidance cost. Letting x^n represent the mean of a variable x given the disutility-of-work parameter n, Kopczuk (2001) shows that the numerator of the right-hand side of equation (8.23) can be re-expressed as follows:

$$\int z(b-1) dF(n,\phi) = \int \int z(b - b^n + b^n - 1) dF(\phi \mid n) dF(n)$$

$$= \int \int z(b - b^n) dF(\phi \mid n) dF(n) + \int \left((b^n - 1) \int z dF(\phi \mid n) \right) dF(n)$$

$$= \int \int z(b - b^n) dF(\phi \mid n) dF(n) + \int z^n (b^n - 1) dF(n). \qquad (8.24)$$

Similarly the denominator can be re-expressed as

$$\int \frac{\partial z^c}{\partial t} dF(n,\phi) = \int \left(\frac{\partial z^c}{\partial t} \right)^n dF(n). \qquad (8.25)$$

Accordingly, by substitution, the optimal marginal tax rate can now be written as

$$t = \frac{\int z''(b'' - 1)dF(n)}{\int (\partial z^c/\partial t)'' dF(n)} + \frac{\int\int z(b - b'')dF(\phi\,|\,n)dF(n)}{\int (\partial z^c/\partial t)dF(n,\phi)}$$

$$= t^* + \frac{\int \mathrm{cov}(z,b\,|\,n)dF(n)}{\int (\partial z^c/\partial t)dF(n,\phi)}.$$

$$(8.26)$$

The term t^* is the optimal marginal tax rate when we ignore differences in avoidance behavior among people having the same disutility of work: that is, it is equivalent to equation (2.20) except for one important difference. The behavioral response that limits progressivity concerns not just wage income, but taxable income. As discussed in chapter 5, this captures the marginal excess burden of raising the tax rate.

The second term captures the impact on optimal progressivity of heterogeneity in avoidance behavior among people having the same disutility of work. If, conditional on n, taxpayers with higher taxable incomes have a lower social marginal utility of income—that is, $\mathrm{cov}(z, b\,|\,n) < 0$—then (making the standard assumption that the denominator, $\int (\partial z^c/\partial t)dF(n,\phi)$, is negative) optimal progressivity rises compared to when we take no account of horizontal differences in avoidance behavior. Intuitively, when $\mathrm{cov}(z, b\,|\,n) < 0$, those with a high taxable income at any given level of ability n are accorded less weight by the social welfare function, increasing the desire for progressive taxation. The opposite is true if $\mathrm{cov}(z, b\,|\,n) > 0$. Thus determining the bias from ignoring horizontal differences in avoidance behavior is an empirical matter. Kopczuk (2001) argues that differences in avoidance cost among taxpayers is the most compelling explanation of heterogeneous avoidance behavior, so that under plausible assumptions low taxable income can signal either low avoidance cost or low ability. Because redistribution is only desirable in the latter case, the informativeness of taxable income as an indicator of individual well-being is lower in the presence of avoidance under these assumptions. This suggests that $\mathrm{cov}(z, b\,|\,n) > 0$, implying standard optimal tax rates (and the optimal extent of progressivity) ignoring heterogeneity in avoidance behavior are overstated.

So how does heterogeneity in avoidance behavior affect its desirability? In the absence of heterogeneity in avoidance behavior, any income distribution that can be achieved in the presence of avoidance can also be achieved with nonlinear taxes alone, but without the social waste of costly avoidance, so avoidance can only be welfare-improving if it relaxes the standard incentive compatibility constraints faced by the social planner.[7] This may be the case if avoidance opportunities are more readily available to those to whom the social planner wishes to redistribute toward, and the loss in revenue due to avoidance is less than the gain from additional redistribution. As Kopczuk (2001) explains, this result is closely related to Akerlof (1978), who shows that making taxable income a function of additional nontax instruments can more precisely target unobservable aspects of taxpayer behavior.[8]

9   Endogenous Elasticity

9.1   Optimal Elasticity

As we argued in chapter 5, the elasticity of behavioral response with respect to a tax rate is a central concept in modern tax analysis. The higher the (compensated) elasticity of a tax base, the higher is the marginal excess burden per dollar raised from that base. Other things equal, the higher is marginal excess burden the lower is the optimal tax rate on a given base.

In most contexts the fact that a behavioral elasticity need not be constant over the range of parameters considered is noted and then put aside, as the insights do not depend on this characteristic.[1] In addition private agents can take actions that affect their elasticity of response to changes in tax rates, or other tax-system instruments. For example, multinational companies can increase their responsiveness to one country's tax policy by placing production facilities in a number of countries, and individuals can do the same by putting wealth in liquid forms such as jewelry, Swiss banks, and human capital including fluency in English.

The dependence of behavioral elasticities with respect to tax rates on other tax-system parameters is a serious substantive issue. To see this, first consider the standard model of optimal progressivity, where the social planner chooses a tax function to maximize social welfare assuming the elasticity of taxable income, which in many models is equivalent to the elasticity of labor supply, a structural preference parameter. The change in focus from labor supply, as in chapter 2, to taxable income, as in chapter 5, is important, because numerous non-rate tax-system aspects under the control of policy makers—such as the breadth of the tax base, opportunities for sheltering, and enforcement effort—may affect the tax-rate elasticity.

138   Chapter 9
Recall that one of the motivating examples for focusing on taxable income and its elasticity, rather than on labor supply alone, is the idea that higher tax rates may reduce labor supply only slightly, but may induce significant shifting into inefficient untaxed fringe benefits, tax shelters, and so on. But tax policy could also directly address these issues by paring tax-exempt activities, restricting shelters, and so on, which could substantially reduce the ETI, which in turn might increase the optimal level of progressivity.

We can explore this issue analytically. Whereas we usually presume that the elasticity of labor supply is an unalterable consequence of individual preferences about leisure versus consumption, Slemrod and Kopczuk (2002) modify the standard problem by allowing the social planner to control a tax-system instrument that affects the elasticity of taxable income with respect to a tax rate, albeit with a resource cost. Slemrod and Kopczuk (2002) provide an instructive example in which the social planner controls the elasticity of taxable income by choosing the set of commodities that are tax deductible, which in their one-period model is equivalent to choosing which commodities are taxed, as in Yitzhaki (1979) and Wilson (1989). This provides a nice link to the literature on the optimal breadth of a commodity tax base we discussed in chapter 8.[2]

In the model of Slemrod and Kopczuk (2002), consumers have Cobb–Douglas utility over a continuum of goods such that

$$u(c) = \exp\left(\int_0^1 \alpha_i \log(c_i) di\right), \tag{9.1}$$

where α_i are consumers' expenditure shares on each good. The vector of tax-system instruments is $\theta = \{t, A, I\}$, where t is a linear tax rate on income, A is a demogrant, and goods $i \in [0, I]$ are subject to tax, with $I = 1$ corresponding to a completely comprehensive tax base. When the tax base consists of goods $i \in [0, I]$, the expenditure share of taxed goods, which we refer to as the tax base, is

$$b(I) \equiv \int_0^I \alpha_i di. \tag{9.2}$$

Taxpayers are assumed to supply one unit of labor inelastically, with a taxpayer of income-earning ability n facing the following budget constraint:

$$\int_0^1 c_i di = n + A - tz_n, \tag{9.3}$$

where before-tax prices have been normalized to unity and with taxable income, z_n, equal to

$$\left(n + A - \int_I^1 c_i di\right),\tag{9.4}$$

where the last term refers to tax-deductible expenses. That the demogrant, A, is included in taxable income is not important to the analysis, and simplifies the analysis somewhat. Because, due to the Cobb–Douglas assumption, the income elasticity of demand for all goods is equal to unity, all consumers choose a consumption bundle in proportion to their income:

$$c_i = \begin{cases} (1-t)\alpha_i (n+A), & i \le I, \\ \alpha_i (n+A), & i > I, \end{cases}\tag{9.5}$$

so that a taxpayer of type n has indirect utility of

$$v(n,t,A,b) = (n+A)(1-t)^b,\tag{9.6}$$

up to a multiplicative constant that has been normalized to one. By reference to equation (8.2), and recognizing that $(1-t)^b \approx (1+t)^{-b}$, we can see that taxpayers' indirect utility varies in the same manner (but in the opposite direction) whether we vary the share of goods that are deductible from taxable income or the share of goods that are subject to a constant tax rate on consumption.[3]

Strikingly, the compensated elasticity of taxable income in this model with respect to the net-of-tax rate simplifies to equal exactly $(1-b)$: the broader is the tax base, the lower is the elasticity. This makes intuitive sense because there are fewer untaxed commodities toward which to substitute when the tax rate rises. As in Yitzhaki (1979) and Wilson (1989), a broader tax base lowers the excess burden of taxation, but this is assumed to raise administrative costs. For any given size of the tax base, b, the commodities minimizing administrative cost are assumed to be included in the tax base, so that administrative cost, $D(b)$, is a smoothly increasing function in the neighborhood of the optimum tax policy.

Now consider which tax policy θ maximizes a social welfare function W given an exogenous distribution of abilities $F(n)$ and the aggregate budget constraint. The Lagrangian for this problem is

$$L = \int (W(v(n,t,A,b)) + \lambda [bt(n+A) - A - D(b) - G])dF(n),\tag{9.7}$$

with the associated FOCs:

$$[\partial A] \quad \int \left(W'(1-t)^b + \lambda [bt - 1]\right)dF(n) = 0,\tag{9.8}$$

$$[\partial t] \quad \int \left(-W'b(n+A)(1-t)^{b-1} + \lambda b(n+A)\right)dF(n) = 0,\tag{9.9}$$

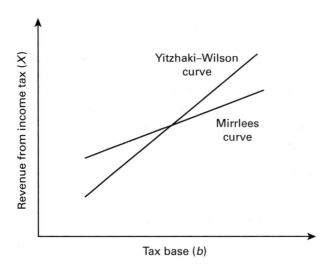

Figure 9.1
Mirrlees and Yitzhaki–Wilson curves and the optimal tax system

$$[\partial b] \quad \int \left(W'(n+A)(1-t)^b \, ln(1-t) + \lambda[t(n+A)-D'(b)] \right) dF(n) = 0. \quad (9.10)$$

Note that choosing b is equivalent to choosing I. The FOCs for (A, t) define the optimal tax policy, holding the breadth of the tax base fixed, as in the Mirrlees (1971) problem, where the base was fixed. Solving for optimal policy at each value of b produces an upward-sloping "Mirrlees" curve in (X, b) space, where $X \equiv tb\int (n+A)dF(n)$ is the amount of revenue raised from distortionary income taxes (see figure 9.1). Because the elasticity of taxable income in this model is decreasing in the breadth of the tax base, ceteris paribus, having a broader tax base implies that it is optimal to have a more progressive tax system, with the amount of revenue raised from distortionary taxes serving as a sufficient statistic for progressivity.

In contrast, taking the demogrant as given and solving the FOCs for (t, b) to characterize the optimal tax policy, as in Yitzhaki (1979) and Wilson (1989), defines the optimal breadth of the tax system holding progressivity constant. Solving for all values of the demogrant, A, produces an upward-sloping "Yitzhaki–Wilson" curve in (X, b) space, defined by an optimality condition almost identical to that derived earlier in equation (8.5) for the Yitzhaki (1979) model. This implies that more egalitarian societies (raising more revenue from distortionary taxes) will have a broader tax base, and so a lower compensated elasticity of taxable income.

The optimal tax policy, θ, is found at the intersection of the "Mirrlees" and "Yitzhaki–Wilson" curves, defining the optimal degree of progressivity and elasticity of the tax base. Slemrod and Kopczuk (2002) prove that in the neighborhood of an optimum, the "Yitzhaki–Wilson" curve cuts the "Mirrlees" curve from below, so that an increase in egalitarianism (which shifts up the Mirrlees curve) will increase the amount of revenue raised from distortionary taxes, broaden the tax base, and lower the compensated elasticity of taxable income at the optimum. Slemrod and Kopczuk (2002) also prove that an increase in the cost of maintaining a broad tax base—that is, increasing $D'(b)$ holding $D(b)$ constant—decreases the optimal progressivity of the tax system and narrows the optimal tax base.

9.2   Fixing the Leak in Okun's Bucket

Behavioral response to higher marginal tax rates involves not only substitution to more lightly taxed goods—as in the example proposed by Slemrod and Kopczuk (2002)—but also increased avoidance behavior. In an income tax context, higher marginal tax rates induce taxpayers to rearrange their affairs to exploit additional deductions and loopholes in the tax code. This sort of socially wasteful activity raises individual taxpayers' after-tax incomes, but does not alter the composition of consumption other than via income effects. How then does the presence of avoidance opportunities affect the optimal progressivity of the income tax code? And given that the availability of avoidance opportunities can be (partly) controlled—at some cost—by tax policy choices, does the level of enforcement affect optimal progressivity?

Slemrod (1994) tackles this question by modifying the standard optimal linear income tax problem to allow taxpayers to engage in avoidance behavior, and by supposing that the social planner controls a costly instrument affecting taxpayers' avoidance behavior. The phrase in the title—"fixing the leak in Okun's bucket"—refers to the important 1975 book by Arthur Okun, *Equality and Efficiency: The Big Tradeoff*. Okun believed that wealth transfers by taxation from the relatively rich to the relatively poor are an appropriate policy for government, but he recognized the loss of efficiency inherent in the distribution process. To make the trade-off vivid, Okun introduced the metaphor of a leaky bucket: "The money must be carried from the rich to the poor in a leaky bucket. Some of it will simply disappear in transit, so the poor will not receive all the money that is taken from the rich" (p. 91). Okun attributed these losses—the leak—to the administrative costs of taxing and transferring as well as to incentive effects.

Economists generally take as given and immutable individuals' preferences (e.g., the substitutability between leisure and other goods). But, from a tax-systems perspective, the leak in the bucket can be repaired to some extent, albeit at some cost. The tax base can be broadened, enforcement can be tightened, avoidance avenues can be eliminated. So the optimal tax-systems problem becomes to jointly determine (1) how many resources to devote to installing efficient administrative processes and broadening the tax base (i.e., fixing the leak) and (2) how progressive a tax system to impose given the optimal amount of inefficiency (i.e., carrying water from the rich to the poor).

Slemrod's 1994 model is a special case of the general framework outlined in chapter 7 and is another example of endogenous elasticities discussed in the previous section, using the following specific functional forms:

$$T(y,s,\theta) = t(y-s) - A,$$

$$\kappa = \kappa(y,s,E),$$

$$D(\theta) = E,$$

where y is earned income, A is a demogrant, t is the marginal tax rate, s is the level of sheltering (evasion or avoidance) chosen by the taxpayer, and E is the level of the tax authority's resources directed to reducing the extent of sheltering. Assuming interior solutions for $\theta = \{A, t, E\}$, and recalling that $z = y - s$ denotes taxable income, equation (7.10) implies that the FOCs for the policy maker are as follows:

$$[\partial A] \quad \int \left(W' \frac{\alpha}{\lambda} + t \frac{\partial z}{\partial A} \right) dF(n) \equiv \int b_n dF(n) = 1, \tag{9.11}$$

$$[\partial t] \quad \int z W' \frac{\alpha}{\lambda} dF(n) = \int \left(t \frac{\partial z}{\partial t} + z \right) dF(n), \tag{9.12}$$

$$[\partial E] \quad \int W' \frac{\alpha}{\lambda} \frac{\partial \kappa}{\partial E} dF(n) = \int \left(t \frac{\partial z}{\partial E} - 1 \right) dF(n), \tag{9.13}$$

where b_n is the net social marginal valuation of income. Combining equations (9.11) and (9.12) and using the Slutsky formula yields the following expression for the optimal linear income tax rate, t:

$$t = \frac{-\text{cov}(b_n, z_n)}{\int -(\partial y^c / \partial t) dF(n) + \int (\partial s^c / \partial t) dF(n)}, \tag{9.14}$$

where $\partial y^c/\partial t$ is the compensated change in earned income with respect to the marginal tax rate, assumed to be negative, and $\partial s^c/\partial t$ is the compensated change in sheltering with respect to the marginal tax rate, assumed to be positive. Equation (9.14) differs from the standard formula by the addition of sheltering terms in both the numerator and denominator (compare equation 2.20). In the numerator, taxable income is now equal to $z = y - s$, rather than $z = y$ in the standard case without avoidance behavior. Supposing that sheltering is concentrated among high-income earners, the correlation between taxable income and the social marginal valuation of income falls ($|\text{cov}(b_n, y_n - s_n)| < |\text{cov}(b_n, y_n)|$), implying a lower optimal marginal tax rate, t. Intuitively, when sheltering behavior is concentrated among high earners, reported taxable income is a less informative measure of a taxpayers' marginal utility of income. Taxpayer resistance to higher marginal tax rates through increased sheltering activity also increases the social cost of redistribution. This effect is captured in equation (9.14) via the addition of the sheltering response $\partial s^c/\partial t$ on the denominator. The more responsive is sheltering behavior to an increase in marginal tax rates, the lower is the optimal tax rate, t.

However, the responsiveness of sheltering to a change in marginal tax rates depends on the level of resources devoted to evasion and avoidance, call it enforcement. This level is chosen such that, at an optimum, the marginal social cost of tighter enforcement is equal to the marginal amount of net revenue collected via tighter enforcement (see equation 9.13). The term on the left-hand side of equation (9.13) represents the cost to taxpayers of tighter enforcement, and the expression on the right-hand side of equation (9.13) is the amount of net revenue collected from a marginal increase in enforcement (recalling that each additional unit of enforcement incurs a dollar of administrative cost). Because the term on the left-hand side of equation (9.13) is positive, the optimal level of enforcement falls short of the revenue-maximizing level. If the social planner neglects this condition, and there is a suboptimal level of enforcement, sheltering behavior will respond too elastically to changes in the marginal tax rate compared to a social optimum. We take this sheltering elasticity to be exogenous, so that equation (9.14) tells us that progressivity will be too low relative to a tax system where the level of enforcement and the marginal tax rate are jointly optimized.

10   Optimal Observability and Complexity

Our analysis of tax systems has focused on the manipulability of a tax base, often summarized by a tax base elasticity that depends on the behavioral response of both real quantities and the reporting of such quantities. The optimal tax-systems approach suggests that another important aspect of tax bases is the observability of the true value by the tax authority. Many tax systems rely on a report by a private party to the government, which may be inaccurate, willfully or inadvertently. But the tax authority can directly ascertain information about the true tax base other than via taxpayer reports. Even if no reports are required, behavior can be camouflaged so as to make observation difficult. Both manipulability and observability are endogenous, subject to actions taken by the taxpayer and his or her agents, as well as by the tax authority. Thus a taxpayer can respond to aspects of a tax system by altering the true value, altering the report to the tax authority, or manipulating the observability. Moving your money from a bank to under your mattress affects the observability but not true wealth (although it may involve forgone interest).

Observability is a tax-system desideratum because it is a constraint on capriciousness—a part of rule of law. But tax rules need not make use of all available information, in order to save resources. Thus, in part, observability is about the cost of obtaining an accurate measurement, and the cost may be directly borne by the tax authority, by the taxpayer, and by a third party.

10.1   Observability

The seminal optimal income tax model of Mirrlees (1971) made stark assumptions about what the tax authority can and cannot observe: income is observable at no cost and neither hours worked nor earning potential (ability) is observable at any cost. In practice, true income is almost never observable without cost. Moreover, both hours and ability can be measured, the former more easily and both with error. How many resources should then a tax authority invest in improving observability?

10.1.1 Optimal Observability in a Linear Income Tax

The observability of a given tax base is not exogenous, but rather depends on aspects of the tax system, including how many resources the tax authority invests in accurate measurement. Kaplow (1996, 1998) explores the role of accuracy and complexity in an optimal income tax, and Slemrod and Yitzhaki (1994) apply the issue to the standard deduction in an income tax, which saves administrative and compliance costs but which does not finely distinguish the true extent of deductible activities.

A recent treatment is Slemrod and Traxler (2010), who formalize this issue in the context of an optimal linear income tax problem when tax liability is assessed with a degree of error that the tax authority can control. Formally, a taxpayer of type n maximizes utility $u = u(c, y/n)$ subject to the budget constraint $c = y - T(\theta)$, with the choices c and y implicitly being a function of n, which parameterizes the taxpayer's disutility of work (or ability). The tax function $T(\theta) = [t(y + v) - A]$ captures the assumption that tax liability is based on a noisy measure of income, $y + v$, rather than true income, y. The error with which income is observed by the tax authority, v, is assumed to have a mean-zero distribution given by $H(v; \sigma)$, with the parameter σ denoting the variance of v, which can be reduced by the tax authority incurring administrative cost $D(\sigma)$, with $D'(\sigma) < 0$, so reducing the variance is costly.[1] Risk-averse taxpayers are assumed to make their before-tax labor income choice prior to the resolution of uncertainty over their tax liability, implying the following expected utility maximization problem for a taxpayer of type n:

$$v(t, A, \sigma, n) = \max_{\{c,y\}} \int u\left(c, \frac{y}{n}\right) dH(v; \sigma) \quad \text{s.t.} \quad c = y - T(\theta). \tag{10.1}$$

Limited observability reduces welfare by exposing risk-averse taxpayers to uncertainty over their after-tax income. The social planner chooses tax policy $\theta \in \{t, A, \sigma\}$ to maximize social welfare, W, subject to an exogenous revenue requirement, G. This problem is almost a special case of the Mayshar (1991) model, discussed in chapter 7, with the exception that individual tax liability is now uncertain. The Lagrangian for the social planner's problem is

$$L = \iint (W(v(t, A, \sigma, n)) + \lambda [T(\theta) - D(\sigma) - G]) dH(v; \sigma) dF(n). \qquad (10.2)$$

The FOCs for the social planner, assuming interior solutions, are

$$[\partial A] \quad \int \left(\int W' \frac{\alpha}{\lambda} dH(v; \sigma) + t \frac{\partial y}{\partial A} \right) dF(n) \equiv \int b_n dF(n) = 1, \qquad (10.3)$$

$$[\partial t] \quad \int \left(\int -W' \frac{\alpha}{\lambda} (y + v) dH(v; \sigma) + \left[y + t \frac{\partial y}{\partial t} \right] \right) dF(n) = 0, \qquad (10.4)$$

and

$$[\partial \sigma] \quad \int \left(\int W \frac{\partial h(v; \sigma)}{\partial \sigma} dv + \lambda \left[t \frac{\partial y}{\partial \sigma} - D'(\sigma) \right] \right) dF(n) = 0, \qquad (10.5)$$

where, as before, b_n is the social marginal valuation of income to a taxpayer of type n, with $\bar{b} = \int b_n dF(n) = 1$. In using this expression and the Slutsky formula for the response of earned income y to the marginal tax rate t, it is possible to express the FOC for the optimal choice of t in the following form:

$$t = \frac{-\text{cov}(b_n, y_n) - \int \psi(n) dF(n)}{\int -(\partial y^c / \partial t) dF(n)}, \qquad (10.6)$$

where $\psi(n) = \int W'v(\alpha/\lambda) dH(v; \sigma)$ is the marginal social cost of the tax system's inaccuracy and $\partial y^c / \partial t$ (assumed to be negative) is the compensated change in earned income y with respect to the marginal tax rate, t. If income is perfectly observable, $\psi(n) = 0$ and the expression reduces to the standard form for the optimal linear income tax (see equation 2.20). But with less than perfect observability, $\int \psi(n) dF(n) > 0$, so optimal progressivity falls. Intuitively, as the marginal tax rate, t, increases, the greater is the dispersion of after-tax incomes among any class of taxpayers with the same type n, and the greater is the after-tax income risk to which taxpayers are exposed. To more clearly see the factors determining the optimal observability of income, the FOC for σ can be re-arranged as follows:

$$\frac{1}{\sigma} = \frac{-\frac{1}{\lambda} \iint W[\partial h(v; \sigma)/\partial \sigma] dv dF(n)}{D(\sigma)\varepsilon_{D,\sigma} - t \int y \varepsilon_{y,\sigma} dF(n)}, \qquad (10.7)$$

where $\varepsilon_{D,\sigma} = -\sigma[D'(\sigma)]/D > 0$ is the elasticity of observability costs with respect to the extent of (the inverse of) observability and $\varepsilon_{y,\sigma} = -(\sigma/y)(\partial y/\partial\sigma)$ is the elasticity of earned income with respect to (the inverse of) observability. The expression on the right-hand side of equation (10.7) is the ratio of the marginal social costs to the marginal social benefits of the revenue raised from altering observability, σ. The higher the costs of inaccuracy, due for example to a more concave social welfare function, the greater is the optimal observability of the tax system. This effect is captured by the numerator on the right-hand side of equation (10.7). The terms in the denominator measure the revenue effects of a marginal increase in observability. The first term reflects the marginal change in administrative costs from a marginal change in observability, with $\varepsilon_{D,\sigma} > 0$ by assumption. The more positive is $\varepsilon_{D,\sigma}$, the lower is optimal observability because it is more costly to improve tax-system accuracy. The second term in the denominator reflects the effect on earned income of a marginal increase in observability: if earned income is increasing in observability, then $\varepsilon_{y,\sigma} > 0$. The bigger is $\varepsilon_{y,\sigma}$, the greater is optimal observability.

10.1.2   Financial Transactions

Information is at the heart of modern tax systems, and its availability shapes tax structures. Gordon and Li (2009) highlight the important role financial transactions play in providing information to tax authorities. When firms or individuals make use of the financial sector there is a paper trail of transactions that can be used to enforce tax laws. By moving to cash transactions, firms can escape much of their tax liability, but at the cost of forgoing the benefits of intermediation, such as interest earned on working capital and access to financing. When the benefits of financial intermediation are small, there is typically a large informal sector operating via cash transactions to evade taxes.

Compared to developed economies, developing countries collect less revenue as a share of GDP, rely more on excise taxes, border taxes such as tariffs, seigniorage, and corporate income taxes to raise revenue than do rich countries. The shortfall in revenue collected by developing economies is not due primarily to lower statutory rates: average maximum consumption, corporate and individual income tax rates are broadly similar. Rather, average rates are much lower due to a large informal sector. It is tempting to take these stylized facts as evidence that developing economy tax systems are suboptimal. Optimal tax theory asserts under certain conditions that inputs to production should not be taxed, implying no tariffs, excise taxes that apply to export sales, or seigniorage revenue. In contrast to developing economies, rich countries generally collect little revenue from corporate income taxes, imposing smaller distortions on saving and investment.

But when the benefits of financial intermediation are low for a substantial share of firms, resulting in a large informal sector, optimal tax systems can be very different than under the informational assumptions made by standard optimal taxation theory. Revenue can only be collected on formal-sector firms, so policy is biased toward taxes that raise revenue from firms using the financial sector and that encourage its use.[2] Seen through this lens, Gordon and Li (2009) argue that developing economy tax systems are not necessarily suboptimal.

The presence of a large informal sector that does not make use of financial intermediation constrains both the amount of revenue that can be collected and the breadth of tax bases. Presuming capital-intensive firms are the most dependent on financial intermediation, corporate income taxes can feature in a second-best optimum because they target the firms that are least willing to give up the benefit of transacting through banks. Excise tax rates should be low for sectors whose decision to formalize is elastic with respect to their tax burden, and conversely for sectors that derive a large benefit from formalization, consistent with often large differences in statutory excise rates across sectors in poor countries. Interestingly, the use of tariffs can be rationalized provided they are used to remove the production distortion created by differential excise tax rates.

Otherwise inefficient instruments such as an inflation tax and red tape can also be seen in a different light once their informational implications are recognized. Money's role as an intermediate production input generally precludes raising revenue from seigniorage in an optimal tax system, but higher inflation rates increase the opportunity cost of holding cash, increasing incentives for firms to formalize. Similarly red-tape costs for informal firms—such as licensing fees for verifiable activities—can raise some revenue and increase the cost of operating informally.

10.2   Complexity

Many observers of tax systems have noted that tax systems are often extraordinarily complicated, although the standard for judging excess is generally not made explicit. Consider the US income tax. In chapter

4 we noted that the resource cost of collecting income taxes—including both the administrative cost and compliance cost—has been estimated to be about 10 percent of revenue collected. In 2005 the number of words in the federal income tax code was 1,286,000, and 5,778,000 for federal tax regulations.[3] Is this appropriate, or excessively complex?

Why many tax systems (but not all—see the US Social Security payroll tax) are so complex is itself a complex question. For issues related to capital income, as we discussed in section 3.3.6, part of the cause is the fundamental incoherence of the income tax base in a world where financial innovations, including derivative securities, can exploit the incoherence to create tax arbitrage gains (e.g., buying and selling equivalent but differentially taxed streams of income). Attempts by the government to patch these tax arbitrage gaps—for example, by attempting to distinguish form from economic substance—may create even more complexity.

The desire for progressivity is another reason for complexity. As Musgrave (1994) has stressed, if a society were willing to settle for having tax burden be approximately proportional to income or consumption, then taxes could be impersonal (e.g., value-added or retail sales tax), and no personal information, including annual income or consumption, need be collected or verified. In contrast to Slemrod and Traxler (2010)—in which inaccuracy in the measurement of tax liability stemming from complexity serves no social purpose—Kleven and Kopczuk (2011) argue that for nonuniversal transfer programs complexity is a policy instrument—like benefit levels and eligibility criteria—that can and should be used to screen deserving from undeserving applicants. An optimal program design sets these instruments to minimize take-up by the undeserving (which they label a type II error, in parallel with the terminology from statistical hypothesis testing) for a given level of incomplete take-up among deserving applicants (a type I error). They find that an optimal nonuniversal transfer program generally features eligibility criteria that alone would result in a high share of type II errors, and instead relies on complexity to deter take-up among the undeserving.

Using the income tax system to achieve nonrevenue, nonprogressivity objectives also complicates the tax system. Subsidizing charitable giving by allowing a deduction requires documentation and occasional verification of donations, subsidizing research requires the same for research expenses, and so on.

Tax complexity can affect the private decisions made by taxpayers, as well as the voting and other social choice behavior of citizens. Each of these issues has been recognized, although the connection between the two has not been given much attention.

10.2.1   Taxpayers as Decision Makers

Accurately calculating one's tax liability in self-assessment income tax systems is difficult for many taxpayers. To be sure, the difficulty is heterogeneous. People differ in their cognitive ability, and the cognitive (and energy) process requirements of tax compliance vary greatly across taxpayers. For those with complicated financial affairs, especially with respect to capital income, it can be very difficult. For those whose income is mostly wages and salary, the process can be very straightforward. Professional (and software) assistance can be purchased.

How does complexity affect individuals' perceptions of their choice set and the (relative) prices among alternative choices? There is a long strand of research about taxpayer perceptions of their average and marginal income tax rate. Sheffrin (1994) reviews studies of American, British, and Canadian taxpayers that find that taxpayers generally underestimate both their total tax liability and marginal tax rates. What is not clear is the connection between knowledge of one's marginal tax rate and the complexity of the tax system. One hypothesis is offered by Liebman and Zeckhauser (2004), who suggest that because of cognitive limitations taxpayers presume that their marginal tax rate is the easier-to-calculate average tax rate; they call this rule-of-thumb behavior "ironing," one of two examples of what they dub "schmeduling," defined as an inaccurately perceived price-cum-taxes schedule. They show that ironing behavior eliminates some of the deadweight loss from high marginal taxes, so that when the optimal tax schedule with non-ironing taxpayers would be convex, superior outcomes are available.

Feldman and Katuščák (2006) use eligibility for the US child tax credit (CTC) to develop an empirical test for whether taxpayers confuse their marginal tax rate with their average tax rate. Introduced in 1998, the CTC is available provided that the dependent child has not had a 17th birthday by the end of the tax year for which the credit is claimed, generating predictable variation in average tax rates across tax filers. Despite the marginal tax rate being unaffected by losing eligibility for the CTC, Feldman and Katuščák find that household labor income falls in the tax year following the loss of CTC eligibility for a dependent. This finding is inconsistent with the standard model: losing CTC eligibility has only a negative income effect, implying an increase rather than a decrease in labor income. But the fall in labor income observed by households losing CTC eligibility is consistent with taxpayers reacting as if their average tax rate is what affects the true after-tax price of leisure.

That taxpayers have cognitive limitations has many implications for tax analysis. One is that the distribution of tax burden may depend on, in addition to the intended characteristics, cognitive ability. Another is that taxpayers who are not so good at addressing tax matters may avoid certain employment statuses, such as self-employment, that require or reward this kind of savvy. Goldin (2012) develops a model of optimal tax salience that recognizes that low-salience taxes introduce two offsetting welfare effects: (1) they reduce the excess burden traditionally associated with distortionary taxation by dampening consumers' substitution away from the taxed goods, and (2) they introduce new welfare costs by causing consumers to make optimization errors when deciding how much to consume. Finally, some equivalences taken for granted by tax theory—for example, that between a labor income tax and a consumption tax—may not obtain because they are perceived differently.[4] Blumkin et al. (2012) find, in a lab-experimental setting, that subjects reduce their labor supply significantly more in response to an income tax than they do in response to an equivalent consumption tax, and speculate that this occurs because subjects underestimate the present value of the taxes levied on future consumption. Sausgruber and Tyran (2005) show, also in an experimental setting, that buyers systematically underestimate the tax burden of an indirect tax levied on sellers but do not do so with an equivalent direct tax.

Chetty et al. (2009) find that posting tax-inclusive prices directly on or near the products, rather than adding taxes at the point of sale, reduces purchases. Their findings come from an experiment at a large grocery retailer in California, at which prices inclusive of the 7.375 percent state sales tax were posted alongside the original before-tax price over a three-week period for three product categories (cosmetics, hair care accessories, and deodorants) comprising about 750 goods in total. Using other products in the same store and two neighboring stores as experimental controls, they estimate that the "tax treatment" reduced demand by 8 percent, from which they conclude, given previously estimated demand elasticities of 1 to 1.5 for the affected products, that most consumers do not take the sales tax into account when making purchase decisions. The median respondent in their survey of grocery shoppers had a high level of knowledge about which products are subject to sales tax, while over three-quarters of those surveyed reported a sales tax rate within 0.5 percentage points of the actual rate. Accordingly, Chetty et al. (2009) suggest their results are driven by salience effects. In all of these examples it is an open question about whether such anomalies would persist over the long run if they have substantial negative consequences for consumers.

Recognizing cognitive biases as well as rules of thumb that economize on cognitive resources has implications for the appropriate econometric methodology for measuring taxpayer responses to fiscal instruments. A first but necessary step is to understand how taxpayers map these instruments into perceived relative prices. This step includes, but is not limited to, understanding which changes are ignored as not salient, possibly because rules of thumb conserve cognitive resources and focus only on changes above a certain level of materiality. The burgeoning literature, both theoretical and empirical, on salience and taxation has not, though, yet been placed in an adequate dynamic context; after all, a series of small tax changes, each ignored, can add up to a major displacement from an optimal choice. Doing so is an important agenda item for future research.

10.2.2 Taxpayers as Voters

Adult consumers are also potential voters, and as such must decide which candidates' tax (and other) positions to favor, including how complex they should be. In their role as voters they are confronted by the difficulty of figuring out what the consequences of alternative tax policies are, both for themselves and for aggregate economic outcomes.

Some context is appropriate. Political science research is fairly persuasive that voters know very little about the details of government generally. Delli Carpini and Keeter (1996), in a comprehensive survey of the political knowledge of voters covering several decades and hundreds of surveys, show that majorities of voters are ignorant of many key aspects of the US political system, such as who has the power to declare war, the respective functions of the three branches of government, and who controls monetary policy. The comprehensive survey done in 2003 by National Public Radio, the Kaiser Foundation, and the

Kennedy School of Government confirms that this statement is certainly true for taxation.

In contrast, the policy implications of this lack of political knowledge are highly controversial among political scientists. For example, Lupia (2001) argues that political knowledge, as commonly measured by scales that count the number of correct responses to a small number of questions about public affairs, represent neither necessary nor sufficient conditions for voter competence in making choices, where a choice is defined to be competent if it is the same choice that would be made given the most accurate information about its consequences. There is little systematic evidence that voters are misled to support policies that are almost certainly not in their interest. However, Slemrod (2006) argues that this is the case with respect to Americans' support for a flat income tax: because many (mistakenly) believe the current US income tax system is regressive, they view, and support, the move to a flat tax as a move toward a more progressive distribution of the tax burden.

Why some taxes levied in some jurisdictions become complex, while others do not, has not been widely studied, hampered by the absence of reliable, comparable measures of complexity across countries. Slemrod (2005) uses the variation in US state income tax systems, and their differential change over time, to examine what engenders tax complexity, measured simply by the number of lines in the income tax forms and the number of pages in the instruction booklets, and discovers some intriguing patterns. The analysis shows that in 2000, states with more professional legislatures, as measured by the salaries paid, tended to have more complex tax systems, as did states with a less active voting population. The former relationship suggests that complexity is one of the things that professional legislatures *do*, although it may also be that states whose voters want more activist policy want professional legislatures and choose more complex tax systems. The latter relationship suggests that a more politically involved citizenry acts as a deterrent to tax complexity.

Graetz and Shapiro (2005) argue that taxpayers' misperception about the level of inequality and their likelihood of being subject to the estate tax played a key role in generating political support in 2001 to legislate for the temporary 2010 estate tax moratorium. The estate tax is highly progressive, taxing wealth upon death of only the wealthiest 1 or 2 percent of the population, making it in theory an unlikely candidate for repeal. The provocative title of their book, *Death by a Thousand Cuts*, conjures up images of a world in which narrow interests take advantage of a diffuse and poorly informed majority to dismantle the progressive taxation system piece by piece.

Professional economists cannot be too smug about voter confusion, of course, because there is much we do not understand ourselves in all areas of economics, with the economics of taxation being no exception. Central questions such as the incidence of the corporate tax and deficit financing, and the long-term growth implications of alternative tax systems, are unresolved and controversial.

Politicians and bureaucrats have an incentive and often the ability to take advantage of taxpayers' behavioral quirks and cognitive limitations.[5] Long (1981) argues that the IRS exploits the unpredictability of tax liability to enhance its powers by using it as a license to decide cases in whatever way serves the government's interest at the time. She also notes that unpredictability makes the IRS's burden in proving criminal intent (rather than inadvertent errors) more difficult. McCaffery (1993-1994) and Krishna and Slemrod (2003) argue that the US income tax has many features that take advantage of taxpayers' cognitive biases to reduce the perceived tax burden, and do so by applying well-known features of what in marketing science is known as "price presentation," such as the use of discounts (as in deductions from a broad measure of income) and of small frequent disbursements (as in employer withholding).[6] The laboratory experiments of Baron and McCaffery (2003) provide some support that such a strategy can be successful, as they demonstrate that people tend to underestimate the total tax burden when it is spread among multiple taxes. The concern that some taxes, such as value-added tax or corporation income tax, are "hidden" from taxpayers is a major reason why some conservatives oppose these taxes: they feel that the hiddenness causes voters to underestimate the true cost of government. As an example, Finkelstein (2009) provides evidence that the switch from manual, per trip, remittance of traffic tolls to automatic electronic charging facilitated toll increases because the tax burden became less salient to driver/voters.

The analogy of tax design to price presentation raises the issue of what is different between the public finance setting and a market environment. Although in democracies there is some degree of political competition, it seems likely that in social choices the intermediation of the market is less relevant, whereas in many cases involving behavioral economics, markets might plausibly arbitrage away, or exploit, irrationalities. But even this is not obvious. As Mullainathan and Thaler

(2001) emphasize, many decisions, such as with regard to retirement savings, are made infrequently, and so learning by doing is not likely to be very important; less-than-rational people "survive" and influence market outcomes.

Some insights from the industrial organization literature shed light on the political economy of complexity. Garrod (2007) remarks that obfuscation is widespread in several markets, including, somewhat surprisingly, Internet retailing, and retail financial products such as index funds, money market funds, credit cards, conventional fixed-rate mortgages, life annuities, and term life insurance. Theoretical research has shown that even competitive markets might not drive out private firms' obfuscation about prices. Although Milgrom (1981) shows that if consumers have the cognitive ability to infer that they should avoid firms with hidden information, then competing firms will fully inform consumers of product information if it is feasible and costless, a more recent literature has established that obfuscation can be profitable in equilibrium with competitive constraints. For example, in the "shrouded attributes equilibrium" of Gabaix and Laibson (2006), firms can obfuscate their prices for a complementary, avoidable add-on to a good, and may optimally do so when there are a sufficient fraction of consumers that myopically do not consider the add-on. Of particular interest for the topic at hand is the result that in equilibrium the sophisticated consumers actually benefit by taking advantage of the lower price for the basic good and not purchasing the add-ons.

One take-away from this literature is that firms may benefit from complicating, or obfuscating, the available information and that this process may benefit sophisticated consumers at the expense of unsophisticated ones. By analogy, an incumbent government may also try to, and may be able to, take advantage of framing difficulties to benefit themselves by reducing the perceived burden of what it does. In the process the more sophisticated of taxpayers may actually benefit. But the people in the government are also "just" people and so may themselves be subject to framing issues. One important and understudied issue is how to model the behavior of policy makers subject to cognitive limitations: are they subject to the same kind of heuristic biases as taxpayers and voters?

11 Notches and Optimal Line Drawing

11.1 Commodity Characteristics

As any tax lawyer will say, real-world, in-the-trenches, scuffling about taxation is largely about drawing and interpreting lines that separate the cases where discretely different tax treatments apply.[1] Is a given donation a deductible charitable donation or not? Are food expenditures a deductible business expense for someone who sells their blood, or not? Is a worker an employee, for which an employer must withhold and remit income and payroll taxes, or an independent contractor, for which no withholding is required? Despite its ubiquity and policy relevance, line drawing is almost completely absent from economic analysis. Why?

Let's begin with commodity taxation. The major reason for ignoring lines is that the modern theory of optimal commodity taxation allows for a different tax on each good, which depends on the nature of utility functions and perhaps also on distributional objectives and the pattern of externality generation. But it is excessively costly to administer a separate tax on each good (or service), especially given that new goods are being created every day. Actual commodity tax systems feature a very small set of rates and each tax rate applies to a wide range of goods.[2] Whenever selective commodity taxation is called for, a non-capricious tax system must have procedures for distinguishing among goods subject to different tax rates. Real-world consumption tax systems do that by appealing to the characteristics of the commodities. For example, the retail sales taxes of US states often exempt food but not restaurant meals, requiring the tax law to draw a line between the two categories. This is done by appealing to a set of characteristics of a restaurant meal, and the line can be fine when, for example, grocery stores sell pre-prepared meals that may or may not be eaten on the premises, or they set up in-store salad bars.

The prominent role of characteristics in actual tax systems is due to several factors. First, the alternative that the standard theory implies— relying on estimates of the matrix of compensated elasticities—is infeasible. These elasticities are notoriously difficult to estimate precisely, and they would certainly not be intuitive to either policy makers or consumers in the way that characteristics-based rules are. Second, a shared characteristic plausibly signals something about the relative substitutability of the goods, and so may serve as a more readily measurable indicator of the ideal, but not observable, distinguishing factor. Third, as noted above, modern economies produce a vast amount of different goods, and the set of available goods is constantly evolving. If tax laws were specified literally in terms of goods and their associated elasticities, then, whenever a new good is introduced in the market, there would be no natural way to assign it to a tax category and the law would have to be re-specified to explicitly deal with the new good. In contrast, a characteristics-based rule for assigning tax rates to goods naturally handles the creation of new goods by limiting the tax policy choice to which characteristics-based category the new good falls in.[3]

Some recent work (Kleven and Slemrod 2011) addresses this set of issues by re-formulating optimal commodity tax theory in the language of characteristics so that it matches up more easily with real tax systems. To do so, they make use of Lancaster's (1966, 1975) idea that it is the characteristics of goods, not the goods themselves, which are the direct objects of utility, and there exists a mapping of each good into characteristics space; we have touched on this idea in chapter 3. They formalize the relationship between characteristics, substitutability, and optimal tax rates, which allows one to explore the notion that shared characteristics can be used to gauge substitutability and hence optimal tax-rate differentials. As expected, the closer two goods are in characteristics space, the smaller is the optimal tax-rate differential.

With this reformulation, one can naturally address another important aspect of reality that has been heretofore ignored by the literature on optimal taxation, tax-driven product innovation, the creation of new products that requires no technical innovation, but which represent a re-packaging of characteristics so as to reduce tax liability. Barzel's (1976) lightbulbs, discussed in chapter 3, are an example. This will occur whenever a tax system includes procedures for assigning goods to tax categories based on observable characteristics—line drawing.

Note that lines create "notches" in choice sets, also called "cliffs," where tax liability changes sharply as the characteristics of a good change trivially but cross the statutory line. Given our assumption that a continuum of tax rates is administratively infeasible, notches in characteristic space are not an idiosyncrasy, but rather an unavoidable and ubiquitous feature of tax systems. For example, car manufacturers have an incentive to redesign vehicles to just qualify for gas-saving subsidies or just avoid gas-guzzler taxes. On Wall Street or in the city of London, tax-driven product innovation is a major pre-occupation, where one objective is to design corporate finance vehicles that qualify for the interest deduction accorded to debt finance but have most or all of the characteristics of an equity security. Of less importance but of interest to punsters,[4] arrow manufacturers in the United States responded to the imposition of an excise tax on arrow shafts measuring 18 inches in length or longer by making arrows measuring 17.9 inches long. Sallee and Slemrod (2012) show that in response to the notched US Gas Guzzler Tax, car manufacturers tended to produce cars with fuel efficiency just above each notch. Our favorite examples, discussed by Harberger (1995), concern the response to high tax rates and tariffs on automobiles. In Indonesia the preferential tax treatment of motorcycles led to the creation of a new type of motorcycle with three wheels and long benches at the back seating up to eight passengers. In Chile the market responded to high taxes on cars, but not on panel trucks, by introducing a redesigned panel truck that featured glass windows instead of wood panels and upholstered seats in the back.

The Kleven and Slemrod (2011) model naturally incorporates product innovation into the optimal tax problem, as it can be shown formally how non-uniform tax systems may give rise to the creation of goods that are socially inferior in characteristics space, such as awkward car-like motorcycles, but that may be privately optimal for tax avoidance purposes. This represents a distortion in the set of available goods, which is different from the demand and supply distortions typically considered by public finance economists. Under certain assumptions regarding the technology by which new goods can be created, the notches associated with line drawing create an incentive to the production and consumption of goods that are just on the low-tax side of a line that separates two tax-rate regions. If administratively feasible, optimal lines are drawn so as to completely avoid tax-driven product innovation. In a world with just two goods and two tax rates, this implies that the line should be "close enough" to the characteristics of the low-tax good. This result harkens back to the Diamond–Mirrlees production efficiency theorem, which says that although taxes inevitably create distortions, it is generally optimal to avoid distortions in how goods are produced and instead accept distortions only to what goods are consumed.

11.2   Notches

11.2.1   Quantity Notches

Lines create notches. Perhaps the simplest type of notch is a discontinuity in tax liability as a function of the size of the base. We need look no further than the US federal income tax code for an example of a—admittedly fairly trivial—quantity notch. People with taxable incomes between $3,000 and $100,000 are permitted to calculate their tax liability via a tax table made up of brackets in increments of $50, so tax liability is discontinuous—albeit only up to a maximum of $17—for each $50 of taxable income earned.[5] Tying eligibility for tax and transfer programs to incremental changes in taxable incomes also creates notches in the income tax code. For example, the US Saver's Credit provides a 50 percent credit on deposits into retirement accounts for married filers earning less than $30,000, but only a 20 percent credit for filers earning $30,001 or more. With contributions eligible for a credit capped at $2,000, there is a notch of up to $600 at a taxable income of $30,000.[6] Similarly the phase-out region for the US child care credit features a notch equal to 1 percent of the value of the credit for each $2,000 of taxable income earned above a certain threshold. The first version of the American Recovery and Reinvestment Act 2009 contained a much larger notch at taxable incomes of $75,000 for singles and $150,000 for couples, entitling only taxpayers earning below these amounts eligibility for an $8,000 first-time-homebuyer credit, but the final version of the Act introduced a kinked (i.e., discontinuous marginal tax rates) phase-out region, eliminating the notch. The UK Working Families' Tax Credit—an income support program for low-wage families with children similar to the US EITC—features a prominent notch at 16 hours of work; a single parent working at least 16 hours per week qualifies for the credit, but fewer than 16 hours entitles the parent to no credit. The notch is large because, provided that the household's income is below a certain threshold, maximum benefits are attainable at 16 hours of work (see Blundell et al. 2000).

Prior to expansions in the 1980s and early 1990s, eligibility for Medicaid coincided with the phase-out threshold for cash payments under the Aid to Families with Dependent Children (AFDC) program. This notch—arising because even one dollar of AFDC income qualified a single-parent family to Medicaid coverage for young children before the eligibility expansions—created strong incentives for women on AFDC to remain below the threshold. Reflecting these incentives, Yelowitz (1995) found that for fully phased-in reforms, severing the link between AFDC and Medicaid eligibility reduced women's probability of AFDC participation by 1.2 percentage points, and increased the probability of labor force participation by 0.9 percentage points.

Quantity notches are not restricted to the income tax base. In many countries, properties below a certain size threshold are exempt from property tax or subject to a lower rate, but taxed properties above the threshold are typically not eligible for a deduction equal to the exempt size threshold, creating a notch. The Israeli *arnona* provides a stark example of this. In 2010 Jerusalem's Zone C properties were subject to a property tax rate of NIS 40.68 per square meter for apartments up to 120 square meters, and NIS 54.70 for those 121 square meters and above, levying a tax of NIS 1682.40 on the first square meter of space above 120.[7]

The desirability of quantity notches in an optimal income tax system depends on the flexibility of the tax instruments available. In a fully nonlinear income tax code, notches are undesirable in the standard model because Mirrlees (1971) shows that optimal marginal tax rates are always non-negative and never greater than 100 percent. Marginal tax rates above 100 percent are redundant because, provided that tax-payers can continuously adjust their taxable income, nobody will face a marginal rate above 100 percent, while the assumption that earnings are nondecreasing in income-earning ability guarantees optimal marginal tax rates are non-negative. But in a world with limited tax instrument flexibility, there is no guarantee that notches are undesirable. As Blinder and Rosen (1985) explain, a notch may be a more efficient means of targeting a favored behavior because the subsidy is large close to the notch but, unlike a linear subsidy scheme does not "waste" revenue on infra-marginal consumers away from the notch.

As discussed in chapter 6, firms below a certain size are often exempt from some taxes for administrative reasons, leading to a notch in firm size, and so few firms on the high-tax side of the cutoff. In Japan small firms receive favorable VAT treatment, while in the United States corporations averaging less than $5 million in gross receipts over the prior three years may use a cash rather than an accrual accounting method and are exempt from the corporate alternative minimum tax.

Although explicit or implicit exemption, or more generally special tax treatment, of small firms might economize on collection costs (both compliance costs borne in the first instance by taxpayers and administrative costs borne in the first instance by the tax authority), it also generally causes production inefficiency, in part, because it provides a tax-related incentive for firms to be small. The trade-off between the costs of collection and production inefficiency has not been closely addressed by the optimal tax literature. In part, this is because nearly all modern tax theory has been developed assuming that the party remitting taxes is economically irrelevant. In addition the seminal Diamond and Mirrlees (1971) theorem on aggregate production efficiency posits that production inefficiencies, including from discriminating among firms in the same sector, should not be tolerated if the government faces no constraints on its ability to levy optimal commodity taxes. But their model of optimal taxation ignores administrative costs and assumes that there are no untaxed profits, due to either constant returns to scale—in which case firm size is indeterminate—or a 100 percent profits tax.

An early paper by Heller and Shell (1974) presents a general framework for analyzing an optimal system of commodity taxes, lump-sum taxes, and firm-specific licensing fees and profits taxes when these tax instruments are costly to administer. But when firm-specific taxes are not available, exemptions from taxation must be based on observed outputs. Keen and Mintz (2004) consider an output cutoff for exempting firms from a value-added tax in the presence of administrative and compliance costs. However, firms expect to earn untaxed profits in their model, in which case the Diamond–Mirrlees theorem no longer holds, and in general, different firms should be taxed at different rates, even without administrative costs.[8]

In contrast, Dharmapala et al. (2011) develop a model in which fixed per-firm administrative costs are solely responsible for the production inefficiencies, and these costs require an expansion in the set of tax instruments. In their main model the three available policy instruments are a constant tax rate on output, a fixed per-firm fee, and an output cutoff below which firms are not taxed. While entry fees have often been viewed as a manifestation of bureaucratic inefficiency or corruption (e.g., Djankov et al. 2002), they show that when all firms in an industry are taxed, optimal policy may involve the use of the fixed fee;[9] the fee basically acts like a Pigouvian tax, internalizing the social costs of tax administration.[10] Each industry in the model is characterized by constant returns to scale technology, and there is an effectively unlimited number of ex ante identical potential producers. Firms "discover" heterogeneous productivities after entering the industry. In this setting the standard rules of optimal commodity taxation hold if there are no administrative costs, isolating the implications of introducing these costs. With administrative costs, Dharmapala et al. (2011) identify cases where it is optimal to exempt small firms from taxation. This creates production inefficiencies that are never part of an optimal tax system in the Diamond and Mirrlees framework. These inefficiencies occur because different firms in the same industry sell output at different prices, and also because some firms obtain the tax exemption by reducing their outputs to inefficiently low levels, creating the missing middle described above.

We emphasize that the central claim—that a missing middle can potentially be generated by optimal tax policies under certain circumstances—is theoretical in nature, rather than empirical (that observed missing middles correspond to existing tax thresholds). However, there is an emerging body of empirical evidence documenting cases in which the distribution of firm size has been affected by various tax and regulatory thresholds. For instance, Onji (2009) analyzes the introduction of a value-added tax (VAT) in Japan in 1989 that incorporated preferential treatment for small firms, with a cutoff for eligibility of 500 million yen in sales, and finds a clustering of firms just below this threshold following the reform. Labor market regulations also often vary by firm size. In Italy, firms with more than 15 employees face significantly more stringent employment protection regulations (and, in particular, higher firing costs). Using different empirical approaches, Garibaldi et al. (2004) and Schivardi and Torrini (2008) find significant effects of this threshold, involving slower firm growth and greater persistence close to the threshold.[11] This evidence provides support for the empirical importance for the distribution of firm size of tax and regulatory thresholds that may be optimal.

11.2.2   Time Notches

In section 3.3.4 we discussed time shifting as an example of avoidance. Abrupt changes in tax policy, often caused by the use of (usually annual) accounting periods, create notches whenever tax liability is nonlinear in taxable income, or tax policy changes are anticipated before their introduction in the new year. For example, the yearly system of accounting used in most income tax codes provides incentives for taxpayers to re-time income realization whenever reporting in one period rather than another avoids incurring taxes at a higher rate. An example of this sort of re-timing was the legislation in 1992 of a higher top marginal income tax rate from 1993, which led many Wall Street firms to accelerate bonus payments so that, in aggregate, about two-thirds were paid as end-of-year bonuses, compared to the norm of two-thirds beginning-of-year bonuses (see Parcell 1995), and Goolsbee (2000) documents a large increase in the taxable exercise of stock options in 1992. The possibility at year-end 2012 (ultimately enacted) of increased tax rates on high-income individuals and dividend receipts generated reports of special dividends and the exercise of stock options. The econometric methodologies developed to learn about behavioral responses from the response to policy notches thus can be applied to the standard identification of time-varying policies, so that the behavior in the neighborhood of the transition date does not bias the estimates of the response to persistent policy changes.

11.2.3 Border Notches

When there are differences in taxes across geographic borders, notches exist because an incremental change in the location of economic activity leads to a jump in tax liability. Consumers living close to borders purchase little on the high-tax side of the border, while corporations choose their location taking jurisdictional differences in tax rates into account. In principle, jurisdictions could remove some of these notches by setting graduated tax rates based on distance to the border. This would favor those living closest to the border, but so does a uniform rate policy in a high-tax jurisdiction because those living nearest the low-tax neighboring region face the smallest transportation costs. As one example, in the United States differences in state sales tax rates create discontinuities at state borders. Agrawal (2011) finds that in order to reduce the extent of cross-border shopping, municipalities on the low-state-tax side of a border choose local sales tax rates that eliminate more than half of the difference in state tax rates.

11.3   Surrogate Tax Bases, Notches, and Behavioral Elasticities

We might usefully denote as a *surrogate* tax base one that does not depend solely on the ultimate arguments of utility, and thus generates avoidance and accompanying excess burden. Substitution across elements of a surrogate tax base does not directly alter one's consumption basket, although, through the function linking the surrogate tax base to the consumption basket, it may alter the effective relative prices of the latter and thereby also change consumption choices. We argue that all real-world tax systems have elements of surrogate tax bases.

In the case of *presumptive* income taxes, one tax base is used to explicitly approximate another, better-if-observable, base. Rajaraman (1995) and Yitzhaki (2007) discuss the various forms presumptive taxes take. A standard type is to use relatively easily measurable inputs and other characteristics of a business to estimate its income, as in the case of the Israeli *tachshiv*.[12]

The ubiquity of surrogate tax bases with notches sheds light on the hierarchy of behavioral responses proposed by Slemrod (1990, 1992), which asserts that, of behavioral responses, timing responses are the most elastic, followed by avoidance/accounting responses, with the least responsive being real responses such as labor supply and saving. Although much evidence is broadly consistent with the hierarchy hypothesis, a satisfactory explanation has not yet been offered. But now consider that the evidence cited in favor of a high elasticity of timing response, exemplified by the striking increase in capital gains realizations in advance of known increases in the capital gains tax, is the response of a surrogate tax base (capital gains do not enter utility functions directly) around a notch, the notch in time at the end of a year. This largely reflects the response to effectively very high tax rates per day of postponement near the year-end notch, plus the fact that the timing of sales does not constrain the time pattern of consumption. Thus the reduced-form estimates of capital gains realization elasticities do not provide direct evidence about parameters relating to the intertemporal elasticity of substitution for consumption. The same is true for the high observed elasticity of response to sales tax holidays or expiring investment incentive provision, where the durability of the consumer or investment good comes into play.

A deep question is the relationship between the pattern of local bunching to fundamental parameters of interest such as the intertemporal substitutability of consumption. Perhaps the most common interpretation of this model arises from considering durability (and storability). In this interpretation consumption goods are durable and are purchased to augment the stocks of household capital. Because the marginal utility of goods purchased is lower, the higher is the carried-over stock, purchases that are closely spaced in time are relatively more substitutable. This implies that the pattern of behavior around a time notch does not directly provide evidence about intertemporal substitut-ability, but about the combination of intertemporal substitutability and the durability (or storability) of the goods in question.

For nondurable and nonstorable goods, an optimizing consumer must be indifferent between purchasing an additional good on the high- and low-tax side of the discontinuity; if there are no changes in demand shifters coinciding with the tax change, the magnitude of the difference in purchases around the notch together with the size of the tax change provides direct evidence on the curvature of consumers' utility, and so the intertemporal elasticity of substitution under stan-dard assumptions. More generally, difference-in-difference methods between goods subject to and exempt from the tax-induced price dis-continuity through time may be used to control for demand shifters. With storable goods, consumption need not occur at the same time that purchases are made, in which case the extent of bunching may be used to jointly estimate storage cost function parameters and the intertem-poral elasticity of substitution. The timing of durable goods purchases depend on both costs of storage (given the low rate of depreciation for durables) and consumers' elasticity of intertemporal substitution, each of which can be separately identified.

Because time is an integral part of the model, and time moves in only one direction, this modeling approach does not readily carry over to notches in other characteristics. There are a number of approaches to modeling environments where the characteristics of products are central. One we have already mentioned is the Gorman–Lancaster approach where characteristics generated by goods, not the goods themselves, are the direct objects of utility, and there exists a mapping of each good into characteristics space. Another approach is based on the Hotelling (1929) spatial model.[13]

Regardless of the desirability of notches as part of an optimal tax system, they can provide an excellent opportunity to identify behavioral elasticities. Compared to the recent literature using kinks to identify tax–price elasticities (e.g., see Saez 2010), notches have received relatively little attention. This is unfortunate because implicit marginal tax rates around notches are much larger than at kinks, providing stronger incentives for taxpayers to overcome frictions that can hamper the identification of elasticities using kinks. Chetty (2012) shows formally that the presence of even relatively small optimization frictions can be consistent with a wide range of intensive margin tax–price elasticities, making the discontinuities created by notches valuable opportunities for econometric identification. The urgency of this agenda is enhanced by the pervasiveness of notches, not only in quantities but in characteristics space, geographic borders, and in the time dimension.

In a recent application of this approach, Slemrod, Weber, et al. (2012) exploit a notch in both price and time for real-estate transfer taxes in Washington, DC, to estimate a medium-term lock-in effect. On January 1, 2003, the housing transfer tax rate increased from 2.2 to 3 percent, but only for houses sold for $250,000 or less, providing two sources of variation on which to base estimates of behavioral response. While they find evidence of substantial transaction price manipulation around the price notch, they find little evidence of sales being re-timed around the time notch. Using their preferred econometric specification, they estimate that a 1 percent increase in the transfer tax rate reduces the rate of sales by 0.2 percent.

Despite the strong bunching incentives created by notches, optimization frictions may still meaningfully attenuate structural elasticity estimates. Exploiting administrative data on income tax filings in Pakistan, which has a tax system featuring notches between each income tax bracket (*average* tax rates are constant within each bracket), Kleven and Waseem (2013) find that about 90 percent of wage earners and 50 to 80 percent of self-employed filers reported incomes in strictly dominated regions. They go on to show that the mass of taxpayers in the dominated region can be used to separately identify the structural and the observed elasticity attenuated by optimization frictions. Roughly speaking, their technique for estimating structural elasticities requires inflating the observed elasticity inferred from a notch by the share of people in the dominated region, so in the case of wage earners in Pakistan the structural elasticity is about ten times larger than the observed elasticity. Despite the observed elasticities being attenuated by optimization frictions, Kleven and Waseem (2013) estimate small structural elasticities; the unusually large marginal tax rates at a notch induce pronounced bunching behavior even with small structural elasticities for taxpayers not subject to prohibitively large optimization frictions.

Part IV   Future Directions and Closing Thoughts

12 Future Directions

12.1 The Role of Information Technology

We have stressed throughout this book that taxation is at its core a problem of information: who has it, the cost of government obtaining more of it, and what restrictions are placed on its use. From that perspective, the ongoing revolution in information technology would be expected to have profound implications for tax systems. And so it does. For tax authorities, computerization facilitates the collection, tracking, and analysis of data to operate existing tax systems. Technology also makes it easier to base tax liability on a wider range of information than otherwise. One of the most famous examples are the Finnish and Danish income-related speeding fines; in 2002 in Finland, a multimillionaire Finn was assessed a speeding fine of $200,000 for driving 50 mph in a 25-mph-limit zone.[1] It has been said that personalized consumption taxes could be implemented by the issuance of smart cards that would have to be provided by consumers when they make purchases. Swiping the card would "tell" the cash register what tax rate should be collected on top of the before-tax price. One would expect that providing the card affords the holder a discount from the standard high rate, and thus an incentive for the card to be used. Of course, as mentioned earlier, such a scheme would run into the classic problem with administering legal drinking ages—the purchaser need not be the consumer; we do not yet have in hand the technology to levy the tax when a good is literally consumed. However, some transactions such as medical services are not easily arbitraged by free-market forces, and seem well suited to personalized taxation using smart cards.[2] Technology already enables the collection of highway and urban road use tolls in London, Singapore, and elsewhere. In Israel, the fast lane on the

[margin note: Digital economy characteristic of the info]

highway between Tel Aviv and Jerusalem features a congestion-related variable fee that is electronically collected and depends in real time on the hour of travel and traffic in the fast lane and other lanes.

Basing tax liability on a tag that is correlated with underlying ability can reduce the reliance on distorting progressive taxes. This notion has been parodied by Mankiw and Weinzierl (2010), who deride the tagging idea by focusing on a tax based on height. Height is positively correlated with income-earning ability. Perhaps even easier to parody, but arguably closer to implementation than a tax collected at the point of goods consumption, is the suggestion by Logue and Slemrod (2008) that tax liability might be related negatively to aspects of a person's genome that probabilistically indicate susceptibility to income-inhibiting afflictions and positively to the presence of a genius gene, should that ever be discovered; we discuss this idea below.

Technology is not a one-way street—it can also facilitate evasion. For obvious reasons, we are not as familiar with technological advances in tax evasion. The relevant role of technology is well illustrated by the case of automated sales suppression devices known as "zappers," which have greatly facilitated a very simple (consumption and income) tax fraud—skimming cash sales at electronic cash registers—by excluding random transactions from the apparent electronic record. As Ainsworth (2008) relates, until recently the largest tax fraud case in Connecticut, also the "largest computer-driven tax-evasion case in the nation," was a zapper case—a dairy skimmed $17 million in receipts and stashed the cash in the Caribbean island of St. Martin. Ainsworth (2008) proposes that in response the tax authority certify tax software. A German working group has developed a proposal to use encryption and smart card access to data preserved in cash registers: upon audit the tax authority can access the records of the cash register with a key to read the data and determine if there has been tampering.[3]

12.1.1 Sales Taxes

The technology-driven rise of mail-order and especially online sales is making it increasingly important for states to collect taxes on products purchased out of state. Consumers purchasing goods tax-free in another jurisdiction for use in their home state are required by state law to remit sales taxes, but in practice, the evasion rate for these so-called use taxes is close to 100 percent. Electronically delivered products, such as movies and music, pose particular problems because even the legal tax obligation is often unclear. For example, if a movie is rented online and viewed off a remote server in a tax-exempt location, is the viewer liable for taxes in their home state, as they would be if they had rented the same movie from a bricks-and-mortar store located in-state? Techno-logical innovation expanding the scope of products represents another challenge for tax authorities. Many new digital products were never foreseen by legislators, receiving tax-exempt status by default and in turn contributing to the rising share of untaxed transactions (McLure 2002).

Having a physical presence in destination states, as many large retailers with online presence do, requires retailers to act as tax-remit-ting agents for their online business to those destinations, dramatically boosting compliance rates for state sales taxes. But with sales tax laws differing both across and within states, some argue that the compliance burden imposed on cross-border retailers can be substantial. Not only do states, counties, and towns typically set different rates of sales tax, jurisdictions frequently differ in their definitions of taxable products, necessitating firms with cross-state operations to manage vast amounts of state and product specific information. Remittance requirements such as filing and tax due dates are also not harmonized, adding to firms' compliance burden. This complexity has led the US Supreme Court to rule that only firms with a physical in-state presence can be legally required to remit retail sales taxes. In response, many states have participated in the Streamlined Sales Tax Initiative, a project aiming to simplify and harmonize tax rules and also modernize the collection of sales taxes with the help of new collection technology, with the ultimate goal of the project being to prompt Congressional legisla-tion permitting states to require out-of-state vendors to remit retail sales taxes (Fox et al. 2008).

To be sure, the added complexity coming from increased cross-border operations and multiproduct retailing has been to some extent mitigated by technological advancement aiding compliance, such as barcode scanners, allowing a rich set of product, tax, and sales data to be managed by firms' business information systems. To the extent that firms' information systems track much tax-relevant information for their own purposes, the marginal cost of tax law complexity may be lower than is apparent at first blush. When state tax authorities can gain access to firms' information systems, auditing cost may also be dramatically lower; with all sales and purchase records quick to recall and electronically searchable, firms' complexity of operations is a smaller barrier behind which to hide noncompliance.

12.1.2   Genes

Basing tax liability on genetic attributes may sound like science fiction, but as Logue and Slemrod (2008) argue, the United States already has a form of genetic endowment tax encoded into law as a consequence of forbidding the use of genetic information by insurers; people with genetic attributes indicating lives free of medical issues are pooled with those susceptible to poor health, providing an implicit subsidy that could be avoided were there no prohibition on insurers using genetic information to price discriminate. Presuming that the social marginal utility of income is higher for those with poor rather than good health status, this cross-subsidization seems desirable on utilitarian grounds. However, as individuals become increasingly aware of their own genetic attributes, self-selection in private insurance markets is likely to lead to their unraveling if explicit bans on the use of genetic information by insurers are maintained.

Under these circumstances it seems plausible, if still a bit far-fetched, that governments would someday elect to base transfers on genetic information to undo perceived inequities in private health insurance markets. But health status is just one element of well-being, so as correlations between genetic attributes and income-earning propensities are identified, transfers made on utilitarian grounds could be made more efficient by the use of genetic information. As we have discussed, tax-system efficiency can be improved by basing transfers on some "tag" that is observable, immutable, and correlated with well-being; because taxpayers cannot do anything to alter their tag, there is no efficiency cost. By using tags, a given extent of redistribution can be achieved at a lower efficiency cost.

The potential consequences for tax theory are profound. Mirrlees's seminal 1971 paper setting out the optimal income tax assumes that while income is perfectly observable, neither the effort nor the innate ability producing that income is observable to the tax authority at any cost. If genetic attributes correlate closely with innate income-earning ability, the moral hazard cost is sharply reduced. The technical challenge for tax theory remains substantial, though, because ability is not one-dimensional, necessitating a mapping from the many personal attributes potentially signaled by genetic information—including, for example, complex reasoning skills, perseverance, trustworthiness, and ability to work with others—into a single, or at least simple, index.

The appeal of an endowment tax to economists—permitting a given level of redistribution to be achieved at minimal efficiency cost—has attracted criticism by some who argue that it mandates certain career choices in order to be able to afford the imposed tax liability. But income effects arise with any tax, so it is not clear why those associated with an endowment tax are any more troubling.

12.1.3 Tax Filing

Third-party information has for the most part been implemented to reduce tax evasion, but is already being used in some countries to reduce taxpayers' compliance burdens. Scandinavian countries have for more than a decade been producing pro-forma returns on behalf of taxpayers containing all sources of income known to tax authorities via third-party information reporting. All that taxpayers have to do before signing and filing their pre-populated return is to make any necessary corrections, amend the return to include sources of income not known to the tax authority, and claim any eligible deductions such as charitable contributions not already included on the form. For many taxpayers there is little information not known to the tax authority that needs to be added by the taxpayer (Bankman 2008).

In the United States, information reporting extends well beyond wage and salary and interest income to many less common income sources, including dividends, capital gains from the sale of publicly traded securities, royalty income, estate and trust income, pensions and annuities, and IRA distributions. The depth of information known to the IRS would enable the creation of pre-populated returns requiring few changes for even many high-income earners, perhaps dramatically lowering the cost of tax preparation currently left to individuals and tax professionals. In the United States, one of the biggest impediments to implementation of pro-forma returns is the timely transfer of information from reporting agents to individuals and the IRS. Currently wage and salary information must be reported to individuals by the end of January, but is not due until later to the federal government, passing first to the Social Security Administration, and only then to the IRS such that little wage and salary information is available in time for the April 15 filing deadline (Bankman 2008).

Even assuming administrative arrangements could be put in place to speed up the transmission of third-party information, some critics argue that the use of pro-forma returns would disconnect citizens from the tax system, with a resulting diminution in political engagement. Bankman (2008) casts doubt on this argument, though, noting that tax filing consists mainly of transcription and arithmetic, doing little to make taxpayers aware of their marginal incentives or of the fairness of the tax system writ large.

Ventry (2011) argues in favor of the United States moving to simplified tax filing along the lines of Scandinavian countries. His proposed "data retrieval" platform would allow taxpayers and tax preparers to view, access, and download tax information from a secure database maintained by the government. Many taxpayers would need to input little additional information. Because privacy barriers currently restrict the ability of private-sector firms to centralize so much tax-sensitive information, he argues that it falls to government to put in place these arrangements to simplify tax filing. Privately marketed tax preparation software is already moving toward replicating government-provided pre-populated returns by collating taxpayers' electronically available pay statements, bank account records, credit card receipts, and so on.

12.2   Privacy

Concerns that the collection of taxes may require an unwarranted invasion of privacy have a long history. Such concerns figured prominently in the objections to the first modern income tax that was introduced in Great Britain in 1799. They underlie the British system under which taxpayers provide tax-relevant information to the government, which in turn provides withholding employers a code that summarizes the extent of deductions but not the specific personal circumstances that determine the extent of deductions. Just as in the case of Facebook, the increased availability of personal information—in this case taxpayer-provided and third-party-provided information—raises sensitive questions about privacy. Citizens may want the tax authority to efficiently process information so as to keep down its operating costs, but many citizens are also wary of the government knowing too much about them—Big Brother syndrome, if you like. Americans seem to be particularly sensitive to these issues, with strict US laws prohibiting sharing of IRS information even with other government agencies and, until very recently, very limited release of even scrubbed data for research purposes. In other countries people are apparently less concerned. In Norway and Sweden (and Japan until 2004), taxable income, tax liability, and taxable wealth are public information available to anyone (now somewhat limited in Norway) on the Internet. In Denmark and Sweden, researchers have access to data from administrative records that include, but are not limited to, tax information on all—not just a sample—of residents.[4] In 2008 the Italian tax authority briefly published information from the universe of 2005 income tax returns, presumably believing disclosure would help citizens identify or shame tax evaders into compliance.

To be sure, digital storage of a vast amount of personal information contained on tax forms has substantially raised the risks of data leaks and privacy breaches. Electronic filing is now widespread, both directly by individuals and via professional preparers, raising opportunities for hackers to access data with a few (illegal) keystrokes. The now widespread information-reporting function taken on mostly by firms adds another opening for data privacy breaches. Even the IRS has had to deal with the loss of computers and storage devices.[5]

As discussed by Schwartz (2008) and Lenter et al. (2003), a presumption in favor of privacy of tax information has not always existed in the United States. President Benjamin Harrison was a strong advocate in favor of disclosure, believing that publicity reduced opportunities for evasion. For a brief period in the 1920s, income tax return information was released publicly. The US Secretary of the Treasury who advocated the repeal of income tax disclosure, Andrew Mellon, articulated an opposing view to Congress in 1925, arguing that the likelihood of honest disclosure to government by taxpayers is *increased* by the promise of confidentiality. Whether or not the disclosure of tax data to government is akin to his interpretation of attorney–client confidentiality is debatable. Corporations may be unwilling to reveal accounting information to competition, but public disclosure requirements for many corporations are mandated by the Securities and Exchange Commission, quite apart from tax considerations.

Regardless of the desirability of publicity—either deliberate or as a result of data leaks—the uniqueness of the information appearing on tax forms is declining as a result of technological progress elsewhere. Property tax information once available only via costly search through paper records is now often available on the Internet, credit-scoring agencies provide numerical summaries of people's creditworthiness, while Internet searches can reveal troves of personal information.

12.3 The Role of Multiple Jurisdictions

For the most part in this book we have addressed tax systems within a single-jurisdiction framework, but along with information technology innovation, globalization is likely to have the biggest impact on tax systems of the future. Recognizing the reality of multiple, sometimes overlapping, jurisdictions raises many fascinating and important issues. Some are now fairly well understood, for example that with multiple jurisdictions cross-border revenue spillovers—vertical, horizontal, and diagonal—and the competition for revenues can lead to suboptimal policies.[6] But there are also tax-system aspects of multiple jurisdictions that are only beginning to be addressed.

One such aspect is that, for some cross-border spillovers, such as cross-border shopping in the presence of differential consumption taxes, the border is a tax notch—the same transaction done one foot apart on one side of the border or another has discretely different tax implications. Thus we would expect bunching of sales, and retail firms, near the borders, and the local response of purchases to sales tax rates may not tell us much about the response of consumption to its price.

Our earlier assertion that the details of tax remittance matter is perhaps obvious in a multi-jurisdiction context when, even if the remitter is indifferent about which Treasury collects the money, the government as an agent of its residents certainly is not. To which government a tax is remitted is no longer a matter of indifference.

Standard models of tax competition that focus on tax-rate setting have been expanded to allow each country two tax instruments—the tax rate and the extent of enforcement. The notion that tax enforcement policy is a separate instrument of tax policy that can play a role in tax competition has been recognized in the work of Cremer and Gahvari (2000). An important insight is that each country has an incentive to enforce its tax base suboptimally, because the resulting reduction in the effective tax rate causes more of the mobile tax base to locate within its borders. Peralta et al. (2006) analyze a two-stage game between asymmetric countries that compete for the profits of a single multinational firm by means of the corporation tax rate and a tax enforcement variable. In their analysis tax enforcement is used as a strategic instrument to influence the rival country's subsequent choice of tax rate.

Two distinct but related aspects of behavior matter—the location of real activity and the location of taxable income. The marginal effective tax rate on new investment depends on the statutory tax rate but also on such tax code parameters as the rate of tax depreciation and investment tax credit, if any. But it is mostly the statutory tax rate that affects the incentives to shift income across countries. Income shifting across

ELJ - Attorney General

Spani. Acquire Jr. sobs. - want-99 goodwill Against Spanish mica

Treasury release of W.P. on state Aid   8/23

Anti-Tax Avoidance

26B - bright.limitat vs. PPT   anti-open
   └ bus. like

Countries want AS much flexibility -

   if view adversarial - bus. vs no. Authats

loose void overstrict -   Alternative

   - basic subopthi - can't avoid overstricty =

   WN Murphy - probabi : downside

not de-smith Aggression - pay more to reduce risk.   - Manage around risk

   - risk appetite -   vi retail banks, not risk-Awk

Transition - reduce arena the magnitude of unactivity.

Peter VanDyk   8/25

> subjectivity
> incidence
> untaxed sectors - huge sector

subjects:
= law untaxable -> rational it it is unattractive.

Tirade - Thresholds   > 50?
principle purpose test - debatable -
P.E. main issue
                          "PE" vs. mtg PE"

                                      tax co - Amalgamating

duty Westminster. tax - cost

Purpose of treaties.. somehow arbitrary - are unattractive
- globalization is still imp'tant"
                        - substantive - abstr.

new;
relatorly

borders can be analyzed in a framework like the one we developed in chapter 3.

One specific aspect of cross-border income shifting is the endogenous formulation of country policies that facilitate this, known as tax havens.[7] A tax haven is a jurisdiction that imposes no or only nominal taxes and offers itself as a place to be used by nonresidents to escape tax in their country of residence. A tax haven can offer this service because its laws and/or administrative practices prevent the effective exchange of information on taxpayers benefiting from the low-tax jurisdiction. An OECD (1998) report concluded that "governments cannot stand back while their tax bases are eroded through the actions of countries which offer taxpayers ways to exploit tax havens [and preferential regimes] to reduce the tax that would otherwise be payable to them," (p. 37) and offered a long list of recommendations concerning domestic legislation, tax treaties, and international cooperation. In 2000, the OECD followed up by publishing the names of 35 countries called "non-cooperating tax havens," which were given one year to enact fundamental reform of their tax systems and broaden the exchange of information with tax authorities or face economic sanctions. By 2005, almost all of the blacklisted tax havens had signed the OECD's Memorandum of Understanding agreeing to transparency and exchange of information.

Notably, the 35 designated tax havens are invariably small. Their average population is 284,000, and is 116,000 if one excludes the only two designated countries (Liberia and Panama) whose population exceeds one million. Although the 35 tax havens represent over 15 percent of the world's countries, their total population comprises just 0.150 percent of the world's population (0.058 percent excluding Liberia and Panama). Of the 35 designated tax havens, 27 are island nations.

Our discussion so far has focused on one aspect of tax-haven operations, that opacity of the exchange of information, or secrecy, facilitates primarily individual tax evasion. Many tax havens also facilitate multinational corporations' (legal) use of financial transactions and accounting maneuvering that move taxable income out of high-tax jurisdictions and into low-tax jurisdictions.[8] An example is the use of so-called hybrid holding companies in low-tax countries that generate interest deductions by making loans to related subsidiaries in high-tax countries. These transactions do not usually involve secrecy per se, although often the income shifting is shrouded by a maze of complicated business relationships and financial flows. The behavior is generally not evasion, but rather legally taking advantage of tax rates that are not harmonized across countries with behavior that was not anticipated by any country.

In sharp contrast to the long-standing concern among policy makers about the deleterious effects of secrecy havens, some recent normative analysis has focused on a potentially beneficial role for income-shifting tax havens. The starting point is the well-known result that under certain conditions a small, open economy should levy no distorting tax on mobile factors such as capital.[9] Countries do, however, levy distorting taxes on mobile capital, and much of the recent theoretical literature conceives of tax havens as a device to save these countries from themselves, by providing them with a way to move toward the nondistorting tax regime they should, but for some reason cannot, explicitly enact. For example, in Hong and Smart (2010), citizens of high-tax countries can benefit from haven-related tax planning because it allows them to tax domestic entrepreneurs (in a lump-sum way) without driving away mobile multinational capital. The presence of the haven reduces the (distorting) effective marginal tax rate of the multinationals, but not the domestic firms, for any given statutory tax rate.

The idea that countries should welcome tax havens as a way to overcome their inability to explicitly differentiate the effective tax rate on mobile and immobile capital must be reconciled with the fact that governments of non-haven countries often expend considerable resources to limit the effect of haven transactions on their own tax revenue. This behavior suggests that these countries do not view havens as a way to overcome exogenous, perhaps politically motivated, constraints on their tax policy.

Slemrod and Wilson (2009) develop a model of tax competition in the presence of "parasitic" tax havens that explains and justifies existing initiatives to limit income-shifting haven activities. In the model tax havens lead to a wasteful expenditure of resources, both by firms in their participation in havens and by governments in their attempts to enforce their tax codes. In addition tax havens worsen tax competition problems by causing countries to reduce their tax rates further below levels that are efficient from the viewpoint of all countries combined. Either full or partial elimination of havens is found to be welfare improving. Indeed, initiatives to eliminate some, but not all, havens can be designed to raise welfare both in the non-haven countries and in the remaining havens.

Slemrod and Wilson (2009) model the decision to become a haven and, in so doing, demonstrate that small countries have a greater incentive to become havens. The model treats tax havens as juridical entrepreneurs that sell protection from national taxation, an example of what Palan (2002) calls the "commercialization of state sovereignty." Slemrod (2008b) pursues the idea of commercialization of state sovereignty and examines becoming a tax haven, facilitating money laundering, and issuing "pandering" postage stamps—stamps issued by countries solely for nondomestic philatelists, answering the question of why Elvis is on Burkina Faso postage stamps. The analysis shows that such commercialization is more likely in countries where it is more difficult to raise revenue in alternative ways, and provides less support for the role of costs of commercialization related to integrity and, for less benign activities, sanctions. The examined examples of commercialization that are more likely to directly raise revenue (stamp pandering and tax havens) are more attractive to poorer countries, and stamp pandering is more attractive to more agricultural countries at a given level of per capita income. It seems that when revenue is difficult to raise in other ways, revenue-raising commercialization of state sovereignty becomes especially attractive. Plausible indicators of the potential effect of sanctions, such as the extent of tourism and trade, do not explain the likelihood of facilitating money laundering or being a tax haven. Only for stamp pandering does foreign aid associate positively, which is consistent with the idea that, for the other two activities, the threat of losing it offsets the otherwise positive effect due to its association with need. Being a tax haven or a stamp panderer is more attractive to small countries, a finding that is consistent with the Slemrod and Wilson (2009) assumption that the cost, but not the benefits, of being a tax haven is unrelated to size.

Recent multinational incentives to restrain tax competition have shifted the focus from tax rates to information exchange agreements, which contribute to the enforcement of residence-based tax systems. Keen and Ligthart (2006) discuss the incentive compatibility of such arrangements.

Finally, consider in a multinational context the extent to which tax liability is statute-limited, or subject to negotiation. One hears that in some countries the tax liability of large multinational companies is not as much a matter of applying the known tax rules to the facts at hand as it is a matter of negotiation with the government, where the terms of the negotiation are not only tax liability but other aspects of the private–public relationship, such as the provision of roads near company facilities. This could possibly explain an apparent anomaly. For many years Japan had a significantly higher statutory corporate tax rate than the United States but, despite that, net income shifting flows apparently were toward, not away, from Japan. This apparently profit-reducing behavior could be explained if tax bills were negotiated in Japan but not the United States, because taxes remitted to Japan implicitly purchased something, whereas taxes remitted to the United States did not.

12.4   The Empirics of Tax Systems

One focus of this book—multiple tax policy instruments—has obvious implications for the scope of empirical tax-systems analysis. We are interested not only in the behavioral response to, say, the top marginal personal tax rate but also the response to the setting of other instruments that relate to the broadness of the base and also the enforcement of the base. In principle, this is not a problem. The economics profession has decades of experience estimating demand systems where there are multiple goods and multiple (tax-inclusive) prices. In practice, there are problems. Some are shared by the econometrics of estimating the effect of tax rates, such as the possible endogeneity of tax instruments; just as tax cuts may follow an economic downturn, so might a relaxation of enforcement.

Some special problems arise when we look beyond tax rates to other instruments. Some non-rate tax policy instruments are not easily quantified, at least on a continuous basis; for example, there is either an information-reporting requirement on dividends, or there isn't. Note, though, that tax rates are often not as well measured as one might imagine; think of coming up with one statutory corporate tax rate in a country where there is a graduated rate schedule, regional variation, and sub-federal rates. Furthermore, what matters for behavior is the *perceived* vector of tax instruments, and there is accumulating evidence that these perceptions are often far from their objective values, whether it be the statutory marginal tax rate or the probability that an act of evasion will be detected.

Regarding the other focus of this book—multiple margins of behavioral response—exactly how to proceed empirically in terms of priorities remains controversial. On the one hand, a message of the literature on the elasticity of taxable income—or, more generally, the tax base elasticity—is that this elasticity that captures all responses is the sufficient statistic for marginal excess burden, and no further inquiry into the anatomy of behavioral response can provide insight. Although the logic of the sufficiency argument is powerful, its limitations are now well understood, and discussed in chapter 5. If we allow the relevance of the anatomy of behavioral responses, we are left seeking a matrix of (compensated) multiple responses to multiple instruments, where the cross-effects are critical and the effective relative prices may depend on the relevant avoidance and evasion enforcement technology. Interactions among instruments are important, in order to point to global optima. Pursuing this goal requires data on the multiple tax policy instruments, and until recently this has been scarce. Dušek's (2006) analysis of the effect of withholding on income and other tax revenues suggests using US state data over time as a means of identification, and that is certainly a promising direction to pursue, as it offers the setting of more homogeneous jurisdictions than countries as well as the opportunity for a long time series. Another promising example is the work of Kopczuk and Pop-Eleches (2007), who utilize state time-series variation in electronic filing and show it had a significant effect on participation in the EITC, suggesting that this effect is due to the impact that electronic filing opportunities had on the tax preparation industry. As discussed in chapter 10, Slemrod (2005) also uses the variation in US state income tax systems over time to examine what engenders tax complexity.

13 Conclusion

Tax systems, their costs, and the behavioral response to them have multiple dimensions. Until recently, standard tax analysis has narrowly focused on tax rates, excess burden, and labor supply response. A narrow focus is not in itself sufficient to generate a call for a redirection of research, because all of modern economic analysis relies on stylized models of the world we live in. In this book we argue that there are good reasons to broaden the standard perspective, at the cost of complicating the analysis.

We hope that our book has shed light on the tax phenomena that began the book. Below we repeat that list, annotated by indicating what general issue they illustrate.

• Motorcycles with three wheels and long benches at the back seating up to eight passengers and panel trucks with glass windows instead of wood panels and upholstered seats in the back are examples of tax-induced product innovation.

• Presumptive business income taxes based not on income but, for restaurants, on the seating square footage and number of tables, substitute a more easily measured surrogate tax base that is correlated with income.

• Simplified tax rules—or no tax at all—levied on businesses below a size threshold economizes on administrative costs but generates production inefficiency, which may be optimal in spite of the injunction of Diamond and Mirrlees (1971).

• That an additional dollar added to the tax authority's budget will generate $7.30 in additional tax revenue says nothing about the wisdom of increasing its budget: it compares the apples of real resources to the oranges of revenue transferred from private to public hands.

• Over 150 countries levy a value-added tax, many at rates well above 10 percent, but none levy a retail sales tax at a rate over 10 percent, testifying that the details of tax remittance matter, and matter a lot.
• With limited withholding and information reporting possible, the self-employed—especially in cash businesses—are the final frontier of tax compliance.
• US corporations found real investments in Puerto Rico in high-margin electronics, pharmaceutical, and high-fashion production attractive because income shifting to low-tax Puerto Rico is facilitated by having real operations there, lowering the true effective tax rate on real investment there.

One conclusion of this investigation is that, for the most part, standard theoretical tools of public economics can be applied insightfully, although the failure to formally integrate concerns about horizontal equity in a satisfactory way is problematic. Due to the practical importance of firms in tax collection, tax-systems theory needs to move beyond constant-returns-to-scale models of production to models where heterogeneity of size naturally arises. Because the collection of information is central to taxation, the Holy Grail would be to insightfully integrate the theory of information into the theory of taxation.

As we seek the Holy Grail, our analysis must move beyond the either-or world of the first wave of optimal tax theory, where some information is available to government perfectly and costlessly, while other information is impossible (i.e., infinitely costly) to obtain. The collection and verification of information is very costly, often at least 10 percent of revenue collected and, even with these resources devoted to collection, tax gaps are large in developed countries and even larger in developing countries. In the real world of taxation much of the action is in between two extremes: information is observable with error, to varying degrees, and its quality depends greatly on the type of administration and enforcement in place.

Policy makers are well advised to recognize the interrelationship among tax rates, bases, enforcement, and administration. There are many alternatives to raise revenue, and many types of costs, some that show up in government budgets and some that do not, and the costs of using one tax instrument often depends on the setting of others. Recognizing that tax policy is really tax-system policy can ward off substantial policy errors, such as forgoing tax rate increases because the existing (suboptimal) base is narrow, and misinterpreting large short-run responses to policy changes as indicative of long-run behavioral response.

Frank Hahn once commented that "Optimum tax formulas are either guides to action or nothing at all."[1] The stylized treatment of information in the literature to this point has afforded tremendous insight into the consequences of taxation and its proper design. We believe that an important next step in completing this task is to pursue the issues this book addresses.

Notes

Chapter 1

1. Other standard assumptions of optimal taxation analysis, such as a benevolent government and a consequentialist and welfarist orientation, have been examined extensively elsewhere, and are not the focus of this book.

2. This name is inspired by the title of Richard Musgrave's 1969 book *Fiscal Systems*, which addresses how fiscal institutions and functions change with their environment, and what similarities remain even though the setting differs.

3. The term "iconic victim," which comes from Loewenstein et al. (2006), refers to vivid examples of the negative consequences of a policy.

4. Casanegra de Jantscher (1990, p. 179).

Chapter 2

1. If the consumer's utility function is continuous, and represents a locally nonsatiated preference relation, then the expenditure function is strictly increasing in utility.

2. That is, $\exists \theta_i$ such that $R_{\theta_i} > 0$ and $\partial v(\theta, A)/\partial \theta_i < 0$.

3. This presentation follows that of Sandmo (1976).

4. This insight is not limited to the special case discussed here with no cross-price demand responses.

5. Negative-definiteness of the Slutsky substitution matrix is a sufficient condition for $S_{11}S_{22} - S_{12}S_{21} > 0$.

6. This logic is not specific to leisure, so applies to any good that cannot be taxed at an optimal rate.

7. This derivation follows that of Atkinson and Stiglitz (1980).

Chapter 3

1. In some cases the distinction is not crystal clear.

2. Note the similarity to the standard model of tax evasion of the effect of taxation on an optimal portfolio, in which a tax increase can increase the demand for the risky asset

(Domar and Musgrave 1944). One difference is that, in a portfolio model, it is arguably inappropriate to ignore the effect of the tax scheme on the variability of government revenues (see Gordon 1985; Gordon and Wilson 1989). This issue can be sidestepped in the context of a tax evasion model, because the "risks" are independent and therefore there is no social risk involved.

It is important to distinguish the effect of a change in the environment on evaded income e versus its impact on evaded tax liability, te. With respect to changes in p and π, there will be no interesting distinction. However, when t increases it is possible that e may decline at the same time te increases.

3. This is a somewhat awkward assumption because evasion is not usually observable to the tax authority.

4. In a model with formal and informal sector work, Sandmo (1981) shows that a change in the audit probability has a complex effect on the mean and variance of the taxpayer's evasion gamble, precluding any clear-cut comparative statics.

5. See Martinez-Vaquez (1996) for a nice discussion of general equilibrium modeling of tax evasion and the informal economy.

6. Erard and Ho (2003) find that noncompliance is highest for occupations that have little income subject to third-party information reporting, and where the time burden of preparing and filing is particularly high. Note that the time burden of filing may in part measure legal ambiguity in the tax code that is strategically exploited by some taxpayers.

7. *The Economist* (2012).

8. Chen and Chu (2005). Kraakman (1986) is the seminal article in the law and economics field on this set of issues.

9. See also Sheffrin (2013).

10. This argument is made by Daunton (1998).

11. These qualitative conclusions survive extending the analysis to panel data.

12. Roughly this procedure involves fitting an equation to estimate the fraction of evasion detected as a function of the auditor's seniority, the complexity of the return examined, and an auditor fixed effect for auditors examining a large enough sample of returns.

13. IRS corporate tax gap estimates are based on recommendations of proposed deficiencies of operational audits, unadjusted for variation in tax liability assessed after any appeals. Any bias due to this procedure may be partly offset by the fact that IRS auditors are not able to detect all underreporting. For a more detailed discussion, see Hanlon et al. (2007).

14. This is consistent with the finding of Hanlon et al. (2007) discussed just above.

15. Saez (2010) describes how bunching behavior at kinks can be used to estimate behavioral elasticities.

16. Kirchler (2007, p. 55) concludes from a review of the literature that most studies find a statistically significant, but weaker, relationship between attitudes and self-reported behavior, and suggests that this implies that the relationship between attitudes and actual behavior "is expected to be even weaker."

17. In other cases the taxpayer knows but it is practically impossible for the tax authority to discover. Consider the tax in the early 8th-century Abbasid caliphate collected from non-Muslims, which caused an apparently large amount of conversion—was the conversion real, or was it feigned to reduce tax burden?

18. This nomenclature is meant to parallel the definition of the excess burden of tax evasion in Yitzhaki (1987).

19. In this analysis we are ignoring the production by firms of consumption goods. It is well known that taxes that distort efficient production are, under some conditions, strictly dominated by a full set of consumption taxes. See Diamond and Mirrlees (1971).

20. We do not restrict the sign of $\partial u / \partial c_i$, but note that requiring $\partial u / \partial c_i \geq 0$, $\forall i$, is without loss of generality because each transformation function h^i can be freely defined.

21. We suppose that taxes cannot be levied on all inputs x, ruling out a lump-sum equivalent uniform tax on all inputs. Similarly we assume that at least one consumption good c_i is impossible to tax when discussing hypothetical taxes on the arguments of a taxpayer's utility function, c.

22. For non-qualified stock options in the United States, the difference between the exercise price and the issue price is taxable at ordinary income tax rates at the time of exercise, and is deductible from the employer's taxable income at the same time.

23. The IRA example makes clear that in certain cases (some of) the avoidance behavior is the result of a conscious tax policy choice, in this case with the intent of increasing saving. Another excellent example is capital gains, where taxation upon realization rather than accrual allows for deferral of tax liability, often into periods of lower taxation, and where gains are completely excused from taxation at death due to the step-up of tax basis.

24. In practice, reducing taxable income using the means described by Stiglitz (1985) may involve a combination of illegal evasion and legal avoidance. In the absence of perfect credit markets, the prohibition on the use of IRA assets as collateral for a loan is likely to be a binding constraint, personal interest expense is in general not tax deductible, and limits apply to tax-favored IRA contributions.

25. It is likely that the Tax Reform Act of 1986 mitigated the avoidance tax gap by reducing the dispersion of marginal tax rates and tightening up the rules about tax arbitrage behavior.

26. Because location of income is not clearly defined, this example is actually one where the legality of a given amount of income shifting is problematic.

27. Recall that in this section we use the term "shelter" to cover both avoidance and evasion, where both have costs that may include expected penalties.

28. When κ_1 is negative, the cost of avoidance is decreasing in labor income, but as long as there are decreasing returns in the avoidance-facilitation role of true income, then $\kappa_{11} \geq 0$. The results that follow do not depend on the sign of κ_1.

Chapter 4

1. Much of tax administration could in principle be privatized. Indeed, privatization of tax collection, often called "tax farming," has a long history dating back at least to

Mesopotamia under Hammurabi. In the Middle Ages tax farming also served as a form of borrowing by the monarch and reducing revenue uncertainty, as the tax farmer would provide an up-front payment. One suspects that the equity of tax collections suffered under tax farming. To the extent that professional tax preparers and proprietary software perform tax administration functions that would otherwise be undertaken in-house by the tax authority, all modern tax systems embody some degree of privatization.

2. We discuss these issues in chapters 7 and 10.

3. A good description of the properties of administrative cost can be found in Shoup et al. (1937, pp. 337–51).

Chapter 5

1. Although our discussion here refers to the taxable income base, the argument for considering all behavioral responses applies to any tax base.

2. Studying a linear tax rate is not restrictive because one can always linearize a taxpayer's budget constraint in the neighborhood of the optimum.

3. We assume that taxpayers' evasion gamble is the only source of income risk.

4. We include $D'(e)$ in B_t because administrative costs change as a consequence of taxpayer behavioral response.

5. Note that no assumption has been made about fines or administrative costs being proportional to the marginal tax rate, so revenue from fines and administration cost is not weighted by the marginal tax rate, t.

Chapter 6

1. Tax systems often contain an indirect incentive for accurate and well-documented withholding. For example, to be sure of being able to deduct wage payments from taxable profits, businesses need to have their payment records in order, or else the deduction may be at risk of challenge.

2. Hall and Rabushka (2007).

3. Notwithstanding all the deficiencies of the communist economic system, in a way it featured the ultimate withholding system: everyone worked for the government and was paid net of tax. Ickes and Slemrod (1992) suggest that the invisibility of the actual tax burden under communism may help to explain the resistance to more transparent tax systems in post-communist countries.

4. We refer to data that precedes the enlargement of the OECD in 2010 to include Chile, Estonia, Israel, and Slovenia.

5. Exact cumulative withholding ensures that at year-end taxpayers have no outstanding over- or underpayment of taxes and transfers. Under Britain's Pay As You Earn system, changes in tax-relevant information are passed from taxpayers to the government to firms, who adjust their employees' withholding accordingly.

6. Combined local and state sales tax rates are above 10 percent in some US states, but the average combined state and local tax rate is below 10 percent in all US states (see Tax Foundation, 2012).

7. See Christensen et al. (2001) and Shaw et al. (2010).

8. For an excellent review of the sorts of special tax regimes that countries apply to small businesses, see International Tax Dialogue (2007).

9. The report is International Tax Dialogue (2007). In contrast, most manufacturing employment in developing countries is in small firms (with less than 10 employees); for example, see Tybout (2000). Gauthier and Gersovitz (1997) document the concentration of tax payments for Cameroon.

10. Although the valuation process that occurs because of the probate process does facilitate estate or inheritance taxation, leading former Prime Minister of the United Kingdom David Lloyd George to say "Death is the most convenient time to tax rich people" (Riddell, p. 23).

11. Cash use in the United States is concentrated in the retail sector; see Humphrey (2004).

12. Recall our discussion in section 3.2.1 of Greek banks using a formula to estimate true business income from often understated reported taxable income.

13. Note that the optimal allocation of tax authority resources between enforcement and information provision can, in principle, be determined by the "equalize-the-MECF" rule derived and explained in chapter 7, although this framework is not able to handle the horizontal equity consequences of these policies.

14. The audit rates for very low, or zero, AGIs are slightly higher than those for individuals with higher income, probably reflecting attention paid to returns with reported business losses.

15. As discussed earlier, others interpret this as evidence that deterrence is not an important factor in explaining tax compliance.

16. See also Alt (1983), who discusses how administrative and compliance cost considerations influence the evolution of tax structures.

Chapter 8

1. Consumers have Cobb–Douglas preferences of the form

$$u(c) = exp\left(\int_0^1 \alpha_i \log(c_i) di\right)$$

with

$$\int_0^1 \alpha_i di = 1,$$

so levying a tax at rate t on the set of goods $i \in [0, I]$, with expenditure shares summing to b, yields revenue equal to

$$bA\left(\frac{t}{1+t}\right).$$

To see this, first note that consumer demand for each of the taxed goods is

$$c_i = \frac{\alpha_i A}{q_i(1+t)}.$$

Revenue raised on each of these taxed goods is tq_ic_i, so total revenue raised is

$$R = A\left(\frac{t}{1+t}\right)\int_0^t \alpha_i di = bA\left(\frac{t}{1+t}\right).$$

2. As Louis Kaplow has suggested to us, in some situations both approaches may apply. For example, consider the case where a taxpayer purchases some goods from tax-compliant stores and others from noncompliant cash-only stores. Then, if the two types of stores carry different products on average, successfully taxing more stores both broadens the taxpayer base and the commodity base.

3. Note that in this model taxing labor is equivalent to a perfectly enforced equiproportionate tax on the other two commodities.

4. Cremer and Gahvari (1994) reach similar conclusions in a model with two types of taxpayers and an endogenous labor supply.

5. Louis Kaplow has pointed out to us that the time inconsistency of this model is not unique, and that the law-enforcement strategies of this type of model seldom are.

6. See also Border and Sobel (1987) and Mookherjee and Png (1989).

7. This result relies on the assumption that taxpayers' avoidance behavior does not reveal information about skills.

8. See Sandmo (1993) for a model where people differ not in avoidance behavior but in their taste for work.

Chapter 9

1. However, see Deaton (1987), who stresses that a global-optimum tax exercise may require knowledge of elasticities at tax rates and therefore prices far from historical observations, requiring strong assumptions about the functional form of demand functions, assumptions that may themselves determine optimal tax rules.

2. See also Kaplow (1990), which we discuss in section 8.1.2, for an analysis of this set of issues in a slightly different analytical framework.

3. This approximation breaks down for larger values of t. Taking a second-order Taylor series approximation to $(1-t)^b$ and $(1+t)^{-b}$ around $t = 0$ yields an absolute difference between the two terms that depends on the tax rate according to bt^2.

Chapter 10

1. The function $D(\sigma)$ is assumed to be continuously differentiable, with $D' < 0 \le D''$.

2. Benshalom (2012) argues, along the same lines, for a tax on cash withdrawals.

3. See taxfoundation.org/article/number-words-internal-revenue-code-and-federal-tax-regulations-1955-2005.

4. The textbook equivalences may also fail because of differences in the administrative and compliance costs. See Slemrod (2008a).

5. To be sure, there are other explanations for tax complexity. Hettich and Winer (1999) argue that complex tax structures emerge as a by-product of the struggle for political

office, in the course of which political parties are forced to propose and implement policies that discriminate or distinguish as carefully as possible among heterogeneous voters. In their view, it is administrative costs that limit the desire of governments to discriminate fully among taxpayers.

6. Kim and Kachersky (2006) critically review the marketing science literature on price salience.

Chapter 11

1. See Weisbach (1999) for an insightful legal-analytical view of line drawing.

2. However, note that technological advances in electronic data management systems—which we discuss in chapter 12—may expand the administratively feasible degree of variation in tax rates across commodity types.

3. Belan et al. (2008) pursue a different strategy to the optimal aggregation of commodities when the goods must be grouped into a few tax-rate classes.

4. Arrows have notches!

5. Slemrod (1985) uses the observation that, of those who used the tax table in 1977, there was a bunching toward the top of the bracket, and he interprets this phenomenon as evidence of tax evasion.

6. Ramnath (2013) provides evidence of bunching in taxable income at notches created by the Saver's Credit.

7. One hears anecdotes about people purchasing two adjacent properties of less than 120 square meters and then breaking down the dividing walls to create one property, while failing to inform the tax authority of this activity.

8. This discussion refers to the second of two models presented by Keen and Mintz (2004). In the first model, firm sales are exogenous, so a cutoff rule does not distort output decisions. (See also Zee 2005 for an extension of this model.) Both models differ from the Dharmapala et al. (2011) analysis by treating net product prices as fixed (a small open economy), assuming an exogenous social marginal value of government revenue, and not allowing a per-firm fixed fee as a policy instrument.

9. Auriol and Warlters (2005) also argue that entry barriers may be optimal in some circumstances, but the reason is very different: the entry barriers generate rents for incumbents that the government can tax.

10. International Tax Dialogue (2007, p. 31) discusses the fixed per-firm fee, also known as a *patente* system, as an example of a presumptive tax regime. If, instead of administrative costs, firms incurred fixed compliance costs in the payment of taxes, then the fee would not be needed because these costs would already be internal to the firm.

11. In addition there is widespread support for the more general notion that the distribution of firm size is influenced by taxation and regulation in developed as well as developing countries. Pagano and Schivardi (2003) document significant differences in firm size distributions across European countries, and attribute these in part to tax and regulatory policies. Henrekson and Johansson (1999) find that Sweden has a particularly small share of medium-sized firms (with 10 to 199 employees), and explain this with reference to tax and regulatory policies favoring larger firms.

12. *Tachshiv* can be roughly translated to mean "standard assessment guide," and refers to the (officially) former Israeli presumptive income tax system for the self-employed (see Yitzhaki 2007).

13. Yet another approach, due to Dixit and Stiglitz (1977), places commodities in groups so that goods are excellent substitutes within the group but poor substitutes for the other commodities not in the group; there are intra- and intergroup elasticities of substitution. This approach has proved useful in understanding patterns of international trade; for example, see Krugman (1980).

Chapter 12

1. Arguably these are also examples of the misuse of technology in taxation. In the standard model of externalities, the optimal Pigouvian tax is the marginal social harm, which is unlikely to be related to the driver's income level.

2. These issues are discussed in Cowell (2008).

3. Working Group on Cash Registers: Interim Report, March 16, 2005 (in German). See the citation in Ainsworth (2008).

4. Note that because administrative data are available only in a few select countries, researchers are in danger of generalizing about behavioral response from data generated from a very special set of countries—there is arguably something about the willingness to distribute information that is correlated with the nature and extent of behavioral response to taxation.

5. This discussion draws on Schwartz (2008).

6. For a survey, see Wilson (1999) and Wilson and Wildasin (2004).

7. See Hines (2010) for a discussion of the nature of tax havens and the policy issues they raise.

8. In this dimension aspects of certain non-haven countries' tax systems, such as Belgium and Netherlands, facilitate tax avoidance by multinational corporations (see Drucker 2013).

9. See, for example, Gordon (1986).

Chapter 13

1. Hahn (1973, p. 106).

References

Agell, Jonas, and Mats Persson. 2000. Tax arbitrage and labor supply. *Journal of Public Economics* 78 (1–2): 3–24.

Agha, Ali, and Jonathan Haughton. 1996. Designing VAT systems: Some efficiency considerations. *Review of Economics and Statistics* 78 (2): 303–308.

Agrawal, David R. 2011. The tax gradient: Do local sales taxes reduce tax differentials at state borders? Working paper. University of Michigan.

Ainsworth, Richard T. 2008. Zappers: Technology-assisted tax fraud, SSUTA, and the encryption solutions. *Tax Lawyer* 61 (4): 1075–1110.

Akerlof, George A. 1978. The economics of "tagging" as applied to the optimal income tax, welfare programs, and manpower planning. *American Economic Review* 68 (1): 8–19.

Allingham, Michael G., and Agnar Sandmo. 1972. Income tax evasion: A theoretical analysis. *Journal of Public Economics* 1 (3–4): 323–38.

Alm, James, Betty R. Jackson, and Michael McKee. 1992. Estimating the determinants of taxpayer compliance with experimental data. *National Tax Journal* 45 (1): 107–14.

Alm, James, Betty R. Jackson, and Michael McKee. 1993. Fiscal exchange, collective decision institutions, and tax compliance. *Journal of Economic Behavior and Organization* 22 (3): 285–303.

Alm, James, and Leslie A. Whittington. 1999. For love or money? The impact of income taxes on marriage. *Economica* 66 (263): 297–316.

Alt, James. 1983. The evolution of tax structures. *Public Choice* 41 (1): 181–222.

Andreoni, James, Brian Erard, and Jonathan Feinstein. 1998. Tax compliance. *Journal of Economic Literature* 36 (2): 818–60.

Artavanis, Nikolaos, Adair Morse, and Margarita Tsoutsoura. 2012. Tax evasion across industries: Soft credit evidence from Greece. Working paper. Booth School of Business, University of Chicago.

Atkinson, Anthony B., and Joseph E. Stiglitz. 1980. *Lectures on Public Economics*. New York: McGraw-Hill.

Auerbach, Alan J. 1985. The theory of excess burden and optimal taxation. In Alan J. Auerbach and Martin Feldstein, eds., *Handbook of Public Economics*, vol. 1. Amsterdam: Elsevier, 61–127.

Auerbach, Alan J., and Kevin A. Hassett. 2002. A new measure of horizontal equity. *American Economic Review* 92 (4): 1116–25.

Auriol, Emmanuelle, and Michael Warlters. 2005. Taxation base in developing countries. *Journal of Public Economics* 89 (4): 625–46.

Auten, Gerald, and Robert Carroll. 1999. The effect of income taxes on household behavior. *Review of Economics and Statistics* 81 (4): 681–93.

Bakija, Jon, and Bradley Heim. 2011. How does charitable giving respond to incentives and income? New estimates from panel data. *National Tax Journal* 64 (2, pt. 2): 35–50.

Baldry, Jonathan C. 1979. Tax evasion and labor supply. *Economics Letters* 3 (1): 53–56.

Baldry, Jonathan C. 1987. Income tax evasion and the tax schedule: Some experimental results. *Public Finance* 42 (3): 357–83.

Ballard, Charles L., John B. Shoven, and John Whalley. 1985. General equilibrium computations of the marginal welfare costs of taxes in the United States. *American Economic Review* 75 (1): 128–38.

Bankman, Joseph. 2008. Using technology to simplify individual tax filing. *National Tax Journal* 61 (4, pt. 2): 773–89.

Baron, Jonathan, and Edward J. McCaffery. 2003. The Humpty Dumpty blues: Disaggregation bias in the evaluation of tax systems. *Organizational Behavior and Human Decision Processes* 91 (2): 230–42.

Bartelsman, Eric J., and Roel M. W. J. Beetsma. 2003. Why pay more? Corporate tax avoidance through transfer pricing in OECD countries. *Journal of Public Economics* 87 (9–10): 2225–52.

Barzel, Yoram. 1976. An alternative approach to the analysis of taxation. *Journal of Political Economy* 84 (6): 1177–97.

Becker, Gary S. 1968. Crime and punishment: An economic approach. *Journal of Political Economy* 76 (2): 169–217.

Belan, Pascal, Stéphane Gauthier, and Guy Laroque. 2008. Optimal grouping of commodities for indirect taxation. *Journal of Public Economics* 92 (7): 1738–50.

Benshalom, Ilan. 2012. Taxing cash. *Columbia Journal of Tax Law* 4 (1): 65–93.

Beron, Kurt J., Helen V. Tauchen, and Ann Dryden Witte. 1992. The effect of audits and socioeconomic variables on compliance. In Joel Slemrod, ed., *Why People Pay Taxes*. Ann Arbor: University of Michigan Press, 67–89.

Bhargava, Saurabh, and Dayanand S. Manoli. 2011. Why are benefits left on the table? Assessing the role of information, complexity, and stigma on take-up with an IRS field experiment. Working paper. University of California, Los Angeles.

Bigio, Saki, and Eduardo Zilberman. 2011. Optimal self-employment income tax enforcement. *Journal of Public Economics* 95 (9–10): 1021–35.

Bird, Richard M. 1983. Income tax reform in developing countries: The administrative dimension. *Bulletin for International Fiscal Documentation* 37: 3–14.

Bird, Richard M. 2002. Why tax corporations? *Bulletin for International Fiscal Documentation* 56 (5): 194–203.

Blinder, Alan S., and Harvey S. Rosen. 1985. Notches. *American Economic Review* 75 (4): 736–47.

Blumenthal, Marsha, Charles Christian, and Joel Slemrod. 2001. Do normative appeals affect tax compliance? Evidence from a controlled experiment in Minnesota. *National Tax Journal* 54 (1): 125–38.

Blumkin, Tomer, Bradley J. Ruffle, and Yosef Ganun. 2012. Are income and consumption taxes ever really equivalent? Evidence from a real-effort experiment with real goods. *European Economic Review* 56 (6): 1200–19.

Blundell, Richard, Alan Duncan, Julian McCrae, and Costas Meghir. 2000. The labour market impact of the working families' tax credit. *Fiscal Studies* 21 (1): 75–104.

Boadway, Robin, and Motohiro Sato. 2000. The optimality of punishing only the innocent: The case of tax evasion. *International Tax and Public Finance* 7 (6): 641–64.

Border, Kim C., and Joel Sobel. 1987. Samurai accountant: A theory of auditing and plunder. *Review of Economics and Statistics* 54 (4): 525–40.

Braithwaite, Valerie A. 2003. A new approach to tax compliance. In Valerie A. Braithwaite, ed., *Taxing Democracy: Understanding Tax Avoidance and Evasion*. Burlington, VT: Ashgate, 1–14.

Breusch, Trevor. 2005. Estimating the underground economy using MIMIC models. Econometrics working paper 0507003. EconWPA. Australian National University.

Burman, Leonard E., and William C. Randolph. 1994. Measuring permanent responses to capital-gains tax changes in panel data. *American Economic Review* 84 (4): 794–809.

Calabresi, Guido. 1970. *The Cost of Accidents: A Legal and Economic Analysis*. New Haven: Yale University Press.

Carrillo, Paul E., M. Shahe Emran, and Anita Rivadeneira. 2012. Do cheaters bunch together? Profit taxes, withholding rates and tax evasion. Working paper. George Washington University.

Casanegra de Jantscher, Milka. 1990. Administering the VAT. In Malcolm Gillis, Carl S. Shoup, and Gerardo Sicat, eds., *Value-Added Taxation in Developing Countries*. Washington, DC: World Bank, 171–79.

Cashin, David. 2012. The intertemporal substitution and income effects of a GST rate increase: Evidence from New Zealand. Working paper. University of Michigan.

Cashin, David, and Takashi Unayama. 2011. The intertemporal substitution and income effects of a VAT rate increase: Evidence from Japan. Discussion paper 11045. Research Institute of Economy, Trade and Industry, Tokyo.

Chen, Kong-Ping, and C. Y. Cyrus Chu. 2005. Internal control vs. external manipulation: A model of corporate income tax evasion. *RAND Journal of Economics* 36 (1): 151–64.

Chetty, Raj. 2009. Is the taxable income elasticity sufficient to calculate deadweight loss? The implications of evasion and avoidance. *American Economic Journal: Economic Policy* 1 (2): 31–52.

Chetty, Raj. 2012. Bounds on elasticities with optimization frictions: A synthesis of micro and macro evidence on labor supply. *Econometrica* 80 (3): 969–1018.

Chetty, Raj, Adam Looney, and Kory Kroft. 2009. Salience and taxation: Theory and evidence. *American Economic Review* 99 (4): 1145–77.

Chetty, Raj, and Emmanuel Saez. 2013. Teaching the tax code: Earnings responses to an experiment with EITC recipients. *American Economic Journal: Applied Economics* 5 (1): 1–31.

Christensen, Kevin, Robert Cline, and Tom Neubig. 2001. Total corporate taxation: "Hidden," above-the-line, non-income taxes. *National Tax Journal* 54 (3): 495–506.

Christian, Charles W. 1993/94. Voluntary compliance with the individual income tax: Results from the 1988 TCMP Study Publication 1500 (Rev. 9–94), Washington, DC: Internal Revenue Service.

Clausing, Kimberly. 2003. Tax-motivated transfer pricing and U.S. intrafirm trade prices. *Journal of Public Economics* 87 (9–10): 2207–23.

Clausing, Kimberly, Leonard Burman, and John O'Hare. 1994. Tax reform and realizations of capital gains in 1986. *National Tax Journal* 47 (1): 1–18.

Clotfelter, Charles. 1983. Tax evasion and tax rates: An analysis of individual returns. *Review of Economics and Statistics* 65 (3): 363–73.

Coase, Ronald H. 1937. The nature of the firm. *Economica* 4 (16): 386–405.

Cole, Adam J. 2009. Sales tax holidays: Timing behavior and tax incidence. Working paper. University of Michigan.

Corlett, W. J., and D. C. Hague. 1953. Complementarity and the excess burden of taxation. *Review of Economic Studies* 21 (1): 21–30.

Cowell, Frank A. 2008. Problems and promise of smart cards in taxation. *National Tax Journal* 61 (4, pt. 2): 865–82.

Cremer, Helmuth, and Firouz Gahvari. 1994. Tax evasion, concealment and the optimal linear income tax. *Scandinavian Journal of Economics* 96 (2): 219–39.

Cremer, Helmuth, and Firouz Gahvari. 2000. Tax evasion, fiscal competition and economic integration. *European Economic Review* 44 (9): 1633–57.

Crocker, Keith, and Joel Slemrod. 2005. Corporate tax evasion with agency costs. *Journal of Public Economics* 89 (9–10): 1593–1610.

Daunton, Martin. 1998. Trusting Leviathan: British fiscal administration from the Napoleonic wars to the Second World War. In Valerie Braithwaite and Margaret Levi, eds., *Trust and Governance*. New York: Russell Sage Foundation, 102–34.

de Mooij, Ruud A., and Gaëtan Nicodème. 2008. Corporate tax policy and incorporation in the EU. *International Tax and Public Finance* 15 (4): 478–98.

Deaton, Angus. 1987. Econometric issues in tax design for developing countries. In David Newbery and Nicholas Stern, eds., *The Theory of Taxation for Developing Countries*. Oxford: Oxford University Press, 92–113.

Delli Carpini, Michael X., and Scott Keeter. 1996. *What Americans Know About Politics and Why It Matters*. New Haven: Yale University Press.

Demirgüç-Kunt, Asli, and Harry Huizinga. 2001. The taxation of domestic and foreign banking. *Journal of Public Economics* 79 (3): 429–53.

Dharmapala, Dhammika, Joel Slemrod, and John D. Wilson. 2011. Tax policy and the missing middle: Optimal tax remittance with firm-level administrative costs. *Journal of Public Economics* 95 (9–10): 1036–47.

Diamond, Peter A., and James A. Mirrlees. 1971. Optimal taxation and public production I: Production efficiency. *American Economic Review* 61 (1): 8–27.

Dickert-Conlin, Stacy, and Amitabh Chandra. 1999. Taxes and the timing of births. *Journal of Political Economy* 107 (1): 161–77.

Dixit, Avinash K., and Joseph E. Stiglitz. 1977. Monopolistic competition and optimum product diversity. *American Economic Review* 67 (3): 297–308.

Djankov, Simeon, Rafael La Porta, Florencio Lopez de Silanes, and Andrei Shleifer. 2002. The regulation of entry. *Quarterly Journal of Economics* 117 (1): 1–37.

Domar, Evsey D., and Richard A. Musgrave. 1944. Proportional income taxation and risk-taking. *Quarterly Journal of Economics* 58 (3): 388–422.

Douglas, Roy. 1999. *Taxation in Britain since 1660*. Houndmills, Basingstoke, UK: Palgrave Macmillan.

Drucker, Jesse. 2013. Yahoo, Dell Swell Netherlands' $13 trillion tax haven. Bloomberg. January 23. Available at: www.bloomberg.com/news/2013-01-23/yahoo-dell-swell -netherlands-13-trillion-tax-haven.html.

Dušek, Libor. 2006. Are efficient taxes responsible for big government? Evidence from tax withholding. Working paper. CERGE-EI.

The Economist. 2012. Wake up and smell the coffee. *The Economist.* December 15.

Erard, Brian, and Chih-Chin Ho. 2003. Explaining the U.S. income tax compliance continuum. *eJournal of Tax Research* 1 (2): 93–109.

Everson, Mark. 2005. Testimony given to the President's Advisory Panel on Federal Tax Reform, March 3, Available at: govinfo.library.unt.edu/taxreformpanel/meetings/meeting-03032005.html.

Farnsworth, Albert. 1951. *Addington, Author of the Modern Income Tax*. London: Stevens and Sons.

Feige, Edgar L. 1989. Monetary methods of estimating informal activity in developing nations. In Alois Wenig and Klaus F. Zimmerman, eds., *Demographic Change and Economic Development*. Berlin: Springer Verlag, 211–32.

Feinstein, Jonathan. 1991. An econometric analysis of income tax evasion and its detection. *RAND Journal of Economics* 22 (1): 14–35.

Feld, Lars P., and Bruno S. Frey. 2002. Trust breeds trust: How taxpayers are treated. *Economics of Governance* 3 (2): 87–99.

Feldman, Naomi E., and Peter Katuščák. 2006. Should the average tax rate be marginalized? Working paper. CERGE-EI.

Feldman, Naomi E., and Joel Slemrod. 2007. Estimating tax noncompliance with evidence from unaudited tax returns. *Economic Journal* 117 (518): 327–52.

Feldman, Naomi E., and Joel Slemrod. 2009. War and taxation: When does patriotism overcome the free-rider impulse? In Isaac William Martin, Ajay K. Mehotra, and Monica

Prasad, eds., *The New Fiscal Sociology: Taxation in Comparative and Historical Perspective.* Cambridge, UK: Cambridge University Press, 138–54.

Feldstein, Martin S. 1972. Distributional equity and the optimal structure of public pricing. *American Economic Review* 62 (1): 32–36.

Feldstein, Martin S. 1976. On the theory of tax reform. *Journal of Public Economics* 6 (1–2): 77–104.

Feldstein, Martin S. 1995. The effect of marginal tax rates on taxable income: A panel study of the 1986 Tax Reform Act. *Journal of Political Economy* 103 (3): 551–72.

Feldstein, Martin S. 1999. Tax avoidance and the deadweight loss of the income tax. *Review of Economics and Statistics* 81 (4): 674–80.

Feldstein, Martin S., and Daniel Feenberg. 1996. The effect of increased tax rates on taxable income and economic efficiency: A preliminary analysis of the 1993 tax rate increases. In James Poterba, ed., *Tax Policy and the Economy*, vol. 10. Cambridge: MIT Press, 89–117.

Fellner, Gerlinde, Rupert Sausgruber, and Christian Traxler. 2013. Testing enforcement strategies in the field: Legal threat, moral appeal and social information. *Journal of the European Economic Association* 11 (3): 634–60.

Finkelstein, Amy. 2009. EZ tax: Tax salience and tax rates. *Quarterly Journal of Economics* 124 (3): 969–1010.

Fox, William F., LeAnn Luna, and Matthew N. Murray. 2008. The SSTP and technology: Implications for the future of the sales tax. *National Tax Journal* 61 (4, pt. 2): 823–41.

Frey, Bruno S. 1997. A constitution for knaves crowds out civic virtues. *Economic Journal* 107 (443): 1043–53.

Gabaix, Xavier, and David Laibson. 2006. Shrouded attributes, consumer myopia, and information suppression in competitive markets. *Quarterly Journal of Economics* 121 (2): 505–40.

Garibaldi, Pietro, Lia Pacelli, and Andrea Borgarello. 2004. Employment protection legislation and the size of firms. *Giornale degli Economisti* 63 (1): 33–68.

Garrod, Luke. 2007. Price transparency and consumer naivety in a competitive market. Working paper 07–10. Centre for Competition Policy, University of East Anglia.

Gauthier, Bernard, and Mark Gersovitz. 1997. Revenue erosion through exemption and evasion in Cameroon, 1993. *Journal of Public Economics* 64 (3): 407–24.

Gillitzer, Christian, and Peer Ebbesen Skov. 2013. A gift to the tax man: Evidence on unclaimed charitable contributions from the introduction of third-party information reporting in Denmark. Working paper. University of Michigan.

Goldin, Jacob. 2012. Optimal tax salience. Working paper. Princeton University.

Goode, Richard. 1968. The tax burden in the United States and other countries. *Annals of the American Academy of Political and Social Science* 379 (1): 83–93.

Goolsbee, Austan. 2000. What happens when you tax the rich? Evidence from executive compensation. *Journal of Political Economy* 108 (2): 352–78.

Gordon, Roger H. 1985. Taxation of corporate capital income: Tax revenues versus tax distortions. *Quarterly Journal of Economics* 100 (1): 1–27.

Gordon, Roger H. 1986. Taxation of investment and savings in a world economy. *American Economic Review* 76 (5): 1086–1102.

Gordon, Roger H., and Wei Li. 2009. Tax structures in developing countries: Many puzzles and a possible explanation. *Journal of Public Economics* 93 (7–8): 855–66.

Gordon, Roger H., and Joel Slemrod. 1988. Do we collect any revenue from taxing capital income? In Lawrence Summers, ed., *Tax Policy and the Economy*, vol. 2. Cambridge, MA: National Bureau of Economic Research, 89–130.

Gordon, Roger H., and Joel Slemrod. 2000. Are "real" responses to taxes simply income shifting between corporate and personal tax bases? In Joel Slemrod, ed., *Does Atlas Shrug? The Economic Consequences of Taxing the Rich*. New York: Russell Sage Foundation and Cambridge: Harvard University Press, 240–80.

Gordon, Roger H., and John D. Wilson. 1989. Measuring the efficiency cost of taxing risky capital income. *American Economic Review* 79 (3): 427–39.

Gorman, William M. 1980. A possible procedure for analysing quality differentiation in the egg market. *Review of Economic Studies* 47 (5): 843–56.

Gorodnichenko, Yuriy, Jorge Martinez-Vazquez, and Klara Sabirianova Peter. 2009. Myth and reality of flat tax reform: Micro estimates of tax evasion response and welfare effects in Russia. *Journal of Political Economy* 117 (3): 504–54.

Graetz, Michael J., Jennifer F. Reinganum, and Louis L. Wilde. 1986. The tax compliance game: Toward an interactive theory of tax enforcement. *Journal of Law, Economics, and Organization* 2 (1): 1–32.

Graetz, Michael J., and Ian Shapiro. 2005. *Death by a Thousand Cuts: The Fight over Taxing Inherited Wealth*. Princeton: Princeton University Press.

Gruber, Jonathan, and Emmanuel Saez. 2002. The elasticity of taxable income: Evidence and implications. *Journal of Public Economics* 84 (1): 1–32.

Grubert, Harry, and John Mutti. 1991. Taxes, tariffs and transfer pricing in multinational corporate decision making. *Review of Economics and Statistics* 73 (2): 285–93.

Grubert, Harry, and Joel Slemrod. 1998. The effect of taxes on investment and income shifting to Puerto Rico. *Review of Economics and Statistics* 80 (3): 365–73.

Hahn, Frank. 1973. On optimum taxation. *Journal of Economic Theory* 6 (1): 96–106.

Hall, Robert E., and Alvin Rabushka. 2007. *The Flat Tax*. Palo Alto, CA: Hoover Institution Press.

Hanlon, Michelle, Lillian Mills, and Joel Slemrod. 2007. An empirical examination of corporate tax noncompliance. In Alan Auerbach, James R. Hines Jr., and Joel Slemrod, eds., *Taxing Corporate Income in the 21st Century*. Cambridge, UK: Cambridge University Press, 171–210.

Hanlon, Michelle, and Joel Slemrod. 2009. What does tax aggressiveness signal? Evidence from stock price reactions to news about tax shelter involvement. *Journal of Public Economics* 93 (1–2): 126–41.

Hanousek, Jan, and Filip Palda. 2004. Quality of government services and the civic duty to pay taxes in the Czech and Slovak Republics, and other transition countries. *Kyklos* 57 (2): 237–52.

Harberger, Arnold. 1995. Tax lore for budding reformers. In Rudiger Dornbusch and Sebastian Edwards, eds., *Reform, Recovery, and Growth: Latin America and the Middle East*. Chicago: University of Chicago Press/NBER, 291–310.

Harris, David, Randall Morck, Joel Slemrod, and Bernard Yeung. 1993. Income shifting in U.S. multinational corporations. In Alberto Giovannini, R. Glenn Hubbard, and Joel Slemrod, eds., *Studies in International Taxation*. Chicago: University of Chicago Press, 277–302.

Hasegawa, Makoto, Jeffrey Hoopes, Ryo Ishida, and Joel Slemrod. 2013. The effect of public disclosure on reported taxable income: Evidence from individuals and corporations in Japan. Working paper. University of Michigan.

Heller, Walter Perrin, and Karl Shell. 1974. On optimal taxation with costly administration. *American Economic Review* 64 (2): 338–45.

Henrekson, Magnus, and Dan Johansson. 1999. Institutional effects on the evolution of the size distribution of firms. *Small Business Economics* 12 (1): 11–23.

Hettich, Walter, and Stanley L. Winer. 1999. *Democratic Choice and Taxation: A Theoretical and Empirical Analysis*. Cambridge, UK: Cambridge University Press.

Hines, James R., Jr. 1999. Lessons from behavioral responses to international taxation. *National Tax Journal* 52 (2): 305–22.

Hines, James R., Jr. 2010. Treasure islands. *Journal of Economic Perspectives* 24 (4): 103–25.

Hines, James R., Jr., and Eric M. Rice. 1994. Fiscal paradise: Foreign tax havens and American business. *Quarterly Journal of Economics* 109 (1): 149–82.

Hinrichs, Harley. 1966. *A General Theory of Tax Structure Change during Economic Development*. Cambridge: Harvard Law School.

HM Revenue and Customs. 2011. Measuring tax gaps 2011. http://www.hmrc.gov.uk/stats/measuring-tax-gaps.htm.

Hong, Qing, and Michael Smart. 2010. In praise of tax havens: International tax planning and foreign direct investment. *European Economic Review* 54 (1): 82–95.

Hotelling, Harold. 1929. Stability in competition. *Economic Journal* 39 (153): 41–57.

Humphrey, David B. 2004. Replacement of cash by cards in U.S. consumer payments. *Journal of Economics and Business* 56 (3): 211–25.

Hurst, Erik, Geng Li, and Benjamin Pugsley. Forthcoming. Are household surveys like tax forms: Evidence from income underreporting of the self-employed. *Review of Economics and Statistics*.

Ickes, Barry, and Joel Slemrod. 1992. Tax implementation issues in the transition from a planned economy. *Public Finance/Finance Publique* 47 (suppl.): 384–99.

Internal Revenue Service, US Department of the Treasury. 2012a. *Internal Revenue Manual*. Available at: www.irs.gov/irm/part20/index.html.

Internal Revenue Service, US Department of the Treasury. 2012b. *Internal Revenue Service Data Book, 2011*. Publication 55B. Washington, DC.

Internal Revenue Service, US Department of the Treasury. 2012c. *The Tax Gap*. Available at: www.irs.gov/newsroom/article/0,id=158619,00.html.

Internal Revenue Service Oversight Board, US Department of the Treasury. 2006. *2005 Taxpayer Attitude Survey*. Available at: www.treasury.gov/irsob/releases/2006/02212006 .pdf.

International Tax Dialogue, with input from the staff of the International Monetary Fund, Inter-American Development Bank, OECD, and the World Bank. 2007. Taxation of small and medium enterprises. Background paper. International Tax Dialogue Conference, Buenos Aires.

Johannesen, Niels, and Gabriel Zucman. Forthcoming. The end of bank secrecy? An evaluation of the G20 tax haven crackdown. *American Economic Journal: Economic Policy*.

Johns, Andrew, and Joel Slemrod. 2010. The distribution of income tax noncompliance. *National Tax Journal* 63 (3): 397–418.

Jones, Damon. 2012. Inertia and overwithholding: Explaining the prevalence of income tax refunds. *American Economic Journal: Economic Policy* 4 (1): 158–85.

Joulfaian, David. 2000. Corporate income tax evasion and managerial preferences. *Review of Economics and Statistics* 82 (4): 698–701.

Kaplow, Louis. 1989. Horizontal equity: Measures in search of a principle. *National Tax Journal* 42 (2): 139–54.

Kaplow, Louis. 1990. Optimal taxation with costly enforcement and evasion. *Journal of Public Economics* 43 (2): 221–36.

Kaplow, Louis. 1996. How tax complexity and enforcement affect the equity and efficiency of the income tax. *National Tax Journal* 49 (1): 135–50.

Kaplow, Louis. 1998. Accuracy, complexity, and the income tax. *Journal of Law, Economics, and Organization* 14 (1): 61–83.

Kaplow, Louis. 2001. Horizontal equity: New measures, unclear principles (commentary). In Kevin A. Hassett and R. Glenn Hubbard, eds., *Inequality and Tax Inequality and Tax Policy*. Washington, DC: American Enterprise Institute, 75–97.

Kaplow, Louis, and Steven Shavell. 2001. Any non-welfarist method of policy assessment violates the Pareto principle. *Journal of Political Economy* 109 (2): 281–86.

Kawano, Laura, and Joel Slemrod. 2012. The effect of tax rates and tax bases on corporate tax revenues: Estimates with new measures of the corporate tax base. Working paper. University of Michigan.

Keen, Michael, and Jenny E. Ligthart. 2006. Incentives and information exchange in international taxation. *International Tax and Public Finance* 13 (2–3): 163–80.

Keen, Michael, and Jack Mintz. 2004. The optimal threshold for a value-added tax. *Journal of Public Economics* 88 (3–4): 559–76.

Kesselman, Jonathan R. 1989. Income tax evasion: An intersectoral analysis. *Journal of Public Economics* 38 (2): 137–82.

Kim, Hyeong Min, and Luke Kachersky. 2006. Dimensions of price salience: A conceptual framework for perceptions of multi-dimensional prices. *Journal of Product and Brand Management* 15 (2): 139–47.

Kimball, Miles S. 1990. Precautionary saving in the small and in the large. *Econometrica* 58 (1): 53–73.

Kimball, Miles S., Claudia R. Sahm, and Matthew D. Shapiro. 2008. Imputing risk tolerance from survey responses. *Journal of the American Statistical Association* 103 (483): 1028–38.

King, Mervyn A. 1983. An index of inequality: With applications to horizontal equity and social mobility. *Econometrica* 51 (1): 99–115.

Kirchler, Erich. 2007. *The Economic Psychology of Tax Behaviour*. Cambridge, UK: Cambridge University Press.

Klepper, Steven, and Daniel Nagin. 1989. The anatomy of tax evasion. *Journal of Law, Economics, and Organization* 5 (1): 1–24.

Kleven, Henrik J., Martin B. Knudsen, Claus T. Kreiner, Soren Pedersen, and Emmanuel Saez. 2011. Unwilling or unable to cheat? Evidence from a tax audit experiment in Denmark. *Econometrica* 79 (3): 651–92.

Kleven, Henrik J., and Wojciech Kopczuk. 2011. Transfer program complexity and the take up of social benefits. *American Economic Journal: Economic Policy* 3 (1): 54–90.

Kleven, Henrik J., Claus T. Kreiner, and Emmanuel Saez. 2009. Why can modern governments tax so much? An agency model of firms as fiscal intermediaries. Working paper 15218. NBER.

Kleven, Henrik J., and Joel Slemrod. 2011. A characteristics approach to optimal taxation and tax-driven product innovation. Working paper. University of Michigan.

Kleven, Henrik J., and Mazhar Waseem. 2013. Using notches to uncover optimization frictions and structural elasticities: Theory and evidence from Pakistan. *Quarterly Journal of Economics* 128 (2): 669–723.

Konrad, Kai A., and Salmai Qari. 2012. The last refuge of a scoundrel? Patriotism and tax compliance. *Economica* 79 (315): 516–33.

Kopczuk, Wojciech. 2001. Redistribution when avoidance behavior is heterogeneous. *Journal of Public Economics* 81 (1): 51–71.

Kopczuk, Wojciech. 2005. Tax bases, tax rates and the elasticity of reported income. *Journal of Public Economics* 89 (11–12): 2093–2119.

Kopczuk, Wojciech, and Cristian Pop-Eleches. 2007. Electronic filing, tax preparers and participation in the earned income tax credit. *Journal of Public Economics* 91 (7–8): 1351–67.

Kopczuk, Wojciech, and Joel Slemrod. 2003. Dying to save taxes: Evidence from estate-tax returns on the death elasticity. *Review of Economics and Statistics* 85 (2): 256–65.

Kopczuk, Wojciech, and Joel Slemrod. 2011. Taxation of family firms. Working paper. University of Michigan.

KPMG. 2012. Corporate and indirect tax survey 2012. KPMG International. Available at: www.kpmg.com/Global/en/IssuesAndInsights/ArticlesPublications/Documents/corporate-indirect-tax-survey.pdf.

Kraakman, Reinier H. 1986. Gatekeepers: The anatomy of a third-party enforcement strategy. *Journal of Law, Economics, and Organization* 2: 53–104.

Krishna, Aradhna, and Joel Slemrod. 2003. Behavioral public finance: Tax design and price presentation. *International Tax and Public Finance* 10 (2): 189–203.

Krugman, Paul. 1980. Scale economies, product differentiation, and the pattern of trade. *American Economic Review* 70 (5): 950–59.

LaLumia, Sara, and James M. Sallee. 2013. The value of honesty: Empirical estimates from the case of the missing children. *International Tax and Public Finance* 20 (2): 192–224.

Lancaster, Kelvin J. 1966. A new approach to consumer theory. *Journal of Political Economy* 74 (2): 132–57.

Lancaster, Kelvin J. 1975. Socially optimal product differentiation. *American Economic Review* 65 (4): 567–85.

Lee, Kangoh. 1998. Tax evasion, monopoly, and nonneutral profit taxes. *National Tax Journal* 51 (2): 333–38.

Legislative Analyst's Office. 2011. California's use tax. Presented to Assembly Revenue and Taxation Committee, Hon. Henry T. Perea, Chair. Available at: www.lao.ca.gov/handouts/Econ/2011/CA_Use_Tax_2_28_11.pdf.

Lenter, David, Douglas Shackelford, and Joel Slemrod. 2003. Public disclosure of corporate tax return information: Accounting, economics and legal issues. *National Tax Journal* 56 (4): 803–30.

Levi, Margaret. 1998. A state of trust. In Valerie Braithwaite and Margaret Levi, eds., *Trust and Governance*. New York: Russell Sage Foundation, 77–101.

Leviner, Sagit. 2008. An overview: A new era of tax enforcement—from "big stick" to responsive regulation. *Regulation and Governance* 2 (3): 360–80.

Liebman, Jeffrey B., and Richard J. Zeckhauser. 2004. Schmeduling. Working paper. Harvard University.

Loewenstein, George, Deborah A. Small, and Jeff Strnad. 2006. Statistical, identifiable, and iconic victims. In Edward J. McCaffery and Joel Slemrod, eds., *Behavioral Public Finance*. New York: Russell Sage, 32–46.

Logue, Kyle D., and Joel Slemrod. 2008. Genes as tags: The tax implications of widely available genetic information. *National Tax Journal* 61 (4, pt. 2): 843–63.

Logue, Kyle D., and Joel Slemrod. 2010. Of Coase, Calabresi and optimal tax liability. *Tax Law Review* 63 (4): 797–866.

Long, Susan B. 1981. The extent of criminal tax violations. *Tax Notes*: 1325–26.

Lupia, Arthur. 2001. What we should know: Can ordinary citizens make extraordinary choices? Working paper. University of California, San Diego. Available at: www-personal.umich.edu/~lupia/what.pdf.

MacKie-Mason, Jeffrey K., and Roger H. Gordon. 1997. How much do taxes discourage incorporation? *Journal of Finance* 52 (2): 477–505.

Maki, Dean M. 1996. Portfolio shuffling and tax reform. *National Tax Journal* 49 (3): 317–29.

Mankiw, N. Gregory, and Matthew Weinzierl. 2010. The optimal taxation of height: A case study of utilitarian income redistribution. *American Economic Journal: Economic Policy* 2 (1): 155–76.

Martinez-Vazquez, Jorge. 1996. Who benefits from tax evasion? The incidence of tax evasion. *Public Economics Review* 1 (2): 105–35.

Mayshar, Joram. 1991. Taxation with costly administration. *Scandinavian Journal of Economics* 93 (1): 75–88.

McCaffery, Edward J. 1993–1994. Cognitive theory and tax. *UCLA Law Review* 41: 1861–1947.

McCulloch, John R. [1845] 1975. *A Treatise on the Principles and Practical Influence of Taxation and the Funding System*. Denis P. O'Brien, ed. Edinburgh: Scottish Academic Press.

McLure, Charles E., Jr. 2002. Thinking straight about the taxation of electronic commerce: Tax principles, compliance problems, and nexus. In James M. Poterba, ed., *Tax Policy and the Economy*, vol. 16. Cambridge: MIT Press, 115–40.

Melumad, Nahum D., and Dilip Mookherjee. 1989. Delegation as commitment: The case of income tax audits. *RAND Journal of Economics* 20 (2): 139–63.

Milgram, Stanley. 1963. Behavioral study of obedience. *Journal of Abnormal and Social Psychology* 67 (4): 371–78.

Milgrom, Paul. 1981. Good news and bad news: Representation theorems and applications. *Bell Journal of Economics* 12 (2): 380–91.

Mirrlees, James A. 1971. An exploration in the theory of optimum income taxation. *Review of Economic Studies* 38 (114): 175–208.

Mookherjee, Dilip, and Ivan Png. 1989. Optimal auditing, insurance, and redistribution. *Quarterly Journal of Economics* 104 (2): 399–415.

Morse, Susan, Stewart Karlinsky, and Joseph Bankman. 2009. Cash businesses and tax evasion. *Stanford Law and Policy Review* 20 (1): 37–68.

Mullainathan, Sendhil, and Richard H. Thaler. 2001. Behavioral economics. In Neil J. Smelser and Paul B. Baltes, eds., *International Encyclopedia of the Social and Behavioral Sciences*. Oxford: Pergamon Press, 1094–1100.

Musgrave, Richard A. 1969. *Fiscal Systems*. New Haven: Yale University Press.

Musgrave, Richard A. 1994. Progressive taxation, equity, and tax design. In Joel Slemrod, ed., *Tax Progressivity and Income Inequality*. Cambridge, UK: Cambridge University Press, 341–56.

National Public Radio, Kaiser Foundation and Kennedy School of Government. 2003. Americans' views on taxes. Available at: www.npr.org/news/specials/polls/taxes2003/index.html.

O'Donnell, Gus. 2004. *Financing Britain's Future: Review of the Revenue Departments. Great Britain Treasury.* Presented to Parliament by the Chancellor of the Exchequer by Command of Her Majesty. London: Stationery Office.

Okun, Arthur M. 1975. *Equality and Efficiency: The Big Tradeoff.* Washington, DC: Brookings Institution.

Oldman, Oliver, and LaVerne Woods. 1983. Would a value-added system relieve tax compliance problems? In Phillip Sawicki, ed., *Income Tax Compliance: A Report of the ABA Section of Taxation Invitational Conference on Income Tax Compliance.* Reston, VA: American Bar Association, 317–38.

Onji, Kazuki. 2009. The response of firms to eligibility thresholds: Evidence from the Japanese value-added tax. *Journal of Public Economics* 93 (5–6): 766–75.

Organisation for Economic Co-operation and Development (OECD). 1998. Harmful tax competition: An emerging global issue. Paris: OECD.

Organisation for Economic Co-operation and Development (OECD). 2009. Withholding & information reporting regimes for small/medium-sized businesses & self-employed taxpayers. Forum on Tax Administration: Compliance Sub-group, Information Note. Available at: www.oecd.org/site/ctpfta/listofftapublications-bysegment.htm.

Organisation for Economic Co-operation and Development (OECD). 2011. Tax administration in OECD and selected non-OECD countries: Comparative Information Series (2010). Available at: www.oecd.org/ctp/administration/CIS-2010.pdf.

Pagano, Patrizio, and Fabiano Schivardi. 2003. Firm size distribution and growth. *Scandinavian Journal of Economics* 105 (2): 255–74.

Palan, Ronen. 2002. Tax havens and the commercialization of state sovereignty. *International Organization* 56 (1): 151–76.

Parcell, Ann D. 1995. *Income Shifting in Response to Higher Tax Rates: The Effects of OBRA 93.* Washington, DC: Office of Tax Analysis, US Department of Treasury.

Peacock, Alan T., and Jack Wiseman. 1961. *The Growth of Public Expenditure in the United Kingdom.* Princeton: Princeton University Press.

Pedone, Antonio. 1981. Italy. In Henry J. Aaron, ed., *The Value Added Tax: Lessons from Europe.* Washington, DC: Brookings Institution, 31–42.

Pencavel, John H. 1979. A note on income tax evasion, labor supply, and nonlinear tax schedules. *Journal of Public Economics* 12 (1): 115–24.

Peralta, Susana, Xavier Wauthy, and Tanguy van Ypersele. 2006. Should countries control international profit shifting? *Journal of International Economics* 68 (1): 24–37.

Phillips, Mark D. 2010. Taxpayer response to targeted audits. Working paper. University of Chicago.

Pirttilä, Jukka, and Hakan Selin. 2011. Income shifting with a dual income tax system: Evidence from the Finnish tax reform of 1993. *Scandinavian Journal of Economics* 113 (1): 120–44.

Pissarides, Christopher A., and Guglielmo Weber. 1989. An expenditure-based estimate of Britain's black economy. *Journal of Public Economics* 39 (1): 17–32.

Pitt, Mark M., and Joel Slemrod. 1989. The compliance cost of itemizing deductions: Evidence from individual tax returns. *American Economic Review* 79 (5): 1224–32.

Plueger, Dean. 2009. Earned income tax credit participation rate for tax year 2005. Internal Revenue Service. Available at: www.irs.gov/pub/irs-soi/09resconeitcpart.pdf.

Polinsky, A. Mitchell, and Steven Shavell. 2000. The economic theory of public enforcement of law. *Journal of Economic Literature* 38 (1): 45–76.

Polinsky, A. Mitchell, and Steven Shavell. 2007. The theory of public enforcement of law. In A. Mitchell Polinsky and Steven Shavell, eds., *Handbook of Law and Economics*, vol. 1. Amsterdam: Elsevier, 403–54.

Pomeranz, Dina D. 2011. No taxation without information: Deterrence and self-enforcement in the value added tax. Working paper. Harvard University.

Rajaraman, Indira. 1995. Presumptive direct taxation: Lessons from experience in developing countries. *Economic and Political Weekly* 30 (18–19): 1103–24.

Ramnath, Shanthi P. 2013. Taxpayers' response to notches: Evidence from the saver's credit. *Journal of Public Economics* 101 (6): 77–93.

Ramsey, Frank P. 1927. A contribution to the theory of taxation. *Economic Journal* 37 (145): 47–61.

Randolph, William C. 1995. Dynamic income, progressive taxes, and the timing of charitable contributions. *Journal of Political Economy* 103 (4): 709–38.

Rice, Eric M. 1992. The corporate tax gap: Evidence on tax compliance by small corporations. In Joel Slemrod, ed., *Why People Pay Taxes: Tax Compliance and Enforcement*. Ann Arbor: University of Michigan Press, 125–61.

Riddell, George Allardice. 1933. *Lord Riddell's Intimate Diary of the Peace Conference and After, 1918–1923*. London: Victor Gollancz.

Robinson, Leslie, and Joel Slemrod. 2012. Understanding multidimensional tax systems. *International Tax and Public Finance* 19 (2): 237–67.

Rosen, Harvey S. 1976. Tax illusion and the labor supply of married women. *Review of Economics and Statistics* 58 (2): 167–72.

Saez, Emmanuel. 2001. Using elasticities to derive optimal income tax rates. *Review of Economic Studies* 68 (1): 205–29.

Saez, Emmanuel. 2010. Do taxpayers bunch at kink points? *American Economic Journal: Economic Policy* 2 (3): 180–212.

Saez, Emmanuel, Joel Slemrod, and Seth Giertz. 2012. The elasticity of taxable income with respect to marginal tax rates: A critical review. *Journal of Economic Literature* 50 (1): 3–50.

Sallee, James M., and Joel Slemrod. 2012. Car notches: Strategic automaker responses to fuel economy policy. *Journal of Public Economics* 96 (11–12): 981–99.

Sanchez, Isabel, and Joel Sobel. 1993. Hierarchical design and enforcement of income tax policies. *Journal of Public Economics* 50 (3): 345–69.

Sandford, Cedric T. 1973. *Hidden Costs of Taxation*. London: Institute for Fiscal Studies.

Sandford, Cedric T. 1995. *Tax Compliance Costs: Measurement and Policy*. Bath, UK: Fiscal Publications.

Sandmo, Agnar. 1976. Optimal taxation: An introduction to the literature. *Journal of Public Economics* 6 (1–2): 37–54.

Sandmo, Agnar. 1981. Income tax evasion, labour supply, and the equity-efficiency trade-off. *Journal of Public Economics* 16 (3): 265–88.

Sandmo, Agnar. 1993. Optimal redistribution when tastes differ. *FinanzArchiv / Public Finance Analysis* 50 (2): 149–63.

Sausgruber, Rupert, and Jean-Robert Tyran. 2005. Testing the Mill hypothesis of fiscal illusion. *Public Choice* 122 (1–2): 39–68.

Schivardi, Fabiano, and Roberto Torrini. 2008. Identifying the effects of firing restrictions through size-contingent differences in regulation. *Labour Economics* 15 (3): 482–511.

Schneider, Friedrich. 2005. Shadow economies around the world: What do we really know? *European Journal of Political Economy* 21 (3): 598–642.

Scholz, John K. 1994. Tax progressivity and household portfolios: Descriptive evidence from the surveys of consumer finances. In Joel Slemrod, ed., *Tax Progressivity and Income Inequality*. Cambridge, UK: Cambridge University Press, 219–67.

Schwartz, Paul. 2008. The future of tax privacy. *National Tax Journal* 61 (4, pt. 2): 883–900.

Scotchmer, Suzanne. 1987. Audit classes and tax enforcement policy. *American Economic Review* 77 (2): 229–33.

Shaw, Jonathan, Joel Slemrod, and John Whiting. 2010. Administration and compliance. In Stuart Adam, Timothy Besley, Richard Blundell, Stephen Bond, Robert Chote, Malcolm Gammie, Paul Johnson, Gareth Myles, and James Poterba, eds., *Dimensions of Tax Design: The Mirrlees Review*. Oxford: Oxford University Press/Institute of Fiscal Studies, 1100–62.

Sheffrin, Steven M. 1994. Perceptions of fairness in the crucible of tax policy. In Joel Slemrod, ed., *Tax Progressivity and Income Inequality*. Cambridge, UK: Cambridge University Press, 309–34.

Sheffrin, Steven M. 2013. *Tax Fairness and Folk Justice*. Cambridge, UK: Cambridge University Press.

Shoup, Carl, Roy Blough, and Mabel Newcomer. 1937. *Facing the Tax Problem: A Survey of Taxation in the United States and a Program for the Future*. Prepared under the auspices of the Committee on Taxation of the Twentieth Century Fund. New York: Twentieth Century Fund.

Silvani, Carlos, and John Brondolo. 1993. An analysis of VAT compliance. Working paper. Fiscal Affairs Department, IMF.

Sivadasan, Jagadeesh, and Joel Slemrod. 2008. Tax law changes, income-shifting and measured wage inequality: Evidence from India. *Journal of Public Economics* 92 (10–11): 2199–2224.

Slemrod, Joel. 1985. An empirical test for tax evasion. *Review of Economics and Statistics* 67 (2): 232–38.

Slemrod, Joel. 1990. Optimal taxation and optimal tax systems. *Journal of Economic Perspectives* 4 (1): 157–78.

Slemrod, Joel. 1992. Did the Tax Reform Act of 1986 simplify tax matters? *Journal of Economic Perspectives* 6 (1): 45–57.

Slemrod, Joel. 1994. Fixing the leak in Okun's bucket: Optimal tax progressivity when avoidance can be controlled. *Journal of Public Economics* 55 (1): 41–51.

Slemrod, Joel. 1995. What do cross-country studies teach about government involvement, prosperity and economic growth? *Brookings Papers on Economic Activity* 2: 373–415.

Slemrod, Joel. 1996. Which is the simplest tax system of them all? In Henry J. Aaron and William Gale, eds., *The Economics of Fundamental Tax Reform*. Washington, DC: Brookings Institution, 355–91.

Slemrod, Joel. 1998. Methodological issues in measuring and interpreting taxable income elasticities. *National Tax Journal* 51 (4): 773–88.

Slemrod, Joel. 2001. A general model of the behavioral response to taxation. *International Tax and Public Finance* 8 (2): 119–28.

Slemrod, Joel. 2003. Trust in public finance. In Sijbren Cnossen and Hans-Werner Sinn, eds., *Public Finance and Public Policy in the New Century*. Cambridge: MIT Press, 49–88.

Slemrod, Joel. 2004a. The economics of corporate tax selfishness. *National Tax Journal* 57 (4): 877–99.

Slemrod, Joel. 2004b. Written testimony submitted to the Committee on Ways and Means, Subcommittee on Tax Simplification. Washington, DC, June 15.

Slemrod, Joel. 2005. The etiology of tax complexity: Evidence from U.S. state income tax systems. *Public Finance Review* 33 (3): 279–99.

Slemrod, Joel. 2006. The role of misconceptions in support for regressive tax reform. *National Tax Journal* 59 (1): 57–75.

Slemrod, Joel. 2007. Cheating ourselves: The economics of tax evasion. *Journal of Economic Perspectives* 21 (1): 25–48.

Slemrod, Joel. 2008a. Does it matter who writes the check to the government? The economics of tax remittance. *National Tax Journal* 61 (2): 251–75.

Slemrod, Joel. 2008b. Why is Elvis on Burkina Faso postage stamps? Cross-country evidence on the commercialization of state sovereignty. *Journal of Empirical Legal Studies* 5 (4): 683–712.

Slemrod, Joel, and Marsha Blumenthal. 1996. The income tax compliance cost of big business. *Public Finance Quarterly* 24 (4): 411–38.

Slemrod, Joel, Marsha Blumenthal, and Charles Christian. 2001. Taxpayer response to an increased probability of audit: Evidence from a controlled experiment in Minnesota. *Journal of Public Economics* 79 (3): 455–83.

Slemrod, Joel, and Wojciech Kopczuk. 2002. The optimal elasticity of taxable income. *Journal of Public Economics* 84 (1): 91–112.

Slemrod, Joel, and Nikki Sorum. 1984. The compliance cost of the U.S. individual income tax system. *National Tax Journal* 37 (4): 461–74.

Slemrod, Joel, Thor O. Thoresen, and Erlend E. Bø. 2012. Taxes on the Internet: Deterrence effects of public disclosure. Working paper. University of Michigan.

Slemrod, Joel, and Christian Traxler. 2010. Optimal observability in a linear income tax. *Economics Letters* 108 (2): 105–108.

Slemrod, Joel, and Caroline E. Weber. 2012. Evidence of the invisible: Toward a credibility revolution in the empirical analysis of tax evasion and the informal economy. *International Tax and Public Finance* 19 (1): 25–53.

Slemrod, Joel, Caroline E. Weber, and Hui Shan. 2012. The lock-in effect of housing transfer taxes: Evidence from a notched change in D.C. policy. Working paper. University of Michigan.

Slemrod, Joel, and John D. Wilson. 2009. Tax competition with parasitic tax havens. *Journal of Public Economics* 93 (11–12): 1261–70.

Slemrod, Joel, and Shlomo Yitzhaki. 1987. The optimal size of a tax collection agency. *Scandinavian Journal of Economics* 89 (2): 25–34.

Slemrod, Joel, and Shlomo Yitzhaki. 1994. Analyzing the standard deduction as a presumptive tax. *International Tax and Public Finance* 1 (1): 25–34.

Slemrod, Joel, and Shlomo Yitzhaki. 1996. The costs of taxation and the marginal efficiency cost of funds. *International Monetary Fund Staff Papers* 43 (1): 172–98.

Slemrod, Joel, and Shlomo Yitzhaki. 2002. Tax avoidance, evasion, and administration. In Alan J. Auerbach and Martin Feldstein, eds., *Handbook of Public Economics*, vol. 3. Amsterdam: Elsevier, 1423–70.

Stiglitz, Joseph E. 1982. Utilitarianism and horizontal equity: The case for random taxation. *Journal of Public Economics* 18 (1): 1–33.

Stiglitz, Joseph E. 1985. The general theory of tax avoidance. *National Tax Journal* 38 (3): 325–38.

Swedish Tax Agency. 2004. *Taxes in Sweden 2003*. Solna: Swedish Tax Agency.

Tait, Alan A. 1988. *Value-Added Tax: International Practice and Problems*. Washington, DC: IMF.

Tanzi, Vito. 1980. The underground economy in the United States: Estimates and implications. *Banco Nazionale del Lavoro Quarterly Review* 135 (2): 427–53.

Tanzi, Vito. 1983. The underground economy in the United States: Annual estimates. *IMF Staff Papers* 30 (2): 283–305.

Tanzi, Vito. 1992. Structural factors and tax revenue in developing countries: A decade of evidence. In Ian Goldin and L. Alan Winters, eds., *Open Economies: Structural Adjustment and Agriculture*, Cambridge, UK: Cambridge University Press, 267–85.

Tanzi, Vito. 1999. Uses and abuses of estimates of the underground economy. *Economic Journal* 109 (456): F338–47.

Tax Foundation. 2012. State and local sales taxes at midyear 2012. Available at: taxfoundation.org/article/state-and-local-sales-taxes-midyear-2012.

Torgler, Benno. 2003. Tax morale, rule-governed behaviour, and trust. *Constitutional Political Economy* 14 (2): 119–40.

Torgler, Benno. 2004. Moral suasion: An alternative tax policy strategy? Evidence from a controlled field experiment. *Economics of Governance* 5 (3): 235–53.

Tybout, James R. 2000. Manufacturing firms in developing countries: How well do they do, and why? *Journal of Economic Literature* 38 (1): 11–44.

Tyler, Tom R. 2006. *Why People Obey the Law.* Princeton: Princeton University Press.

Usher, Dan. 1986. Tax evasion and the marginal cost of public funds. *Economic Inquiry* 24 (4): 563–86.

Ventry, Dennis J., Jr. 2011. Americans don't hate taxes, they hate paying taxes. *University of British Columbia Law Review* 44 (3): 835–89.

Wagner, Adolph. [1883] 1958. *Finanzwissenschaft*, 3rd ed. Leipzig. Excerpted in Richard A. Musgrave and Alan T. Peacock, *Classics in the Theory of Public Finance*. London: Macmillan.

Webber, Carolyn, and Aaron B. Wildavsky. 1986. *History of Taxation and Expenditure in the Western World*. New York: Simon and Schuster.

Weisbach, David A. 1994–1995. Tax responses to financial contract innovation. *Tax Law Review* 50: 491–544.

Weisbach, David A. 1999. Formalism in the tax law. *University of Chicago Law Review* 66: 860–86.

Weiss, Laurence. 1976. The desirability of cheating incentives and randomnness in the optimal income tax. *Journal of Political Economy* 84 (6): 1343–52.

Wilson, John D. 1989. On the optimal tax base for commodity taxation. *American Economic Review* 79 (5): 1196–1206.

Wilson, John D. 1999. Theories of tax competition. *National Tax Journal* 52 (2): 269–304.

Wilson, John D., and David E. Wildasin. 2004. Capital tax competition: Bane or boon. *Journal of Public Economics* 88 (6): 1065–91.

Yaniv, Gideon. 1988. Withholding and non-withheld tax evasion. *Journal of Public Economics* 35 (2): 183–204.

Yaniv, Gideon. 1992. Collaborated employee–employer tax evasion. *Public Finance* 47 (2): 312–21.

Yelowitz, Aaron S. 1995. The Medicaid notch, labor supply, and welfare participation: Evidence from eligibility expansion. *Quarterly Journal of Economics* 110 (4): 909–39.

Yitzhaki, Shlomo. 1974. A note on "Income tax evasion: A theoretical analysis." *Journal of Public Economics* 3 (2): 201–202.

Yitzhaki, Shlomo. 1979. A note on optimal taxation and administrative costs. *American Economic Review* 69 (3): 475–80.

Yitzhaki, Shlomo. 1987. On the excess burden of tax evasion. *Public Finance Quarterly* 15 (2): 123–37.

Yitzhaki, Shlomo. 2007. Cost–benefit analysis of presumptive taxation. *FinanzArchiv: Public Finance Analysis* 63 (3): 311–26.

Zee, Howell. 2005. Simple analytics of setting the optimal VAT exemption threshold. *De Economist* 153 (4): 461–71.

Index

Accidental evasion, 130

Addington, Henry, Prime Minister, 94

Administrative costs, 5, 7–10, 12, 16, 57, 69–77, 84, 86, 88, 98–100, 105, 116–17, 121–24, 126, 129, 132, 139, 142–43, 146, 148, 150, 162–63, 185, 192n3 (chapter 4), 192n4 (chapter 5), 192n5 (chapter 5), 193n16, 194n4 (chapter 10), 194–95n5, 195n10

Agell, Jonas, 63

Agha, Ali, 40

Agrawal, David R., 164

Ainsworth, Richard T., 172, 196n3

Akerlof, George A., 136

Allingham, Michael G., 24

Allingham–Sandmo model, 24–31, 42–43, 47–48, 85, 109, 130

Alm, James, 32, 51, 58

Alt, James, 193n16

Andreoni, James, 43–44

Arm's-length prices, 59–61, 64, 70, 73, 103

Artavanis, Nikolaos, 36–37

Atkinson, Anthony B., 20, 134, 189n7

Audit class, 88, 132

Audit coverage, 43, 72, 130
  individual income tax, IRS, 107 table 6.1

Audit experiment
  Denmark, 37, 48
  Minnesota, 37, 49

Audit rate, 48, 93, 107–109, 128, 193n14

Audits, 6, 32, 34, 37–38, 43, 45–47, 106, 108, 128–130, 132, 190n13

Auerbach, Alan J., 14, 119–20

Auriol, Emmanuelle, 195n9

Auten, Gerald, 90

Avoidance. See Tax avoidance

Bakija, Jon, 58

Baldry, Jonathan C., 44, 137

Ballard, Charles L., 70

Bankman, Joseph, 175

Baron, Jonathan, 155

Bartelsman, Eric J., 60

Barzel, Yoram, 55, 57, 158

Becker, Gary S., 24, 130

Beetsman, Roel, M. W. J., 60

Behavioral economics, 13, 155

Behavioral response, 9, 15–17, 53–54, 57–58, 64, 69, 85–86, 89–90, 133, 135, 137, 141,145, 164–65, 167, 183, 185, 187, 196n4
  hierarchy, 12, 165
  multiple margins, 7, 79–83, 182–83

Belan, Pascal, 195n3

Benshalom, Ilan, 194n2 (chapter 10)

Beron, Kurt J., 48

Bhargava, Saurabh, 106

Big Brother syndrome, 176

Bigio, Saki, 132

Bird, Richard M., 72, 99

Blinder, Alan S., 161

Blough, Roy, 192n3 (chapter 4)

Blumenthal, Marsha, 50, 52, 76

Blumkin, Tomer, 152

Blundell, Richard, 160

Bø, Erlend E., 104

Boadway, Robin, 130

Border, Kim C., 194n6

Borgarello, Andrea, 163

Braithwaite, Valerie A., 105

Breusch, Trevor, 41

Brondolo, John, 40

Bunching, 48, 51, 165–67, 178, 190n15, 195n5 (chapter 11)

Burman, Leonard E., 58
Business tax evasion
  Allingham–Sandmo model, 30
  managerial preference, 30
  principal-agent aspect, 31
  proposed deficiency, 46
  Sarbanes–Oxley Act of 2002, 31
  stock-market response, 30
  tactical opening bid, 45

Calabresi, Guido, 98–99
Capital gains, 6, 11, 44, 58, 62, 23n62, 101, 103, 165, 175
Capital gains realizations, 58, 165
Capital gains tax rate, 58
Capriciousness, 69, 72, 145
Carrillo, Paul E., 51
Carroll, Robert, 90
Casanegra de Jantscher, Milka, 189n4 (chapter 1)
Cash, 9, 23, 30, 38, 41, 61, 63, 96, 101, 149, 160–61, 171–72, 193n11, 194n2 (chapter 8), 194n2 (chapter 10)
  cash business and cash economy, 40, 103–104, 186
  cash transactions, 104, 148
Cashin, David, 62
Chandra, Amitabh, 58
Characteristics, 5, 9, 35, 37, 44, 46, 48, 55–57, 63, 75, 119, 132, 152, 157–59, 165–67
Cheapest-cost harm avoider, 99
Chen, Kong-Ping, 190n8
Chetty, Raj, 27, 79, 84–85, 88, 105–106, 152–53, 166
Christensen, Kevin, 193n7
Christian, Charles W., 45, 50, 52
Chu, C. Y. Cyrus, 190n8
Clausing, Kimberly, 58–59
Cliffs, 159. *See also* Notches
Cline, Robert, 193n7
Clofelter, Charles, 44, 48
Coase, Ronald H., 73, 98–99
Coase theorem, 98
Cognitive ability, 151–52, 156
Cognitive biases, 4, 153, 155
Cognitive limitations, 9, 11, 151–52, 155–56
Cole, Adam J., 62
Collection cost, 61, 76, 100, 121–22, 162
Commercialization of state sovereignty, 181

Complexity, 8, 12, 45, 70–74, 77, 84, 86, 98, 106, 117, 124, 126, 129, 139, 142, 151, 154, 156, 162–63, 173, 183, 185, 190n12, 194–95n5, 195n10
  accuracy, 146
  arbitrage, 150
  progressivity, 150
  transfer program screening, 150
Compliance costs, 5, 7, 16, 27, 57, 69, 98, 115, 117, 121, 146, 150, 162, 193n16, 194n4 (chapter 10), 195n10
  corporations, 76, 99–100
  magnitude, 76
  psychological cost, 75
  survey evidence, 74–75
  voluntary avoidance, 77
Computers, 10, 62, 72, 76, 171–72, 177
Consumption-income gap, 35
Corlett, W. J., 17
Corporate income tax, 30, 45, 64, 76, 83, 108, 148–49
Corporation, C form, 53, 59, 83
Corporation, S form, 53, 59, 83
Cowell, Frank A., 196n2
Cremer, Helmuth, 178, 194n4 (chapter 8)
Crocker, Keith, 31
Cross-border spillovers, 84, 164, 178–79
Cutoff, 133, 161–63, 195n8

Data retrieval platform, 176
Daunton, Martin, 190n10
de Mooij, Ruud A., 59
Deadweight loss, 13–14, 111, 151
Deaton, Angus, 194n1 (chapter 9)
Deduction, 39, 41, 44, 47, 54, 75, 90–91, 101–102, 122, 141, 146, 150, 155, 159, 161, 175–76, 179, 192n1 (chapter 6)
Delli Carpini, Michael X., 153
Demirgüç-Kunt, Asli, 60
Demogrant, 14, 19–20, 80, 133, 138–40, 142
Depreciation, 6, 11, 110, 166, 178
Deterrence, 24, 31, 33, 42–43, 47–48, 51–52, 105, 127, 160, 162, 193n15
Dharmapala, Dhammika, 73, 132, 162–63, 195n8
Diamond, Peter A., 4, 55, 160, 162–63, 185, 191
Diamond–Mirrlees. *See* Production efficiency theorem
Dickert-Conlin, Stacy, 58

Difference-in-difference estimates, 35, 88–90, 166
Disclosure, 46, 104–105, 177
Discriminant formula (DIF), 133
Distribution, 4, 8, 13–14, 19, 23, 40, 49, 51, 63, 82–83, 89, 100–101, 118–20, 131–32, 135, 139, 141, 146, 152, 154, 157, 163, 175, 195n11
Dixit, Avinash K., 196n13
Djankov, Simeon, 162
Domar, Evsey D., 189–90n2
Douglas, Roy, 94
Drucker, Jesse, 196n8
Dual income tax
  Finland, 59
Duncan, Alan, 160
Dušek, Libor, 98, 183

Earned Income Tax Credit (EITC), 74, 95, 105–109, 160, 183
  information provision experiment, 106, 117, 193n13
Economist, The, 190n7
Efficiency cost, 7–8, 13–15, 23, 54, 69–70, 77, 81–84, 86–88, 98, 116, 121, 124, 127, 174
Elasticity, 7–8, 12, 17, 27, 29, 35, 49, 62, 90, 124, 145, 148, 165–67, 182
  endogenous, 137, 143
  optimal, 137–41
Elasticity of taxable income, 12, 81–83, 86, 139–41, 182
  Chetty critique, 27, 84–88,
  estimates, 88–91
  evasion, 7, 79
  identification, before–after comparisons, 88
  identification, panel data, 88–91
  identification, shares analysis, 88–89
  optimal elasticity, 137–41
  sufficiency, 80
  tax base breadth, 84 (*see also* Optimal elasticity)
Electronic filing, 177, 183
Emran, M. Shahe, 51
Enforcement, 5, 7–8, 10–12, 20, 26, 28, 31–32, 35, 38–39, 45, 47, 50, 72, 86, 93, 100, 102, 105, 124–30, 137, 141–42, 178, 181–83, 186, 193n13
  revenue-maximization, 3, 127, 129, 131, 143, 185

Entrepreneurs, 132–33, 180–81
Erard, Brian, 43–44, 190n6
Evasion, 5–7, 9–12, 23–44, 46–53, 66–67, 69, 84–88, 97–105, 109, 115, 125, 127–31, 142–43, 175, 177, 179–80, 182–83, 189–90n2, 190n3, 190n4, 190n5, 190n12, 191n18, 191n24, 191n25, 192n3 (chapter 5), 195n5
  accidental, 130
  Allingham–Sandmo model, 24–31, 42, 47, 109, 130
  by line item, 47
  by income source, 41–43
  dependent children, 101
  general equilibrium effects, 29, 38
  inadvertent, 33–34, 155
  informal economy, 27, 41
  labor supply, 27–30
  marginal tax rate, bunching, 48–49, 51, 195n5, 195n6 (chapter 6)
  non-standard theories, 31–33
  optimal randomness, 129–30
  prudence, precautionary labor supply, 28
  risk aversion, 24–29, 33, 42, 87–88, 109
  risk-bearing cost, 7, 26–27, 87–88, 128–29
  role of authority, 32–33
  sales suppression software, 10, 23, 172
  tax morale, 24, 31, 33, 50
  television license, Austria, 49–50
  traces-of-income, 34–37, 60
  value-added tax, Chile, 50
  zappers, 23, 172
Everson, Mark, 45–46
Excess burden, 7–8, 13–14, 16–17, 23, 25, 54–57, 63, 69, 79, 87–88, 121–25, 128–29, 135, 137, 139, 152,164, 183, 185, 191n18
  tax evasion, 7, 23, 25, 69, 79, 87–88, 125, 129
Externalities, 13, 73, 83–84, 91, 122, 196n1 (chapter 12)

Family firms, 104
Farnsworth, Albert, 94
Feenberg, Daniel, 83
Feige, Edgar L., 41
Feinstein, Jonathan, 38, 43–44, 48
Feld, Lars P., 42
Feldman, Naomi E., 36, 52, 151–52
Feldstein, Martin S., 79, 83, 90, 118–19

Fellner, Gerlinde, 49–50
Field experiments, 37, 49, 51–52
Financial instruments, 61
Financial sector, 36–37, 148–49
Financial transactions
  informal economy, 148
  information, 61–62, 148–49, 179
Finkelstein, Amy, 155
Firms, 4–5, 30, 40–47, 50–51, 59–61, 64,
    104, 148–49, 156, 161–64, 173, 176–78,
    180, 186, 191n19, 192n5 (chapter 6),
    193n9, 195n10, 195n11
  administrative cost, 73, 77, 132, 162–63,
    185
  exemption, 100, 162–63
  licensing fees, optimality, 149, 162
  missing middle, 73, 132, 163
  optimal boundary between, Coase, 73,
  tax collection and remittance, 9–10,
    93–100, 162
Fiscal externalities, 83–84, 91
Fox, William F., 173
Frey, Bruno S., 32, 42
Frictions, 84, 166–67
  adjustment, 84
  optimization, 167

Gabaix, Xavier, 156
Gahvari, Firouz, 178, 194n4 (chapter 8)
Ganun, Yosef, 152
Garibaldi, Pietro, 163
Garrod, Luke, 156
Gauthier, Bernard, 193n9
Gauthier, Stéphane, 195n3
Genetic endowment tax, 174
Gersovitz, Mark, 193n11
Giertz, Seth, 79, 81, 86, 90–91
Goldin, Jacob, 152
Goode, Richard, 111
Goolsbee, Austan, 58, 84, 164
Gordon, Roger H., 59, 63, 148–49,
    189–90n2, 196n9
Gorman, William M., 56, 166
Gorodnichenko, Yuriy, 35
Graetz, Michael J., 131, 154
Gruber, Jonathan, 90–91
Grubert, Harry, 60, 64

Hague, D. C., 17
Hahn, Frank, 187, 196n1 (chapter 13)
Haig–Simons income definition, 54
Hall, Robert E., 94, 192n2 (chapter 6)

Hanging with zero probability, Becker
  130
Hanlon, Michelle, 30, 46, 190n13, 190n14
Hanousek, Jan, 52
Harberger, Arnold C., 159
Harris, David, 60
Hasegawa, Makoto, 104
Hassett, Kevin A., 119–20
Haughton, Jonathan, 40
Hearth tax, 23
Heim, Bradley, 58
Heller, Walter Perrin, 96–97, 162
Henrekson, Magnus, 195n11
Heterogeneity, 45, 75, 106, 133–35, 186
Hettich, Walter, 194–95n5
Hines, James R., Jr., 60, 196n7
Hinrichs, Harley, 70
HM Revenue and Customs, 40
Ho, Chih-Chin, 190n6
Hong, Qing, 180
Hoopes, Jeffrey, 104
Horizontal equity, 69, 105, 119–20, 186,
    193n13
  rank reversals, 119
Hotelling, Harold, 166
Household survey
  evasion, 34, 36
Huizinga, Harry 60
Humphrey, David B., 193n11
Hurst, Erik, 36

Ickes, Barry, 192n3 (chapter 6)
Incidence, 26, 63, 96–97, 99, 155
Income shifting
  facilitation, 64–67, 191n28
  general model, Slemrod, 64–67 (see also
    Facilitation)
  geographic, 59–60, 64, 179–81
  implicit subsidy, 64, 66
  over time, 57–58, 62
  Puerto Rico, 3, 60–61, 64–66, 186
  real activity, 64–67, 178–79
  tax base, 83–84
Individual income tax, 38, 41–42, 70,
    107–108
Individual Retirement Account (IRA), 62
  avoidance, 62, 191n23, 191n24
Inflation tax, 149
Informal economy, 27–28, 40–41, 190n5.
    See also Underground economy
Information,
  provision of, 105–106, 117, 193n13

Information reports, 9, 42–43, 47, 50, 95, 100–102
Information technology, 72, 171–72, 177
Intangible capital, 60
Internal Revenue Service (IRS), 3, 6, 31, 38–39, 42–46, 48, 51, 76, 101, 106–109, 127–29, 155, 175–77, 190n13
International Tax Dialogue, with input from the staff of the International Monetary Fund, Inter-American Development Bank, OECD, and the World Bank, 193n8, 193n9, 195n10
Internet, 7, 63, 104–105, 156, 176–77
Intra-firm transactions, 59
Intrinsic motivation, 32
Invariance proposition, 99
Inverse elasticity rule, 17, 121
Invoice-credit method of VAT, 50, 94
Ironing, 151
Ishida, Ryo, 104
Israeli *tachshiv*, 165, 196n12

Jackson, Betty R., 32, 51
Johannesen, Niels, 102
Johansson, Dan, 195n11
Johns, Andrew, 43–44
Jones, Damon, 95
Joulfaian, David, 30
Juridical entrepreneurs, 181

Kachersky, Luke, 195n6 (chapter 10)
Kaplow, Louis, 119–20, 125, 146, 194n2 (chapter 8), 194n5 (chapter 8), 194n2 (chapter 9)
Karlinsky, Stewart, 40, 103–104
Katuščák, Peter, 151–52
Kawano, Laura, 109–10
Keen, Michael, 162, 181, 195n8
Keeter, Scott, 153
Kesselman, Jonathan R., 29
Kim, Hyeong Min, 195n6 (chapter 10)
Kimball, Miles S., 28, 109
King, Mervyn A., 119
Kirchler, Erich, 190n16
Klepper, Steven, 47
Kleven, Henrik J., 37–38, 44, 48, 57, 104, 150, 158–59, 167
Knudsen, Martin B., 37–38, 48
Konrad, Kai A., 52
Kopczuk, Wojciech, 58, 84, 91, 104, 110, 133–36, 138, 141, 150, 183
KPMG, 96

Kraakman, Reinier H., 190n8
Kreiner, Claus T., 37–38, 48, 104
Krishna, Aradhna, 155
Kroft, Kory, 152–53
Krugman, Paul, 196n13

La Porta, Rafael, 162
Lab experiment, 32–33, 38, 51, 152
Labor supply, 7, 12, 19–20, 27–29, 53, 65–67, 80–81, 83–85, 116, 125, 130–31, 137–38, 152, 165, 185, 191n4
Laffer curve, 90, 110, 130
Laibson, David, 156
LaLumia, Sara, 101
Lancaster, Kelvin J.,
Lancaster–Gorman preferences, 56, 158, 166
Laroque, Guy, 195n3
Lee, Kangoh, 30
Legislative Analyst's Office, 63
Legitimacy, 32, 69
Lenter, David, 104, 177
Levi, Margaret, 32
Leviner, Sagit, 105
Li, Geng, 36
Li, Wei, 148–49
Liebman, Jeffrey B., 151
Ligthart, Jenny E., 181
Lines, 9, 154, 157, 159–60
Line drawing, 9, 157–60, 151n1
optimal, 157–60
Loewenstein, George, 189n3 (chapter 1)
Logue, Kyle D., 98–99, 172, 174
Long, Susan B., 155
Looney, Adam, 152–53
Loopholes, 4, 7, 84, 133, 141
Lopez de Silanes, Florencio, 162
Loss carryback, 109
Loss carryforward, 109
Lump-sum taxes, 5, 13–14, 16, 123–24, 128, 162
Luna, LeAnn, 173
Lupia, Arthur, 154

MacKie-Mason, Jeffrey K., 59
Maki, Dean M., 58
Manipulability, 145
Mankiw, N. Gregory, 172
Manoli, Dayannand S., 106
Marginal efficiency cost of funds, 15, 81–82, 84, 87–88, 98, 116, 121, 124
Market transactions, 9, 73, 103–104

Martinez-Vazquez, Jorge, 190n5
Mayshar model, 65, 115, 146
McCaffery, Edward J., 155
McCrae, Julian, 160
McCulloch, John R., 95
McKee, Michael, 32, 51
McLure, Charles E., Jr., 173
Mean reversion, 89–90
Mechanical burden, 16, 81, 85, 128
Meghir, Costas, 160
Melumad, Nahum D., 131
Milgram, Stanley, 33
Milgrom, Paul, 156
Mills, Lillian, 46, 190n13, 190n14
Mintz, Jack, 162, 195n8
Mirrlees curve, 140–41
Mirrlees, James A., 4, 55, 72, 140–41, 145, 160–63, 174, 185, 191n18
Misperception, 154
Mobility, 73
Money laundering, 181
Mookherjee, Dilip, 131, 194n6
Morck, Randall, 60
Morse, Adair, 36–37
Morse, Susan, 40, 103–104
Mullainathan, Sendhil, 155
Multinational corporations, 59–60, 103, 137, 178–81, 196n8
Multiple jurisdictions, 164, 172–73, 177–82
Multiple tax instruments, 109–10, 115–19
Murray, Matthew, N., 173
Musgrave, Richard A., 70, 150, 189n2 (chapter 1), 189–90n2
Mutti, John, 60

Nagin, Daniel, 47
National Public Radio, Kaiser Foundation, and Kennedy School of Government,
National Research Program (NRP), 38–45, 47
Nero, 95
Neubig, Tom, 193n7
Newcomer, Mabel, 192n3 (chapter 3)
Nicodème, Gaëtan, 59
Nonstandard theories of tax evasion
  intrinsic willingness, 24, 31–32
  lab experiment, 32–33, 51
  legitimacy, 32
  obedience, 33
  personal morality, 32
  Stanley Milgram, 33

Noncompliance, 6, 26–27, 34, 37–38, 40, 42–50, 101, 105, 107, 173, 190n6
Noncompliance rate, 36, 40, 42–43, 45–47
Notches
  border, 164, 178
  desirability, 161, 166
  disclosure threshold, 104–105
  earned income tax credit, 160
  income tax, Pakistan, 167
  income tax, United States, 160, 195n6 (chapter 11)
  Israeli *arnona*, 161
  labor market regulations, 163
  Medicaid notch, 160–61
  optimization frictions, 166–67
  quantity, 160–63, 167
  time, 163–64
  UK working families tax credit, 160
  US child care credit, 160

Obedience, 33
Obfuscation, 156
Observability, 9–10, 12, 97, 100, 104, 124–27, 186
  optimal, 145–48
O'Donnell, Gus, 39
O'Hare, John, 58
Okun, Arthur M., 141–42
Okun's bucket, 141–43
Oldman, Oliver, 40
Onji, Kazuki, 163
Optimal audit rules, 131–33
  Corlett–Hague rule, 17–18
  Ramsey, 16–17, 55
  uniform, 5, 16, 122, 126
Optimal commodity taxation, 5, 9, 12, 16–18, 55, 57, 121–27, 162–63
  characteristics/line drawing, 157–60
Optimal linear income tax, 16, 18–20, 134, 141–42, 146–47
  Atkinson–Stiglitz representation, 20, 134, 189n7
Optimal tax base, 6, 122–24, 141
OECD (Organisation for Economic Co-operation and Development), 40, 60, 70–72, 95, 101, 109, 179, 192n4 (chapter 6)

Pacelli, Lia, 163
Pagano, Patrizio, 195n11
Palan, Ronen, 181
Palda, Filip, 52

Parcell, Ann D., 164
Pareto distribution, 82
Pareto principle, 13, 120
Partnership, 59, 83
Patriotism, 52
Peacock, Alan T., 94
Pedersen, Soren, 37–38, 48
Pedone, Antonio, 40
Penalties, 6, 10, 24–26, 28–29, 31, 33, 42,
   45, 47, 51, 59, 88, 93, 95, 106–109, 119,
   128, 130–31, 191n27
  Yitzhaki form, 25–26, 109
Pencavel, John H., 130
Peralta, Susana, 178
Personalized taxation, 171
Persson, Mats, 63
Phillips, Mark D.
Pigouvian tax, 73, 162, 196n1 (chapter 12)
Pirttilä, Jukka, 59
Pissarides, Christopher A., 34, 36
Pitt, William, the Younger, 94
Plueger, Dean, 106
Polinsky, A. Mitchell, 130
Pomeranz, Dina D., 50
Pop-Eleches, Cristian, 183
Png, Ivan, 194n6
Pre-populated return, 95, 175–76
Presumptive tax, 37, 165, 185, 195n10,
   196n12
Price presentation, 155
Privacy, 10, 12, 176–77
  Big Brother syndrome, 176
Production efficiency, 5, 162
Production efficiency theorem, 160
Progressivity. See Tax progressivity
Public disclosure, 46, 104–105, 177
Pugsley, Benjamin, 36
Purchases, 9, 50, 54, 56–57, 95, 101, 123,
   125–27, 152, 165, 171, 178, 194n2
   (chapter 8)
  timing, 62–63, 166

Qari, Salmai, 52

R&D, 59–60, 64, 110
Rabushka, Alvin, 94, 192n2 (chapter 6)
Rajaraman, Indira, 165
Ramnath, Shanthi P., 195n6 (chapter 11)
Ramsey, Frank P., 16–17, 55, 123
Randolph, William C., 58
Randomized field experiment, 37–38,
   49–50, 105

Real behavioral response, 5, 53–54, 57, 69,
   133
Reciprocal altruism, 32
Redistribution, 8, 20, 117, 122, 131,
   133–36, 143, 174. See also Tax
   progressivity
Reinganum, Jennifer F., 131
Remittance, 5–7, 10, 51, 69, 74, 93–100,
   102, 105, 155, 178
  Calabresi, 98–99
  optimality, Coase theorem, 73, 98–99
  responsibility for, 63, 93–100
  retail sales tax, 6–7, 63, 93–94, 96–97,
    173, 186
  statutory incidence, 93, 96, 99, 110
  value-added tax, 3, 7, 9, 94, 96, 186
Retail sales tax, 3, 6–7, 9–10, 54, 62–63, 94,
   96–97, 103, 122, 150, 152–53, 157,
   164–65, 172–73, 178, 186, 192n6
  harmonization, 173
Return-free tax system, 95
Revenue-maximizing, 110, 127, 131, 143
Rice, Eric M., 46, 60
Riddell, George Allardice, 193n10
Risk aversion/risk bearing, 7, 24–30, 33,
   42, 87–88, 109, 128–29, 146–47
Rivadeneira, Anita, 51
Robinson, Leslie, 72, 111
Role of firms, 9, 93–100
Role of information, 12, 43, 171–72
Rosen, Harvey S., 67, 161
Ruffle, Bradley J., 152

Sabirianova Peter, Klara, 35
Saez, Emmanuel, 37–38, 48, 79, 81–82, 86,
   90–91, 104–106, 166, 190n15
Sahm, Claudia R., 109
Salience, 67, 152–53, 195n6 (chapter 10)
Sallee, James M., 101, 159
Sanchez, Isabel, 131, 133
Sandford, Cedric T., 74–75
Sandmo, Agnar, 24, 189n3 (chapter 2),
   190n4, 194n8
Sarbanes–Oxley Act of 2002, 31
Sato, Motohiro, 130
Sausgruber, Rupert, 49–50, 152
Schivardi, Fabiano, 163, 195n11
Schmeduling, 151
Schneideer, Friedrich, 41
Scholz, John K., 58
Schwartz, Paul, 177, 196n5
Scotchmer, Suzanne, 132

Self-employed, 3, 26, 34, 36–37, 42–43, 45, 48–50, 59, 103, 132–33, 152, 167, 186
Services, 5, 30, 40, 52, 57, 60, 62, 111, 122, 171, 196n12
 tax base, 8, 122, 157
Selin, Håkan, 59
Shackelford, Douglas, 104, 177
Shan, Hui, 58, 167
Shapiro, Ian, 154
Shapiro, Matthew, 109
Shavell, Steven, 120, 130
Shaw, Jonathan, 193n7
Sheffrin, Steven M., 151, 190n9
Shell, Karl, 162
Sheltering, 64–66, 79–80, 84, 88, 115, 137, 142–43
Shleifer, Andrei, 162
Shoup, Carl, 192n3 (chapter 4)
Shoven, John B., 70
Silvani, Carlos, 40
Sivadasan, Jagadeesh, 59
Slemrod, Joel, 15, 30–31, 34, 36–37, 41, 43–46, 49, 52–53, 57–60, 63–65, 72–73, 75–76, 79, 81, 84, 86, 90–91, 98–99, 104, 109–11, 128, 132, 138, 141–42, 146, 150, 154–55, 158–59, 162–63, 165, 167, 172, 174, 177, 180–81, 183, 190n13, 190n14, 192n3 (chapter 6), 193n7, 194n4 (chapter 10), 195n5, 195n8
Small businesses, 40, 45, 73, 76, 100, 193n8
Small, Deborah A., 189n3 (chapter 1)
Smart cards, 10, 63, 171–72
Smart, Michael, 180
Sobel, Joel, 131, 133, 194n6
Social welfare function, 19, 116–19, 126, 134–35, 139, 148
Sorum, Nikki, 76
Speeding fine
 Income-related, 171
Stiglitz, Joseph E., 20, 61–62, 129–30, 134, 189n7, 191n24, 196n13
Streamlined Sales Tax Initiative, 173
Strnad, Jeff, 189n3 (chapter 1)
Surrogate tax base, 164–67, 185
Swedish Tax Agency, 39

Tait, Alan A., 40, 75
Tagging or Tag, 172
 endowment tax, 174–75
 genetic, 174
Tanzi, Vito, 41, 111

Tauchen, Helen V., 48
Tax arbitrage, 53, 61–63, 150, 155, 171, 191n25
Tax avoidance, 5–8, 11–12, 23, 31, 49, 53–57, 61–67, 77, 79–80, 84, 89, 97–98, 102, 115, 141–43, 159, 163–65, 183, 191n23, 191n24, 191n25, 191n28, 194n7, 194n8, 196n8
 birth, 58
 capital gains tax, 57–58
 characteristics, 56–57
 death, 58
 definition, 11, 53, 61
 desirability, 28, 33, 135–36
 excess burden of, 54–57, 69
 facilitation, 64–67
 heterogeneous behavior, 133–36
 lightbulbs, 57
 marriage, 58
 non-qualified stock options, 58
 optimal progressivity, 135–36, 141–42
 re-classification, 141, 143
 re-timing, 62–63, 163
 Slemrod–Yitzhaki definition, 53
 Stiglitz, 61–62, 191n24
Tax base, 5–8, 10, 12, 40, 55, 57–59, 70, 73–74, 79–91, 103, 109–10, 116–17, 121–25, 132, 137–42, 161, 164–67, 172, 178–79, 182, 185, 192n1 (chapter 5)
 breadth, 8, 20, 84, 91, 121–23, 125, 137–38, 140
Tax base elasticity, 7–8, 12, 79–91, 145, 182
Tax collection agency
 optimal size, 127–31
Tax competition, 178, 180–81
Tax-driven product innovation, 57, 158–59
Tax evasion gamble, 25, 64
Tax evasion penalty, 24–25, 28–29, 47, 59, 119, 128, 130–31
 fraud, 31, 33, 108–109, 172
 minor offense, 33, 109
Tax farming, 191n1
Tax filing, 10, 76, 173, 175–77, 183
Tax Foundation, 192n6, 194n3 (chapter 10)
Tax gap, 34, 38–39, 63, 186, 191n25
 corporate income tax, 39, 45, 45n
 individual income tax, 39, 41–43
 value-added tax, 40
Tax handles, 70

Tax havens 60, 179–81, 196n7
  desirability, 180
  information sharing, 102, 179
  secrecy, 179–80
Tax holidays, 62, 165
Tax illusion, 67
Tax morale, 24, 31, 33, 50
Tax progressivity, 4, 20, 44, 133, 135,
    137–38, 140–41, 143, 147, 150. *See also*
    Redistribution
Tax salience, 67, 153
  optimal taxation, 152
Tax-driven product innovation, 57,
    158–59, 185
Taxpayer ignorance, 33–34
Taxable income, 7, 12, 24, 27, 41, 43,
    48–49, 53–54, 61, 66, 79–91, 94, 103–104,
    122, 130–31, 134–43, 160–61, 163, 176,
    178–79, 182, 191n22, 191n24, 192n1
    (chapter 5), 193n12, 195n6 (chapter 11)
Taxpayer Compliance Measurement
    Program (TCMP), 38, 40, 46, 48
Taxpayer perceptions, 5, 9, 33, 151
Taxpayers as voters, 153–56
Tax remittance, 5–7, 10, 51–63, 69, 74,
    93–100, 102, 105, 155, 173, 178, 186
Thaler, Richard H., 155
Thin capitalization, 109
Thoresen, Thor O., 104
Time shifting, 57–58, 62, 163
Torgler, Benno, 52
Torrini, Roberto, 163
Traces, 60
Traces-of-income approach
  charitable giving, 36
  Greek banks, 36–37, 193n12
  Pissarides, 34, 36
  Russian flat-tax reform, 35
Transfer pricing, 59–60, 64, 103
Traxler, Christian, 146, 150
Tsoutsoura, Margarita, 36–37
Tybout, James R., 193n9
Tyler, Tom R., 32
Tyran, Jean-Robert, 152

Unayama, Takashi, 62
Underground economy, 28–29, 40. *See also*
    Informal economy.
  currency, 41
  electricity consumption, 41
Use taxes, 47, 63, 172
Usher, Dan, 79

Value-added tax (VAT), 3, 7, 9, 40, 50, 62,
    72, 74, 94, 96, 103, 150, 155, 161–63,
    186
van Ypersele, Tanguy, 178
Ventry, Daniel J., Jr., 176
Vertical equity, 20, 69, 199

Wagner, Adolph, 111
Wagner's law, 111
Warlters, Michael, 195n9
Waseem, Mazhar, 167
Wauthy, Xavier, 178
Webber, Caroline, 23, 52
Weber, Caroline E., 34, 37, 41, 58, 167
Weber, Guglielmo, 34, 36
Weinzierl, Matthew, 172
Weisbach, David A., 61, 195n1
Weiss, Laurence, 129–30
Whalley, John, 70
Whiting, John, 193n7
Whittington, Leslie A., 58
Wildasin, David E., 196n6
Wildavsky, Aaron B., 23, 52
Wilde, Louis L., 131
Wilson, John D., 73, 124, 132, 138–41,
    162–63, 180–81, 189–90n2, 195n8, 196n6
Winer, Stanley L., 194–95n5
Wiseman, Jack, 94
Withholding, 42–43, 45, 57, 70, 77, 93–96,
    98, 101, 155, 157, 176, 186, 192n1
    (chapter 6), 192n3 (chapter 6)
  approximate, 95
  exact, 95, 192n5 (chapter 6)
  over-withholding, 95
  reverse withholding, Ecuador, 50–51
  size of government, Dušek, 98, 183
Witte, Ann Dryden, 48
Woods, LaVerne, 40

Yaniv, Gideon, 77
Yelowitz, Aaron S., 161
Yeung, Bernard, 60
Yitzhaki, Shlomo, 15, 25–26, 53, 85, 87,
    109, 122, 126, 128, 130, 138–41, 146, 165,
    191n18, 196n12
Yitzhaki–Wilson curve, 140–41

Zappers, 23, 172
Zeckhauser, Richard J., 151
Zee, Howell, 195n8
Zilberman, Eduardo, 132
Zucman, Gabriel, 102